Speaking to Life's Problems

SPEAKING TO LIFE'S PROBLEMS

by

Lloyd M. Perry

and

Charles Sell

MOODY PRESS

CHICAGO

© 1983 by
THE MOODY BIBLE INSTITUTE
OF CHICAGO

All Scripture quotations in this book are from the *New American Standard Bible*, © 1960, 1962, 1963, 1968, 1971, 1973, 1975, and 1977 by the Lockman Foundation, and are used by permission.

Library of Congress Cataloging in Publication Data

Perry, Lloyd Merle.
    Speaking to life's problems.
    Includes bibliographies.
    1. Preaching. 2. Pastoral psychology. 3. Meditations.
4. Homiletical illustrations. I. Sell, Charles M., 1933-
II. Title.
BV4211.2.P447 1983   251   83-917
ISBN 0-8024-0170-8

1 2 3 4 5 6 7 Printing/EB/Year 87 86 85 84 83

Printed in the United States of America

Contents

Scripture and Subjects for
Meditation and Ministry

Introduction

Good preaching can be an important factor in the revitalization of the twentieth-century church. People are crying out as they did in years past, "Is there a word from the LORD?" (Jer. 37:17).

Edgar Jackson says in his book *Psychology for Preaching* that "Jesus spent little time sawing sawdust. He ripped into the real problems of people and of His age. He generated participation and response."[1] God had one Son, who came to earth as a preacher and teacher. He was touched with the joys, hopes, and pains of the people. He mingled with them in the crowds and ministered to them as individuals. He brought a word to the people from God the Father designed to make the loads lighter and the days brighter.

Biblically oriented life-situation preaching will never go out of style, for it is designed to help people resolve the tensions, relieve the pressures, and disperse despair. The preacher strives to reach into the core of distress in personal, modern living and apply the healing of the gospel. The material in this book can help revolutionize a pastor's preaching and bring worthwhile rewards to his parishioners. A wide variety of instructional and inspirational material related to the diseases of the soul will serve to provide some answers for the problems of daily living.

The goals of pastoral care and prophetic preaching are quite compatible. Pastoral preaching should develop as a man of God becomes involved in the lives of the members of his congregation. He will become saturated with their situation and will then prayerfully seek to relate the revelation of God to the exigencies of the people.

Good literature and good preaching both deal with people. A

---

1. Edgar N. Jackson, *How to Preach to People's Needs* (New York: Abingdon, 1956), pp.12-13.

preacher should study human nature and combine that study with a thorough knowledge of Scripture. He will not displace the gospel of Matthew with the good news from Menninger, nor will he give Rogers the priority over Romans. He will start where the people live and, under the guidance of the Holy Spirit, help those in need find a biblical solution. A preacher can speak with power and conviction when he believes in the authority of Scripture and its ability to provide help for individuals in need. The helpful biblical preacher must go beyond the Greek aorist and the Old Testament Jebusites and seek to provide practical help for the people where they are living day by day. A lesson provides information, but a sermon should provide both information and application. A sermon should be noted for biblical truth and contemporary relevance. Good preaching should seek the confrontation of the living God with living people through the living Word.

The illustrations, quotations, and counseling analyses will provide help for a lay reader, Sunday school teacher, or preacher. The scriptural resources, including the biblically oriented devotionals dealing with personal problems, will provide spiritual guidance and inspiration. Such problems as anxiety, depression, fear, guilt, and loneliness touch many lives. Those are not theoretical problems, but rather problems that are practical, living, and urgent. God can provide help from the Bible through the ministry of the Holy Spirit. The Bible has built-in application for the real questions and practical personal problems of daily living. Let's give God a chance!

Part 1

A Preaching Perspective

From the example of Jesus can be drawn certain requisite presuppositions for preaching as a form of group soul-healing. There was always the recognition of problems and the possibility of solution. There was always understanding of the cause-effect relationship in living, so that the emphasis was on helping the individual to face the future, rather than condemning past behavior. Yet there was a consciousness of the power of a sense of guilt over both body and mind, and the need for soul-purging through forgiveness. Further, there was a strong sense of the need for healing action that could fix new habit patterns in the life of the healed individual. And at the core of his preaching was a sense of concern, even compassion, that made the individual in the group feel that here was a friend to be trusted and followed.[1]

1. Edgar N. Jackson, *How to Preach to People's Needs* (New York: Abingdon, 1956), pp. 12-13.

1

Preaching on Problems

There is a problem in every pew. Our people need help. We have said through the years that Jesus saves, keeps, and satisfies. Our people are now asking that we make good on our proclamation. Therefore, we must feed the appetite we have created. Preaching must recognize people and their problems. The preacher stands between the demands of God and the needs of man. When faith and the issues of life come together, light comes. It is as though two great electrodes have met and the fire has ignited.

Let us say that a hypothetical minister serves a congregation of five hundred adults representing a cross section of the American population. Based on various research studies, it could be estimated that approximately twenty-five of his members have been hospitalized for major mental illness in the past, twenty-four are alcoholics, another fifty are severely handicapped by neurotic conflicts, and another one hundred afflicted by moderate neurotic symptoms.[2]

One hundred fifteen members of this hypothetical congregation would answer "yes" to the question, "Have you ever felt you were going to have a nervous breakdown?" Seventy would have sought professional help for a personal or marital problem in the past.[3] Approximately six of the parishioners will be hospitalized for mental illness in any given year. One member of his congregation will attempt suicide every other year. Eight members will be involved in a serious crime in a given year. If the married persons in the congregation were

2. W. L. Holt, Jr., "The Mental Disease Problem as Seen by the Practicing Physician," *Health Week*, November 1955, pp. 17-18.
3. Gerald Gurin, et al., *Americans View Their Mental Health* (New York: Basic Books, 1960), p. 304.

asked to rate the relative happiness of their nuptial relationship, fewer than half would rate it as "very happy."[4]

One study of a cross section of the American adult population revealed that one out of every seven Americans has sought professional help concerning a personal problem. Of those, 42 percent went to clergymen, 29 percent went to family doctors, 18 percent to psychiatrists and psychologists, and 10 percent to a special agency or clinic.[5] The pastor has a unique opportunity. Of all the counselors in modern society, he is the only one who also preaches. He appears before his people once a week with the opportunity to speak to them on the issues of life.

According to some experts, the approximately 235,000 parish clergymen are seeing approximately 6,570,000 persons each year. It would require approximately 65,000 specialists to replace the counseling done by those parish ministers. The wise preacher will use this opportunity in the pulpit to establish a precounseling relationship.

Killinger makes the following claim:

> The sermon ought always to constitute a precounseling situation and prepare the way for the most effective personal confrontation between the minister and the counselee. It should set up a relation of confidence between the clergyman and the person in the pew so that the person in the pew realizes that he may approach the clergyman about any problem, however delicate or distasteful, and find reflected in him the same kind of magnanimity and graciousness of spirit as that characterizing the gospel he proclaims.[6]

Leslie J. Tizard believes that if people do not come to the minister with their personal problems, he should ask himself this question: "What is wrong with my preaching?"[7] There are always some people in every congregation who need to talk over their difficulties with one who is understanding and helpful. The preacher can win the troubled person's confidence by conveying certain things in his pastoral sermons. He must show through the way he preaches, by the things he

4. Howard J. Clinebell, Jr., *The Mental Health Ministry of the Local Church* (Nashville: Abingdon, 1972), p. 22.
5. Gurin, *Americans View Their Mental Health*, p. 307.
6. John Killinger, *The Centrality of Preaching in the Total Task of Ministry* (Waco, Tex.: Word Bks, 1969), p. 63.
7. Leslie J. Tizard, *Preaching: The Art of Communication* (New York: Oxford U., 1959), p. 95.

says, and the revelation of his personality that he is approachable, human, and knows his job.

The help that can be given in any one sermon is limited for two reasons. First, a sermon deals with personal problems in a general way only. And second, the wrong person does the talking in preaching. Pastoral preaching, however, can do these things: prepare the way for personal dealing; assure people that they are not alone in their difficulties and troubles; help people to see the constructive possibilities in every experience; and give the assurance that God is available.

THE NATURE OF LIFE-SITUATION PREACHING

One of the best discussions of life-situation or pastoral preaching is that of Ilion T. Jones.[8] Such preaching is directed to people in definite situations with specific needs. Jones shows how both a loose definition and a narrower definition are implied by different authors and preachers. He points out that life-situation preaching is considered by some to be identical with topical preaching. But Jones argues that topical preaching can rightly be called life-situation preaching only when it deals helpfully with the practical problems and questions people face.[9] He also distinguishes life-situation preaching from preaching on contemporary social problems.[10]

Other labels have been used to refer to life-situation preaching. Frank Hill Caldwell points out that the life-situation sermon is also identified as the "problem-solving sermon." He quotes Harry Emerson Fosdick, who made the following statement:

> Start with a life issue, a real problem, personal or social, perplexing the mind or disturbing the conscience: face that problem fairly, deal with it honestly, and throw such light on it from the Spirit of Christ that people will be able to go out able to think more clearly and live more nobly because of that sermon.[11]

"Bifocal preaching" is the term that James T. Cleland uses. He talks about the "Good News immersed in a contemporary situation." According to Cleland, "The preacher is obviously aware of the contemporary situations which confront his people: individual and

---

8. Ilion T. Jones, *Principles and Practices of Preaching* (New York: Abingdon, 1956), pp. 39-43.
9. Ibid., pp. 40-41.
10. Ibid., p. 41.
11. Frank Hill Caldwell, *Preaching Angles* (New York: Abingdon, 1954), p. 109.

social, national and international. . . . He is aware of the milieu in which they live both from his reading and from his pastoral visiting. The preacher then relates those situations to the 'Good News' or some aspect of it."[12]

The life-situation preacher is symbolized by Casey, a character in John Steinbeck's *Grapes of Wrath*. The author portrays a preacher named Casey, who goes up and down the road and sees the empty houses from which families are moving west. Casey decides he must leave, too, because "I got to go where folks is going." Pastoral preaching is specific preaching that attempts to deal with where people are "going" in life.[13]

George M. Gibson speaks of "personal-problem preaching." He observes that "the preacher who knows and loves his people will have them in mind whenever he preaches and will deliberately plan some sermons directly around their personal needs."[14]

Charles F. Kemp has written *Pastoral Preaching*, which is a sequel to his book *Life-Situation Preaching*. Written seven years later, it is, in essence, another volume of life-situation sermons. He defines pastoral preaching as "an attempt to meet the individual and personal needs of the people by means of a sermon."[15]

Edmond Holt Linn's book is a study of the method of preaching used by Harry Emerson Fosdick. Linn describes Fosdick's search for a kind of preaching that would be satisfactory to the known needs of the audience.

> This would be personal counseling on a group basis, a conversational message from soul to soul. Here, he felt, was the answer to his searching. A great gulf between the needs of individuals and the unsearchable riches of Christ could be bridged by sermons based on the idea of personal counseling. Fosdick called this development of preaching as counseling the "project method." It is also known as the "counseling sermon."[16]

Many authors have defined life-situation preaching specifically. Robert J. McCracken gives a specific definition. He includes the preaching of Jesus as an example.

---

12. James T. Cleland, *Preaching to Be Understood* (New York: Abingdon, 1964) p. 37.
13. Robert D. Dale, *Growing a Loving Church* (Nashville: Convention, 1974), p. 37.
14. George M. Gibson, *Planned Preaching* (Philadelphia: Westminster, 1954), p. 74.
15. Charles F. Kemp, *Pastoral Preaching* (St. Louis: Bethany Press, 1963), p. 12.
16. Ibid., p. 15.

Seeking to avoid the remoteness and irrelevance, not to say unreality, which are the bane of much biblical exposition, it starts with people where they are, which was what Jesus did over and over again. The point of departure is a live issue of some kind. It may be personal or social; it may be theological or ethical. Whatever it is, the preacher makes it his business to get at the core of the problem, and, that done, he goes on to work out the solution, with the biblical revelation, and the mind and Spirit of Christ, as the constant points of reference and direction.[17]

It is the view of Halford E. Luccock that the life-situation sermon is the kind of sermon "which originates in the experience of the people to whom it is preached, with the specific aim of bringing help to that situation."[18] Such preaching begins with the problems of people. Luccock goes on to say that that kind of preaching "cuts across the traditional classifications of sermons into doctrinal, biblical, ethical, or topical."[19]

Ilion T. Jones says that "every preacher should certainly do some preaching on personal problems, if for no other reason than to give variety to his preaching."[20] Such preaching is preventive as well as remedial. "By preaching sermons that deal with personal needs, or by dealing with biblical statements concerning spiritual growth, the church is often able to prevent problems that might otherwise arise."[21] Collins believes that "the prevention of problems may be even more important than the solving of problems, and such preaching will contribute to the greater psychological stability of people in the church."[22] If the preacher does that, he will be a therapist engaged in "the cure of souls." David A. MacLennan uses the word "cure" to describe this function of the pastor-preacher.[23] That is the name by which a priest is known in French Canada and in all other places where French is spoken.

Unfortunately, many sermons do not enhance personality health. A

17. Robert J. McCracken, *The Making of the Sermon* (New York: Harper & Brothers, 1956), p. 62.
18. Halford E. Luccock, *In the Minister's Workshop* (New York: Abingdon-Cokesbury, 1944), p. 51.
19. Ibid., p. 54.
20. Jones, p. 41.
21. Gary Collins, *Man in Transition: The Psychology of Human Development* (Carol Stream, Ill.: Creation House, 1971), p. 21.
22. Gary Collins, *Search for Reality: Psychology and the Christian* (Wheaton, Ill.: Key, 1969) p. 198.
23. David A. MacLennan, *A Preacher's Primer* (New York: Oxford U., 1950), pp. 48-49.

cartoon depicting a woman shaking hands with a minister as she left the church had this caption: "Thank you for your sermon. It was like water to a drowning man."

Preaching on personal problems need not differ greatly from the rural parish to the city or suburban parish. Arthur W. Hewitt pointed that out when he made the following statement:

> My deepest conviction is that the church of God is one, in whatever variation of circumstance it may be found; that the principles of preaching and of pastoral work are the same for city and country—for love is the same, and hearts are the same.[24]

William L. Malcomson suggests that the kind of preaching needed today is "invitational preaching."[25] Such preaching must start with human need or men's problems, focus on the gospel in the Bible, and end in an invitation.

Whether one calls preaching to meet people's needs "invitational" preaching, "life-situation" preaching, "problem-solving" preaching, "therapeutic" preaching, or "pastoral" preaching, the name is not as important as the content. What matters is that shortly after the sermon begins, one listener after another finds "the preacher bowling down his alley."[26]

The church's task has been divided into three categories: (1) *kerygma* (teaching and preaching the gospel), (2) *koinonia* (the establishment of a fellowship with a vertical dimension), and (3) *diakonia* (the implementation of the faith in loving service). Although pastoral counseling is primarily an expression of *diakonia*, the ministry of service, it is also a means of communicating the gospel and establishing *koinonia*.

DANGERS OF LIFE-SITUATION PREACHING

The preacher must be careful lest he divulge, in his preaching, information that his parishioners have shared with him in confidence. There is also the danger of starting a sermon on the discussion of a problem for which the sermonizer has no solution. As he deals with a life-situation problem from the pulpit the sermonizer must beware of

---

24. Arthur W. Hewitt, *God's Back Pasture: A Book of the Rural Parish* (Chicago: Willett, Clark & Co., 1941), p. 20.
25. William L. Malcomson, *The Preaching Event* (Philadelphia: Westminster, 1968) pp. 115-20.
26. J. Winston Pearce, *Planning Your Preaching* (Nashville: Broadman, 1979), p. 76.

handling it inadequately, for to do so might cause far more damage than good. He must remember that to merely talk about a problem does not solve that problem. Instruction and illustration are insufficient without personal application.

The sermonizer must also avoid the tendency to substitute psychology for Christianity. We attend church to hear something about a God who makes sense out of no sense, a God who cares for us in spite of everything, and who says "I love you and forgive you." Instead, the sermon frequently is a psychological dissertation lacking biblical foundation and content. The preacher should beware of setting himself up as a psychoanalyst rather than guiding those with special needs to professional help. He should refer anyone who shows signs of possible neurological disease to a physician.

The preacher's message may be distorted by some emotional need of his own demanding satisfaction. He should ask himself, "Am I preaching on the needs of my people, or on my own needs?" There is always the danger of dealing with a problem that is not actually faced by the local congregation. Too many problem-centered sermons might put problems into people's minds that were not there previously. A listener might begin to imagine the symptoms of the problem under discussion.

Life-situation preaching is an attraction for the preacher; therefore, he should beware lest he fall into the trap of preaching only this type of sermon. Too much of life-situation preaching might force the people to give too little attention to God and His provision for their needs. Because of the abundance of materials available to the preacher from extrabiblical sources that deal with each kind of problem, there is the danger of allowing biblical and doctrinal content to be crowded out of the sermon to the detriment of the congregation. An overemphasis on the problems of life-situation preaching could make the preacher wholly occupied with the issues of time rather than the issues of eternity. He would thereby become merely timely, not timeless.

There is the danger of confusing Christian morality with natural virtue. Such preaching can result in only mild editorializing on a problem, with a religious flavor added. The preacher must never come to the point where he feels that life-situation preaching adequately takes the place of pastoral care. The two go together.

A need exists for studying the Bible in the light of people's problems. The individual who aspires to be a preacher must feel the needs of mankind until such needs become an oppression to his soul. But how can a man preach effectively to people he does not know?

How can he bring the gospel he is commissioned to declare to bear upon experiences with which he is not acquainted? A prerequisite to success in the pulpit is a knowledge of the human heart. The physician must understand, not merely the nature of the remedies that he is to employ, but also the symptoms and workings of the diseases that he desires to cure. He must "walk the hospitals" as well as study the pharmacopoeia.

Healthy prescription always depends on good diagnosis, and a preacher who does not know both the ideal man and the actual man is no more fitted to preach than a physician is to practice who is not familiar with anatomy and physiology, both normal and abnormal.

The gospel is a remedial measure, and therefore, it is essential that its preachers should be acquainted with the nature of man, as well as with the means which, as the instrument in the hands of God's Spirit, he is to use for its transformation and renewal. Hence, he who wishes to become an efficient minister must be a diligent student of people.

The knowledge of mankind may come from many sources—the characters of the Bible, the people whose lives are described in secular history, the characters of secular literature. But the most productive source of all is man himself. To know people deeply, the minister must live among them, observing every phase of human behavior. Only by living close to people can he learn the innermost workings of their minds and know how to take aim with the message of God.

The interpretation of religious truth involves the understanding of the minds to be reached as well as of the truth to be declared. A preacher may have a clear and right understanding of religious truth, but he will still fail in the interpretation of it if he does not know and estimate the state of mind before him. Of the criticisms leveled at the ministry, none is more serious than that which charges that the minister is too preoccupied with books.

Phillips Brooks laid down three rules that bear upon the preacher's need of a knowledge of his people.

These three rules seem to have in them the practical sum of the whole matter. I beg you to remember them and apply them with all the wisdom that God gives you. First, have as few congregations as you can. Second, know your congregation as thoroughly as you can. Third, know your congregation so largely and deeply that in knowing it you shall know humanity.[27]

27. Phillips Brooks, *Lectures on Preaching* (New York: Dutton, 1898), p. 190.

Also, from *The Cure of Souls* we read:

> The minister ought to be soaked in life; not that his sermon may never escape from local details, but rather that, being in contact with the life nearest him, he may state his gospel in terms of human experience.[28]

"The proper study of mankind is man." The preacher will obtain his best material from his reading in human nature. The pastoral and preaching offices are indubitably intertwined. We must know some people to preach to anybody; and we must know our own people to preach to them. We must start where people live, then lead the questioning soul to the doctrinal and biblical sources, instead of the traditional expository type of preaching that spends the first paragraphs explaining the Hebrew and Greek roots while the listeners' minds are in greener pastures. The sermon must arrest the attention of the hearers with a real issue of life.

This preaching does not begin with large religious doctrines and then bring them down to their particular applications. It begins with the living person and his confused but vital impulses; and it explores their possibilities, until at last it shows the frustration of the irreligious life and reveals the great highroads of religious faith.

All preaching, if it is to be genuine preaching, should be to personal needs. It is the transmission of God's truth through a person to a person. Preaching includes instruction, interpretation, and inspiration, but we must be sure to include application. The wise preacher will not only study books but people as well.

THE BIBLE AND LIFE-SITUATION PREACHING

Dr. Jay Adams has provided some helpful guidance for the use of Scripture in counseling, which is also applicable to life-situation preaching.[29] *Moralistic* use of the Scriptures usually involves at least two faults. The first is a failure to show that the intended action must be done, not merely to remove some grief or trouble from the counselee, but primarily to please God. Second, the Scriptures are used moralistically when biblical principles or practices are enjoined to achieve a reformation apart from the saving work of Jesus Christ.

---

28. John Watson (Ian Maclaren), *The Cure of Souls* (New York: Dodd, Mead & Co., 1896), p. 55.
29. Jay Adams, *The Use of the Scriptures in Counseling* (Grand Rapids: Baker, 1975), pp. 89-91.

Illustrational use of the Scriptures consists of prooftexting ideas set forth by the preacher or someone else.

Prescriptional use of the Scriptures reminds us that the Scriptures cannot be given out to a counselee as if they were a magic potion that (understood or not) will do him good. On the contrary, they must be explained and concretely applied to the specific problems he encounters.

The *abstract* use of the Scriptures is closely related to the last error mentioned above. Setting forth principles and truths alone is often insufficient. The counselee usually does not know how to apply them to his life. While it is important to teach principles so that they may be known and later applied in various circumstances, it is essential to show how those principles work in the present.

The proper use of the Scriptures in counseling and preaching is very effective and satisfying, because by such usage one does many things at once. He brings God's sure Word to bear on the listener's problem. He honors God by pointing away from human wisdom to Him. He shows the counselee the rich wealth of information contained in the Bible, thus encouraging him to turn more often to that source. He instructs the listener in the ways and means of personally using the Bible in days ahead. Thus, by the use of the Scriptures problems may be solved and prevented from recurring in the future.

The Preaching Program and Life-Situation Preaching

A minister had a series of life-situation sermons on Sunday evening in a semiresidential, urban area on the general theme of "Good News."[30] The Sunday bulletin announced specific days in which that minister would be available for consultation. The thought was that persons wishing to see him should telephone for an appointment. After the second sermon, and for the remainder of the series, he received many requests for interviews. The notes in the bulletins and the series of messages together were the steps that opened the door for a counseling ministry.

Andrew W. Blackwood said that "in summer more than any other season good people suffer from disorders of the soul."[31] If the pastor takes his vacation during August, then the months of June and July are

---

30. Simon Doniger, *The Application of Psychology to Preaching* (Great Neck, N.Y.: Pastoral Psychology, 1952), pp. 12-13.
31. Andrew W. Blackwood, *Planning a Year's Pulpit Work* (Grand Rapids: Baker, 1975), p. 187.

especially suited to inspirational messages. That is the time for the "pastoral sermon," the name that Blackwood employs for the life-situation sermon, meaning "one in which he employs some portion of the Bible in meeting the needs of the Christian soul."[32] That is a good way to attack the summer slump in a church's program. A series of these messages at that time could be an annual affair.

Pearce suggests eight different plans that a pastor can use in planning his preaching, one of which is preaching to meet people's needs.[33] Because every congregation is made up of diverse characteristics and different needs, the plan of preaching should take those facts into consideration. Pearce suggests a whole year's preaching program based on the people's needs.[34]

Sangster believed that many advocates were too critical of pure exposition. Overly critical advocates may be right in suggesting another approach, but they err "in supposing that their approach is the only one."[35] There must be a balance in the pastor's preaching program, so life-situation preaching must be kept in its place.

> Personal problems can never be the whole staple of a congregation's diet. There are not enough of them (thank God) for fifty-two Sundays each year after year . . . and if there were, they would leave people terribly preoccupied with themselves. Imagine it! No exposition of the Word: no high doctrine; none of the deeper philosophic problems; no evangelism.[36]

The Holy Spirit should be relied on for His part in planning the preaching program. Blackwood has written a "creed of the pastor-preacher," in which one of the statements is: "I believe in prayer for the leading of the Holy Spirit that I may sense the needs of the people in this community, and make ready to meet their needs through the prayers of the sanctuary, and through the preaching of God's Word."[37] Thomas Hywel Hughes has given an excellent treatment of the relationship of the Holy Spirit to preaching, including its planning.[38]

32. Ibid., p. 189.
33. Pearce, pp. 74ff.
34. Ibid., p. 83.
35. William E. Sangster, *The Craft of Sermon Construction* (Grand Rapids: Baker, 1972), p. 121.
36. Ibid., p. 124.
37. Carl F. H. Henry, ed., *Contemporary Evangelical Thought* (Great Neck, N.Y.: Channel, 1962), p. 311.
38. Thomas Hywel Hughes, *The Psychology of Preaching and Pastoral Work* (New York: Macmillan, 1941), pp. 115-22.

COUNSELING AND LIFE-SITUATION PREACHING

The minister as counselor is perhaps the one role in which the relations between religion and mental health are most sharply illuminated. Wayne Oates suggests that helpful messages of comfort, reassurance, inspiration, and teaching can frequently be communicated more effectively through preaching than through counseling.[39] Those who view preaching as counseling are not saying that preaching merely opens the way for subsequent counseling sessions. Nor are they saying that preaching involves wise counsel along with proclamation, exhortation, instruction, and prophetic witness. Rather, they are saying that preaching is fundamentally an act of pastoral counseling.

Many of life's problems are insoluble on their own terms. Triumph comes as a result of the transformation of the person so that he can creatively deal with any situation (Phil. 4:13). Pastoral counseling is rightly understood only in the context of pastoral care. Most ministers who take counseling seriously find that it deepens their preaching. In his Yale lectures on preaching some ninety years ago, Phillips Brooks declared, "The work of the preacher and the pastor really belong together, and ought not to be separated."[40]

In counseling, the relationship between counselor and counselee communicates the love of God. In preaching, that same love of God is announced in a clear, decisive proclamation. Thus, pastoral counseling and preaching communicate the same reality, but preaching does it through the spoken word, while counseling does it through the relationship of counselor and counselee. If the preacher will talk in terms of everyday feelings, habits, aspirations, commonplace life situations, and familiar biblical scenes and sayings rather than in technical formulations of a theological or psychological nature, he can accomplish a great deal to help his people to a better understanding of themselves and better adjustment to each other.[41]

The churches have face-to-face relationships with over 120,000,000 adults and youth—more than any other institution in our society. In the study referred to at the beginning of the chapter, University of Michigan investigators found that fifty-four percent of the Protestants who attend church at least once a week went to a minister when they sought personal help. Even among those who attend church less

39. Wayne E. Oates, *The Christian Pastor*, rev. ed. (Philadelphia: Westminster, 1964), pp. 62-65.
40. Brooks, p. 75.
41. Thomas A. C. Rennie and Luther E. Woodward, *Mental Health in Modern Society* (New York: The Commonwealth Fund, 1948), pp. 262-63.

frequently, 33 percent who went for help chose a clergyman.[42] In light of those findings there is no doubt that ministers occupy a central and strategic role as counselors in our society.[43]

What do preaching and pastoral counseling methods have in common? A good approach to that question is to identify similarities in the sermon and the counseling session. Admittedly, we do not normally think of the sermon and the counseling session as similar. The sermon is public; the counseling session is private. The sermon is delivered to a congregation; the counseling session involves ministry to as few as one parishioner. The sermon regularly is given on a Sunday morning. The counseling session is specially arranged. The list of differences could go on and on. Are there any similarities? Yes. An important similarity, often unrecognized, is that both the sermon and the counseling session have a formal structure. When the minister enters the pulpit to deliver his sermon, the congregation expects to be spoken to for a reasonably predictable period of time. When pastor and parishioner set up a counseling session, they expect to talk together for about an hour and then take their leave of each other. During the sermon, the congregation remains silent while the preacher talks. During the counseling session, pastor and parishioner converse with each other.

In their compendium of pastoral care source material from the pages of church history, William A. Clebsch and Charles R. Jaekle identify four pastoral care functions: healing, sustaining, guiding, and reconciling.[44] Each function has its counseling aspect in that within each, one-to-one or small group relationships are used to help people handle problems constructively and improve their relationships.

Many ministers have experimented with techniques for creating homiletical dialogue, direct feedback, and grass roots congregational involvement. For a number of years, Leslie Weatherhead had a question-and-answer period following his Sunday evening sermon. Post-sermon discussion groups immediately following the service and during the week is a device frequently used. During series of sermons on Christian beliefs, it is also useful to have a five-minute period for question writing immediately after the sermon.

A sermon is group counseling when it communicates to a supportive

---

42. Gerald Gurin, *An Introduction to Pastoral Counseling* (New York: Basic Books, 1960), p. 319. (Some of the respondents had gone to more than one source of help.)
43. Ibid., p. 319.
44. William A. Clebsch and Charles R. Jaekle, *Pastoral Care in Historical Perspective* (New York: Aronson, 1964), p. 33.

religious group the healthy values of the tradition. Many people who have unreliable inner controls need periodic reinforcement of their value structure to help them maintain constructive limits in their behavior.

In his autobiography, Harry Emerson Fosdick describes the focus of effective preaching:

> Every sermon should have for its main business the head-on constructive meeting of some problem which was puzzling minds, burdening consciences, distracting lives, and no sermon which has met a real human difficulty, with light to throw on it and help to win a victory over it, could possibly be futile.[45]

Fosdick recalls the decisive turning point in his own preaching. He had known for some time that counseling could achieve results. He writes: "It was a great day when I began to feel that a sermon could be immediately creative and transforming."[46]

The sermon offers a minister one of his most valuable opportunities to enhance the mental and spiritual health of his people. As in group counseling, effective preaching offers an efficient means of helping a number of individuals simultaneously. From a mental health viewpoint, the sermon has both preventive and therapeutic potentialities. It offers the minister a superb opportunity to communicate the Christian message in a supportive, life-affirming, and growth-stimulating way.

Preaching is proclaiming the good news of transforming love, but the proclamation can be heard only if it is directly related to the dilemmas, problems, and decisions that people face in their daily living. A church should become an island of sanity in our neurotic society, avoiding thing-centeredness and keeping people at its heart.

45. Harry Emerson Fosdick, *Living of These Days: An Autobiography* (New York: Harper & Brothers, 1956), p. 94.
46. Ibid., p. 99.

In our time we have been uprooted from our former homeland, adrift in a mobile and changing society. We are lonely in crowds who seem not to care, pushed to and fro by machines to serve and be served, until we, too, become mechanical. We meet other persons as strangers, but mostly by external contacts passing by or bouncing away as if we were rubber balls. We are hollow men who do not know the inner life of other persons, and so we give attention mainly to the external appearance. Estranged from them or used by them, we are empty within ourselves, lost souls for whom no one seems to care. The need has never been so urgent for someone to care. How can a pastor care for his people in such a world?[1]

1. Paul E. Johnson, "Where We Are Now in Pastoral Care," *Christian Advocate*, 23 September 1965, p. 7.

2

A Historical Perspective

It is difficult to trace the historical roots of life-situation preaching. The title given to such preaching is an invention of the twentieth century, and the clarification of the meaning of the term *life-situation* is difficult. It appears to include several different kinds of emphases.

The authors of this book have chosen to emphasize the matter of preaching on personal problems. When some authors have attempted to comprise a list of life-situation preachers they have included preachers who emphasized ethical preaching, pastoral preaching, and political preaching. A quick glance at the history of preaching gives evidence of those categories. (We should point out here that we do not endorse the theology of all the preachers mentioned below.)

ETHICAL PREACHING

Ethical preaching was characteristic of the Moderates, a liberal party of the Scottish church in the late seventeenth and early eighteenth centuries. "They dwelt upon self-improvement and the development of moral virtues and civic righteousness."[2]

Webber points out that "at recurring intervals it has been the fashion of the day to preach sermons that are entirely ethical, and when little or nothing is said with regard to sin and salvation."[3] One such man who appeared during the eighteenth-century Evangelical Awakening in Scotland was James Robe. He "sought to bring about an improvement in the lives of the people by preaching sermons on good conduct."[4]

2. F. R. Webber, *History of Preaching in Britain and America*, 3 vols. (Milwaukee: Northwestern Publishing House, 1953), 2:200 (see also p. 204).
3. Ibid., 2:215.
4. Ibid., 2:221.

Webber shows that "the same disregard for evangelical truth that was known as Moderatism in Scotland, had its equivalent in Ireland and England."[5] John Abernethy is cited as one example of that tendency in Ireland. In his preaching "one finds a disproportionate attention to the ethical and a neglect of the evangelical element."[6]

In the late eighteenth century, after the Great Awakening in America, "there was more of an ethical note in the average sermon than there had been in the past."[7] After the American Revolution there was a notable development in American preaching.

> In many instances there is less doctrinal preaching, and rather there is an indication of stress upon the ethical and practical. The American pulpit, which had always been influenced by Europe, is beginning to make a contribution of its own to the history of preaching, and an American style is in the process of development.[8]

That development was carried well into the nineteenth century by such men as William E. Channing and Russell Bigelow.[9]

EARLY ETHICAL PREACHERS

Clement of Rome (A.D. 30-100). Clement is remembered for his ethical preaching. He provided through his preaching consolation for those in the midst of trials.

Quintus Tertullian (A.D. 150-220). Tertullian gave beautiful treatises on moral and spiritual subjects. His messages on patience and penitence were especially noteworthy.

POLITICAL PREACHING

The issue of slavery in the mid-nineteenth century made political preachers out of many. In the years prior to the Civil War, Webber sees a renewed emphasis.

> During colonial days, doctrinal preaching was the rule. . . . Sermons in condemnation of slavery became common after the Revolution. . . . During the anti-slavery controversy, which reached a critical stage

5. Ibid., 2:625.
6. Ibid., 2:625-26.
7. Ibid., 3:80.
8. Ibid., 3:135-36.
9. Ibid., 3:198ff.

between 1840 and 1860, the old prejudice against the "preacher in politics" began to break down. . . . During the anti-slavery agitation, a precedent was established which was to lead, before the end of the century, to the crusading type of clergyman, and his vigorous denunciation of national and municipal corruption. The Christian pulpit, which had limited itself so largely to spiritual interests, was in a period of transition, and the immediate problems of local, national and world politics were destined to become frequent subjects of discussion.[10]

POLITICAL PREACHERS

Cotton Mather (1663-1728). Mather preached on social and personal issues. He is especially remembered for his emphasis on political morality.

Henry Ward Beecher (1813-1887). Beecher is remembered for his preaching against the social vices of his day. He was also a leader in the anti-slavery movement. His sensitivity to the feeling of his audience prompted him, on many occasions, to preach to their personal needs.

Louis Bourdaloue (1632-1704). Bourdaloue was one of the great French preachers. His preaching on moral issues was interspersed with heavy logic. His preaching against the practices of the French court made a strong assault on the conscience of the listeners.

PASTORAL PREACHING

PASTORAL PREACHERS

Berthold of Regensburg (1220-1272). Berthold was a practical German preacher who attacked the sins of all classes during the period of a great interregnum in Germany. He made use of dialogue and honestly attempted to preach to people's needs.

John Wycliffe (1329-1384). Wycliffe is remembered as a practical preacher who gave himself to the care of souls.

Jacques Saurin (1677-1730). Saurin preached practical sermons that were directed to the heart, aimed at regulating the actions of life.

10. Ibid., 3:325-26.

Charles Jefferson (1860-1937). Jefferson believed that his mission was to the sick. He recognized, however, that all sick people are not afflicted with the same sickness, and therefore, all do not require the same treatment. He entered into the great realm of pastoral service. He was convinced that there were many cases of arrested religious development, instances of moral paralysis, and attacks of spiritual prostration. He felt that many of those cases could be relieved and cured if the minister had a better understanding of the nature of the soul and the remedies offered to human minds in Jesus Christ.

Walter Russel Bowie (1882-1968) was a representative of those men who used the Bible to give understanding and meaning to life. He felt an inner compulsion to know each individual of his congregation. It was his conviction that when a preacher is preparing a sermon, every thought that passes through his mind ought to be warmed by the recollection of those who may be listening to what he says. It was his practice as pastor to go to the church sanctuary during the week and to kneel by the pews and pray for the ones who would be sitting there at the next worship service. He was convinced that a pastor should always keep in mind what the message will mean to his people when preached to them.

Phillips Brooks (1835-1893). Brooks believed that the work of the preacher and pastor ought never to be separated. They are not two tasks, but one. He was extraordinarily sensitive to human needs. That was evidenced by the way he spent his afternoons— calling upon his people, especially the poor, the sick, and the troubled. On one occasion, he said that he wished he could do nothing else but make pastoral calls. When people were in trouble, he would go and sit with them for hours, listening to them talk. Not only did he go to the people, but they came to him from near and far in great numbers. They came with personal problems, family problems, and religious problems, seeking counsel, comfort, and advice. His home was a refuge for all who were troubled. He once stated that if he could not see people individually, he could not preach, for his sermons dealt with life. Lord Bryce said of him: "He speaks to his audience as a man might speak to a friend."

Horace Bushnell (1802-1876). Bushnell was a faithful pastor. Through his preaching, writing, and personal counseling he was able to help many find faith in Christ. He frankly admitted that pastoral work was difficult for him. Nevertheless, he sensed its importance, cultivated its art, and in spite of all his writings and other activities, never neglected it. He only wished that he could have devoted more time to it. It was his heart's desire to know all his people personally. He made it his aim to visit them all at least once a year. It was his custom for many years to spend one evening a week at his church office where he was available to anyone who wished to consult him about any personal or religious matter.

LIFE-SITUATION PREACHING

Life-situation preaching by name is a fairly recent kind of preaching. In one sense, preachers have always been concerned with the needs of men. The gospel is designed for such needs. Charles F. Kemp argues that the great interest in the 1940s and 1950s in this kind of preaching was caused by the pastoral psychology movement, which was due to the development of the psychological and sociological studies of man, and resulted in a growing interest in counseling. Pioneer work in this field was done by such men as Richard Cabot, Russell Dicks, Anton Boisen, Seward Hiltner, and others. Preachers began to see the sermon as a tool with therapeutic value, if applied to the problems of the people in the pew.

A survey of sixty-eight homiletics textbooks, written by American-born teachers of homiletics between 1834 and 1954, indicated that the life-situation sermon *per se* was not referred to in those texts prior to 1944. It also pointed out that the four outstanding books dealing with this kind of preaching were: *In the Minister's Workshop*, by Halford Luccock; *The Preparation of Sermons*, by Andrew Blackwood; *You Can Preach*, by Gerald Jordan; and *Preaching Angles*, by Frank Caldwell.[11]

Halford Luccock, in his book *In the Minister's Workshop*, says that the life-situation sermon originates in the experience of the people to whom it is preached, with the specific aim of bringing help to their life situation. This whole approach has a close kinship to the dictum of the Dewey pedagogy that thinking begins with a felt difficulty.

In the Dewey method there are five steps: (1) a felt difficulty, (2) location and definition of that difficulty, (3) suggestions of possible solutions, (4) development of suggestions by reasoning, and (5) further

11. Lloyd M. Perry, "Trends and Emphases in the Philosophy, Materials and Methodology of American Protestant Homiletical Education as Established by a Study of Selected Trade and Textbooks Published Between 1834 and 1954" (Ph.D. dissertation, Northwestern University, 1961).

observation and exploration leading to acceptance or rejection of the selected solution. Preaching that begins with problems bothering people or the predicaments they are in follows this model most noticeably by beginning with a felt difficulty. Preaching that begins with life situations and is carefully aimed at them starts with the great initial advantage that there is a present need.

The first few decades of the twentieth century have seen a proliferation of life-centered preaching.[12] In fact, Webber says that "in our day it has become the fashion to discuss personality problems in the pulpit."[13] He intimates that this trend has been aided by liberal higher criticism of Scripture.[14] Webber advances the thesis that there are periods of spiritual advancement and decline in the history of preaching.[15] If a chart of this advance and decline were made[16] it could be predicted that, as a general rule, the prominence of life-situation preaching would be at a time when there was a dip in the chart.

Ronald E. Sleeth, in *Proclaiming the Word*, suggests further causes for this fairly recent shift in American preaching.[17] Two articles in *Baker's Dictionary of Practical Theology* also suggest that life-situation preaching is especially prominent in our age.[18]

LIFE-SITUATION PREACHERS

John A. Hutton (1848-1947). Hutton preached counseling from psychology, although the field was new. He was a skilled spiritual analyst and was able to search the hearts of his listeners and reveal their sinfulness in a manner most terrifying.

Harry Emerson Fosdick (1878-1969). Fosdick was a minister of life-situation preaching. It was his conviction that every sermon should have for its main business the solving of some important problem that was puzzling minds, burdening consciences, or distracting lives. On Saturday morning, he would sit down in his study and rethink his whole sermon as if the congregation were visibly before his eyes. He would often pick out individuals or groups of individuals, and imaginatively try his course of thought on them. He said, "Somewhere in this

12. Webber, 3:612, 615-16, 622.
13. Ibid., 3:653-54 (see also 2:153).
14. Ibid., 1:616.
15. Ibid., 3:619.
16. Ibid., 2:650.
17. Ronald E. Sleeth, *Proclaiming the Word* (Nashville: Abingdon, 1964), pp. 91ff.
18. Ralph G. Turnbull, ed., *Dictionary of Practical Theology* (Grand Rapids: Baker, 1967), pp. 17, 55.

congregation there is one person who desperately needs what I am going to say. O, God, help me to get at him." Through the years, he combined an effective counseling program with great preaching.

Norman Vincent Peale (1898-   ). Peale limits his sermons to personal problems.

Jack Finegan (1908-   ). Finegan spent most of his life in a university atmosphere, in contact with students. He held many private interviews with students and dealt honestly and fairly with the issues they faced. He also wrote and published many books and articles that were geared to meet the needs of young people.

The late Dr. John Osborn, one of the leaders of the Seventh Day Adventist denomination, did a special research project on the history of preaching in an attempt to determine the prevalence of life-situation preaching. There were seven preachers that he felt should be added to the list already given.

Albert W. Beaven (1892-1943). Beaven developed what he called "preventive preaching." This kind of preaching enabled him to reach many who would never have come to his study for a private conference. It was of special interest to the younger people of his congregation. Many of them were willing to let him help them solve their problems of the home and marriage. Every year, for fourteen years, he preached a series of what he called "fireside sermons." Those messages dealt with issues centered on the home. It was his philosophy that it is wise to provide help before difficulties arose. He made use of questionnaires distributed to the members of his congregation in which he asked such questions as, "What in your judgment is the great element making for happiness in home life?" In response to that particular question, the majority said that religion lived daily in the home was the greatest element.

John Sutherland Bonnell (1893-   ). Bonnell combined his public preaching ministry with an extensive program of personal counseling. As a leader in the pastoral psychology movement he used the resources of both psychology and religion. His philosophy might be summarized by the assertion that it is in the Christian gospel that one can discover the secret of living victoriously in an age of pressure, fear, and tension. As a young man he served as an attendant in the wards of a mental hospital of which his father was superintendent. That experience provided an apprenticeship for the ministry and led him into the field where psychology and religion can be united in ministering to people.

Robert McCracken (1904-1973). McCracken stated that all sermons should come to grips with the religious and moral difficulties confronting men and women in the modern world. He felt that his first business as a preacher was to seek answers for the people's problems with biblical revelation being the constant point of reference and direction. His writings and sermons grew out of his everyday contact with people and their problems.

Ralph Sockman (1859-1970). Sockman expressed his point of view in these words: "It has been said that science has added years to our lives. It is the task of the church to add life to our years." Through radio preaching and numerous books he extended his influence far beyond his parish. His philosophy of pastoral ministry was: "The preacher will prepare his sermon with the needs of his people in mind." In his preaching he provided special help for those members of his congregation who were a bit older. It was his conviction that to prevent an introspective self-centeredness and preserve the full orb of the Christian message, life-situation preaching should be blended with Bible exposition and doctrinal preaching.

Leslie Weatherhead (1893-1976). Weatherhead was the well-known pastor of the City Temple Church in London. He is recognized as one of the pioneers in the study of the relationship of psychology and religion. He conducted a psychological clinic in connection with his church in London in which he used medicine and psychotherapy along with the resources of religious faith.

In addition to those above, there have been several others in the course of the history of preaching who have been recognized for making additional contributions to what we now call life-situation preaching. A survey of the sermons preached by Charles Reynolds Brown (1862-1950), Arthur Gossip (1873-1954), F. W. Gunsaulus (1856-1921), Hugh Latimer (c. 1485-1555), and George W. Truett (1867-1944) show that those men preached many sermons dealing with the personal problems of the members of their congregations. That is evident in such sermon titles as "Religious Quitters," by Brown; "How to Face Life with Steady Eyes," by Gossip; and, "The Privilege of and Peril of Opportunity," by Truett.

Neil B. Wiseman compiled a series of nine essays under the title *Biblical Preaching for Contemporary Man.* One of those essays was written by Darrell Luther, pastor of the Detroit First Church of the Nazarene. The essay was entitled *Making Life-Situation Preaching Biblical.* It is interesting to note that this is a twentieth-century attempt to place life-situation preaching within a biblical context. Such an approach is similar to the approach advanced in this book in which the authors attempt to correlate transactional and relational biblical theology.

The emphasis that had been maintained for years on transactional theology gradually diminished, and relational theology came into prominence. It was during that period that Halford Luccock and others developed life-situation preaching. The emphasis on personal problems was also evident in the preaching of preachers to follow who did not carry the life-situation label.

Several devotional and homiletical writers of the twentieth century wrote on personal problems, but avoided the term *life-situation preaching.* Their avoidance may have been due to their desire to avoid stressing relational theology to the exclusion of transactional theology.

Roy L. Laurin was one of those writers who dealt with the themes of life-situation preaching but avoided the label. Dr. Laurin was vice-president and director of the Fuller Evangelistic Foundation and executive vice-president of the board of trustees of Westmont College. He served regular pastorates for twenty years. For fifteen years he was actively engaged in Bible work in Southern California. His book entitled *Meet Yourself in the Bible* consists of twenty-eight devotionals that provide sermonic material for life-situation preaching. Laurin deals with such subjects as the conquest of temptation, the conquest of inferiority, and the conquest of adversity. Another of his books, *Help Yourself to Life*, carries on the same sermonic thrust by dealing with such titles as "How to be Prepared for Life's Crises" and "How to Prepare for Life's Service." He is best remembered for his "Life" series of devotional expositions. They include such titles as "Life Endures" on 2 Corinthians, "Life Begins" on the epistle to the Romans, "Life at Its Best" on 1 John, and "Life Matures," an exposition of 1 Corinthians. His approach is one that can be termed life-situational.

Guy H. King has produced a number of books dealing with life-situation themes. They have been reprinted by the Christian Literature Crusade of Pennsylvania. His book on the epistle of James is entitled *A Belief That Behaves*, and his book on the epistle to the

Philippians is entitled *Joy Way*. A great portion of the devotionals in those books deal with life-situation themes.

Clarence E. Macartney served in the Presbyterian ministry from 1905 until his retirement in 1953. During those years he served as pastor of three great churches: First Church in Patterson, New Jersey; Arch Street Church, Philadelphia; and First Church of Pittsburgh. He was a very prolific writer of messages. Two of his books emphasize what we would term *life-situation preaching*. They are entitled *You Can Conquer* and *Facing Life and Getting the Best of It*. He deals with such topics as "Getting the Best of Fear," "Getting the Best of Loneliness," and "Getting the Best of Anger."

Louis H. Evans was pastor of the largest Presbyterian church in the world, the First Presbyterian Church of Hollywood, California, having more than 6,000 members. One of his books of messages was entitled *Make Your Faith Work*. Those messages were based on the epistle of James. He dealt with such life-situational themes as "How Do You Face Life's Trials?" "Are You Prejudiced?" and "Are You Conceited?"

Batsell B. Baxter served as pastor of several parishes in the Church of Christ denomination. His book entitled *When Life Tumbles In* is subtitled *Conquering Life's Problems*. The following sermon topics indicate his attraction to life-situational themes. He has messages on the "Escape from Guilt," "The Deadening Effort of Frustration," and "The Burden of Guilt."

Christ confronts persons through preachers who, making themselves willing habitations for him, proclaim God's demands and promises no matter what the personal cost may be. That is how the church was planted in a pagan world, renewed in the sixteenth century, empowered to ameliorate social conditions in eighteenth-century England, and enabled to resist, sporadically, the might of the Nazi state. Those critics who argue that preaching is one function of ministry, which, like General Custer on the plains of Dakota, made its last stand at the close of the nineteenth century, are guilty of superficial judgment.[1]

1. Wallace E. Fisher, *Preaching and Parish Renewal* (Nashville: Abingdon, 1966), p. 19.

3

A Theological Perspective

To understand relational theology, it is helpful to contrast it with transactional (or traditional) theology. Transactional theology emphasizes in its preaching and teaching the great transactions of God for and in man (e.g., the cross, the resurrection, Pentecost, justification, and regeneration). Those mighty acts of God demand a response of faith, love, and obedience as well as gratitude. It was on this kind of theology that most older evangelicals were raised.

On the other hand, relational (or interpersonal) theology emphasizes in its preaching and teaching the place of individuals and the quality of their relationships in the four major areas of interpersonal relationships: family, church, work, and community or club. It is concerned with the specific kinds of problems Christians face in their own lives and with their personal relationships. The feeling is that if a Christian is a failure in those relationships, he will be distressed and in turmoil. Bruce Larson states that life is centered in relationships; therefore, the kingdom of God is, in truth, the kingdom of right relationships. In his opinion relational theology is a return to biblical theology, for the incarnation enabled a relationship to take place between God and man whereby we can love God and our brother. Moreover, the Sermon on the Mount makes pleas for a new relationship with God, others, and ourselves.

There are two focuses in this theology. The first is on self. There is a stress on the need for a Christian to understand himself. What is his self-image? What is his personal integrity? What are his personal quirks? Christianity is seen as helping one become a better person. The second focus is on interpersonal relationships (family, church, work, and club or community).

Relational theology originates from a twofold nonbiblical root: Friedrich Schleiermacher and Sören Kierkegaard. Schleiermacher located that which is genuinely religious in the feelings; that is, the feeling of absolute dependence. Kierkegaard's emphasis was on subjectivity and a personal encounter with the Word before being able to speak of it as true.

There are several trends in our modern culture which Bernard Ramm suggests as reasons for the development of relational theology. There has been an enormous increase in psychological and psychiatric knowledge. That has spilled over into the church in several ways, including the development of a small group theory that is ideally suited to the local church. Transactional theology has failed to help people handle their personal problems and the quality of their relationships, while the new humanism has increased in importance, emphasizing persons, authentic living, and freedom from conformity. There has also been new interest in Eastern religions, which emphasize religion as a quality of one's psychological life rather than a belief in fixed doctrine. Classical leaders in the movement of relational theology have been Leslie Weatherhead, Harry Emerson Fosdick, and Norman Vincent Peale. Contemporary evangelical leaders include Keith Miller, Bruce Larson, Paul Tournier, Eugenia Price, and Eileen Guder.

The effect of relational theology is exhibited in the church in several ways. Scripture is used as a *point of departure* for a new understanding of self and others. Small groups are being widely used to "rap" about problems; the emphasis being on interpersonal relations. There is greater concern for the *application* of texts to one's own situation than for the understanding of the *interpretation* of the text. Christian education materials have become more concerned with relationships than with facts of the Bible and meanings of Christian doctrine. There is also a greater emphasis being placed on counseling. Churches will often employ a counseling psychologist whose services are available to all members. Bible conferences now schedule psychologists as speakers. Seminaries and Bible schools have departments of psychology and pastoral counseling.

Relational theology has had both positive and negative influences on the church. On the positive side, there has been an increased appreciation of *both* special and general revelation as a means of communicating God's truth. Those in this movement look to both theology *and* psychology for a better understanding of human beings and their behavior. A new stress on good interpersonal relationships has also been made in the church. The church is to be a loving and caring community concerned about healing hurts and preventing potential problems. Such a community is a good witness to those on the outside! In worship an attempt has been made to get away from what Larson calls "sacred sterility" with the following results. There is an emphasis on fellowship, a willingness to accept something less than functional perfection in worship, and an objection to a special prayer language. Use of modern versions of the Bible is encouraged as well as contemporary music forms. The building is of little importance since the church is the people. The church has the opportunity to minister to the *whole person*. There is a desire, not only to get people into heaven, but also to minister to all the needs and relationships of the whole person. The new emphasis on confession can be healthy as well. Freud's contention that pent-up guilt is damaging is the ground for encouraging confession, thus providing freedom from guilt in the life of the church.

A new emphasis is placed on lay ministry with the acknowledgment that God does not speak through the clergy alone. The lay people are, therefore, encouraged to actively fulfill their functions in the universal priesthood by ministering to one another. This theology is a help to the clergy in that it allows them to be open and honest about their failures. There is no longer a need to build the false appearance of moral and spiritual perfection. The minister can fail and still be a minister. He can even seek help from his congregation.

On the other hand, there are also certain weaknesses or dangers in relational theology. Typically, there is a lack of clarity in the area of authority. For many within this movement, there is a belief in only a limited inerrancy of the inspiration of Scripture. For others, psychology or human reasoning (although not admitted in theory) take precedence over Scripture. For all, experience is of such an importance that it judges or interprets Scripture. Such a hermeneutic leads to subjectivism.

There is also a deemphasis on doctrine, church discipline, and ethics, since relationships are to triumph over those. The church is a *loving* community, not a judging or believing community. However, love without correct doctrine and the means to enforce it will ultimately lead to heresy. For example, Harold Kuhn writes that "this can lead to the danger of a purely relational atonement," and a subjectivistic view of Christ's atoning death.[2] God removed obstacles that are much greater than the attitudes of sinful men and women. The

---

2. Bruce Larson, *The Relational Revolution* (Waco, Tex.: Word Bks., 1976), p. 84.

tendency to hold that acts are neither good nor evil in themselves, but only in relation to the individuals performing them, is destructive and leads to varied views of redemption that differ from historic Christianity.

That the pastor is to "lead from weakness" in this theology overlooks the Bible's teaching that the minister is to exhibit spiritual maturity and be an example. There is no uplifting example; nothing to reach for. All are on the same level, and that level is inevitably lowered. Even in matters of worship there is an imbalance, since relational theology focuses so totally on the personal relationship. There is a failure to emphasize sufficiently the God-centered nature of worship, praise, prayer, and ministry. And a real danger exists that the truth and the God of transactional theology might be lost in the concern for relationships. It must be remembered that with God, relationships are *always* based upon His great acts in history. The emphasis on love (even unconditional love) and grace with the consequent deemphasis on the justice and holiness of God is dangerous. While love and grace are truly attributes of God's nature, they should be understood in the context of God's holiness and justice. God's love never comes at the expense of His holiness and justice.

There is also the danger of allowing our human situation to set the agenda and conclusion instead of God's Word to man. The minister can become a pulpit psychologist rather than a proclaimer of God's Word, with the worship service and the sermon degenerating into group therapy rather than a word from God. Values and ethical norms could become humanistically rather than theologically grounded. We must act the way we do as Christians, not because it is the most helpful way to foster relationships, but because God's Word says so.

In reality, the relational camp (particularly among evangelicals) is not trying to deny the Word of God or bypass it. Instead, it is seeking what they consider a needed balance of more experiential Christianity in contrast to some evangelicals who have all the right doctrine but no emotional response to it. For that concern we should be happy. It shows a sensitivity to the increasing depersonalization of our culture, to the existential value of truth in the Bible, and to the need for all individuals to let the Spirit of God work His truth into the reality of their lives and relationships.

So often the question we ask of Scripture determines the answers we think we receive. Theologians of hope and liberation ask questions about cultural oppression, and then assume that the Bible is concerned with little else. "Human potential" and "self-actualization" psychologists ask questions about human value and self-image, and then assume that the Bible is mainly for help in that area. And on it goes. Relational theology has, in many cases, made the wrong response to those who are concerned with doctrine. Instead of encouraging them to follow through in the work of exegesis to the equally important principlization and application, they have gone too far the other way in making application the end-all. They have cooked the meat of the Word sometimes beyond recognition, only to be left with the mere juices from which to make a soupy broth. Gimmicky methods, theological naivete, indifference, and horizontal narrowness have often shut off the watershed teachings of Scripture.

Seeking to avoid the remoteness, irrelevance, unreality, which are the bane of much biblical exposition,
it [life-situation preaching] starts with people where
they are, which was what Jesus did over and over
again. The point of departure is a live issue of some
kind. It may be personal or social; it may be
theological or ethical. Whatever it is, the preacher
makes it his business to get at the core of the
problem, and, that done, he goes on to work out
the solution, with Biblical revelation, and the mind
and spirit of Christ, as the constant points of reference and direction.[1]

1. Robert J. McCracken, *The Making of the Sermon* (New York: Harper & Brothers,
1956), p. 62.

4

A Homiletical Perspective

The complexity of present-day living presents untold problems. The demand for counseling help, the aversion to facing reality, and the amount of pills and sedatives being taken bear testimony to the abundance of problems. Few would question the need for providing help for those afflicted. Although the need is evident, the provision is limited. There are not enough counselors to go around. The church must face the possibility of doing something tangible about this challenge. The preacher must be aware of the possibilities and limitations of psychology, the contributions that Scripture has to offer, and he must also have a method for presenting that material to his listeners. It is to this question of methodology for presenting counseling help from the pulpit that we address ourselves.

General Structure

Harold W. Ruopp[2] has suggested a pattern for life-situation preaching that merits notice. He writes that the life-situation preacher should build his sermon over this pattern: 1) We are here; 2) How did we get here?; and 3) How do we get out of here?

Point one becomes his introduction in which he defines and describes the situation to be dealt with. He must convey to his listeners that he understands their hurt and that he cares about them. Point two must be thought out by the preacher, and may or may not be mentioned in the sermon itself. Point three must never be omitted. Here he deals with "how" or "the way out," and must give his audience specific suggestions. The solution must be functional.

More than any other individual, Harry Emerson Fosdick influenced

2. Harold W. Ruopp, "Life-Situation Preaching," *The Christian Century Pulpit,* 12 (May 1941):116.

the development of life-situation preaching. He rejected expository preaching, because he felt it did not deal with people's needs. He also rejected topical preaching, which many suggested as an alternative. For forty years his ministry was successful in terms of the crowds who came to hear him preach and the thousands who heard him coast to coast on "National Vespers."[3]

His introductions were successful in making the problem familiar. After identifying the problem in a general and specific way, he would discuss the symptoms or the causes of the problem. His diagnosis included many examples from real life, and suggested the need for a solution. Sometimes he listed the way the problem was commonly handled before he gave a detailed consideration of the most successful solution to the problem. Results were often visualized to help convince one that the solution would work. Each sermon contained practical suggestions. He usually concluded by relating how religious faith was the foundation on which the best solution could be built. However, there was not much gospel or revelation from Scripture in his messages. The Bible was resorted to only for occasional illustrations or bits of philosophy.

Fosdick subordinated his pulpit to his counseling ministry.[4] In his autobiography, he stated that: "Every sermon should have for its main business the head-on constructive meeting of some problem which was puzzling minds, burdening consciences, distracting lives, and no sermon which so met a real human difficulty, with light to throw on it and help to win a victory over it, could possibly be futile."[5]

A complete discussion of the method of Fosdick's "counseling sermon" is given by Edmund Holt Linn.[6] Linn shows how "the need of the listener affects nearly everything about preaching method, content, organization, language and delivery."[7] Fosdick took the position that preaching was an act of counseling. He believed that sermons should try to face the real problems of people. A sermon should help them meet their difficulties, answer their questions, and confirm their noblest faith.

3. Harry Emerson Fosdick, *On Being a Real Person* (New York: Harper & Brothers, 1943), pp. 188-209.
4. John Killinger, *The Centrality of Preaching in the Total Task of the Ministry* (Waco, Tex.: Word Bks., 1969), pp. 54-55.
5. Harry Emerson Fosdick, *The Living of These Days: An Autobiography* (New York: Harper & Brothers, 1956), p. 94.
6. Edmund Holt Linn, *Preaching as Counseling: The Unique Method of Harry Emerson Fosdick* (Valley Forge, Pa.: Judson, 1966), p. 8, n. 3.
7. Ibid., p. 27.

Edmund Linn discussed Fosdick's method by giving the following seven characteristics of the counseling sermon.

1. It should express clear convictions based on personal experience.
2. It should be presented as though it were being given to one person.
3. It should relate to where people are in life.
4. It should deal fairly with objections.
5. It should apply the gospel.
6. It should retain the values of older methods.
7. It should make a directed effort.

If he uses those characteristics the preacher will have to make every effort to learn the personal strengths and weaknesses of his people.[8]

In 1956 Robert J. Hastings preached a series of messages on personal problems at the University Baptist Church in Carbondale, Illinois.[9] He began each sermon with a description of the problem. Occasionally he started with a biblical text. Sometimes he began by examining the problem's evidences or its consequences. In the development of the sermon he considered alternative solutions to the problem. He evaluated each alternative and showed its relative merits, from the worst solution to the best. At other times he made a list of steps or suggestions for overcoming the problem. His sermons were packed with interesting illustrations, but his preaching was sub-Christian and not biblical. His work was an application of psychology to human weaknesses and problems with only passing reference to Scripture.

A contrasting methodology is that of J. Dwight Pentecost. "In the Word of God are the records of men who wrestled with just such problems, and in this volume we look into their experiences. A study of the Word convinces one that 'whatsoever things were written aforetime were written for our learning' and that God has revealed His answer therein."[10] He examines man's problems in the light of God's Word. He analyzes the fears and frustrations of Bible characters, explains the point of Scripture passages, and uses modern-day illustra-

8. Donald Capps, *Pastoral Counseling and Preaching: A Quest for an Integrated Ministry* (Philadelphia: Westminster, 1980), pp. 14-17.
9. Robert J. Hastings, *How to Live with Yourself* (Nashville: Broadman, 1966), pp. 11-60.
10. J. Dwight Pentecost, *Man's Problems; God's Answers* (Chicago: Moody, 1971), p. 9.

tions from real life. He sees man's problems as opportunities for God to build character. He begins by giving a description or a definition of the contemporary situation. He then moves into the Scriptures to seek a solution. A consideration of the causes of the problem is only incidental, for the scriptural antidotes receive his major attention. The solution may be found in one passage of Scripture or in several passages and is given in terms of principles or steps. He sees some of man's problems as the Bible sees them: as sins. He relates his analyses and solutions to the old and new natures within the Christian. The answer to the problem may be found in a study of the life of Christ, the character of God, or a biblical command. His sermons are full of biblical illustrations related to life.

Charles W. Koller taught homiletics in Chicago for many years. During that time he developed a sermonizing methodology that has found wide acceptance with many preachers. He referred to his sermon outline as the basic or foundational outline. This was developed in his work *Expository Preaching Without Notes*. He estimated that after one has been trained in that basic method, about 75 percent of his sermons subsequently preached will follow that pattern.

The basic pattern has undergone several revisions and additions through the years by many homileticians. One of the latest revisions appeared in the book *Biblical Preaching for Today's World*. This basic pattern can be used profitably when preaching on a problem.[11]

Ilion T. Jones argues, "No single type of sermon structure can be specified exclusively as a life-situation sermon. Any sermon, regardless of its form, can be such a sermon if directed to human situations."[12]

The methods should be varied. The life problem that is being addressed should not always be found in the introduction. The way the introduction starts does not determine whether or not a sermon is a life-situational one, but the general aim of the message does. It is possible to accumulate sermon ideas by keeping eyes and ears open to human need.[13]

THE BIBLICAL BASE OF THE SERMON

Preaching that is relevant must speak to life situations, but it must also be biblically based. It must involve itself with analysis of the

11. Lloyd M. Perry, *Biblical Preaching for Today's World* (Chicago: Moody, 1973), pp. 42-63.
12. Ilion T. Jones, *Principles and Practices of Preaching* (New York: Abingdon, 1956), p. 40.
13. Ibid., pp. 230-34.

human situation, illustration of the principles of the gospel in terms of contemporary life, and application of the Word of God to the specific situation. When the accent is on biblical preaching, it is "a healthful corrective of the errors into which topical, life-situation, moralistic preaching drifted."[14]

Many authors are agreed that there must be a biblical approach to life-situation preaching. Killinger believes that Fosdick made a mistake by focusing only on people.[15] There must also be a focus on God. He gives a geometrical description of preaching as an ellipse, not a circle, with the two focuses being God and people. Preaching must be from God for people. Fosdick seemed to be focusing only on people.

J. Winston Pearce would agree with Killinger about the starting point of such sermons:

> The basic and ultimate source of the sermon . . . is God, not the preacher. The preacher is a channel for the message, not its source. The Bible is his text, not the latest book on psychology. This plan of preaching does not dispense with the Bible; it is difficult to think of any kind of preaching that calls for a more constant and skillful use of the Bible.[16]

Dwight E. Stevenson argues that "life-situation sermons and biblical sermons need not—indeed, they cannot—exclude each other."[17]

Our sermons cannot reflect profound knowledge of the first century and abysmal ignorance of the twentieth century. No one can be true to the biblical text and ignore the congregation. The biblical word is never a word in abstraction. It is always a specific word to a specific situation to incarnate His ultimate revelation. However it is done, application to life is essential to proclamation.

According to Sleeth, the main problem with most life-situation preaching is that there is confusion between content and form.[18] Because he believes that such a sermon has a specific content, his approach is in danger of becoming intellectual, analytical, and primarily psychological. As a result, he ends up only giving good advice and

---

14. Kyle Haselden, *The Urgency of Preaching* (New York: Harper & Row, 1963), p. 74.
15. Killinger, pp. 54-60.
16. J. Winston Pearce, *Planning Your Preaching* (Nashville: Broadman, 1967), p. 82.
17. Dwight E. Stevenson, *In the Biblical Preacher's Workshop* (Nashville: Abingdon, 1967), p. 213.
18. Ronald E. Sleeth, *Proclaiming the Word* (Nashville: Abingdon, 1964), p. 98.

not good news. "This approach often fails to confront people with God, and keeps both the problem and solution on the human plane."[19] It is wrong to assume that biblical preaching is exclusive of relevant, person-centered preaching.[20] It is in the Bible that man is confronted with his real problems.

> You will meet people in this Book who have the same hopes and aspirations, the same dilemmas and disillusionments which surge through you. Modern anxieties, uncertainties, and misgivings they experienced too. The difficulties and the blasted hopes which are so commonplace in life today they knew all about. If people want to know how to meet life in times like that, they can go back to find how men and women long ago met life in those same settings.[21]

It is the written Word that God uses in the hearts of people to accomplish His purposes. The Bible teaches this truth (see John 6:63; Rom. 1:16; Titus 3:5; James 1:18; Heb. 4:12).

Locate a passage of Scripture that deals with the problem for which you are seeking a solution. Be sure that the passage has at least one possible solution rather than just a reference to the problem. One of the best ways of locating such a passage is to trace the life of a Bible character. Relive with that Bible character some of his experiences and the problems he faced. This is really one type of biographical preaching.

Examine the context of the incident to discover what brought on the problem. Did the individual bring the problem on himself through his own actions, or was he a victim of circumstances beyond his control? Attempt to classify the problem you have discovered in that Bible character's experience. Is it an economic, sociological, physical, or psychological problem? Is it found in our day? What modern labels have we attached to that problem? Those psychological and sociological labels might include inferiority complex, guilt complex, psychological depression, and so on. If the individual in the Scriptures with the problem were living today, where would he seek a solution? Would he be likely to find a solution through meditation, education, consulta-

---

19. Ibid., p. 96.
20. Ibid., p. 101.
21. Joseph R. Sizoo, *Preaching Unashamed* (New York: Abingdon-Cokesbury, 1967), p. 213.

tion, or reading? Did the solution within the Scripture passage come to the individual out of everyday circumstances, or was there an element of the miraculous involved? Could we rightfully expect a repetition of that miraculous work in our day? What would probably have happened to the individual if a solution had not been found?

The sermonizer will not only want to study the problem that is presented in the passage, but he will also want to make a study of the date, place, author, purpose, and outline of the passage. Such gathering of biblical data is discussed fully in *Biblical Sermon Guide* by Lloyd M. Perry.[22]

We have now surveyed the problem and the passage. Our next step is to organize our material for presentation in a logical, persuasive, and biblical outline. We are going to present the timeless truths found within the biblical problem situation in such a way that the listeners may glean some help toward solving the similar problem they may face.

The Modification Sermon

The problem in the preaching passage should be isolated as the subject for your sermon. Do not include the name of a person or place in your subject because that would detract from its timelessness. The subject should be stated in contemporary terms, but its presence should be self-evident within the passage.

The next step is the delineation of the theme. The theme will indicate the course the message is to follow. It will be in the form of a phrase and will clearly show that the sermon deals with solving the problem noted in the subject.

This kind of preaching is referred to as *propositional preaching* because the next step is to put the theme into a declarative sentence that will be the essence of your sermon. It will affirm that God, through His Word, does provide help to those seeking a solution to the particular problem at hand. It will not state or imply that the sermon is presenting the only cure for the problem or that it is presenting the complete cure. Rather, it will provide help toward a complete solution. Biblical solutions to problems should take into consideration the whole context of Scripture rather than presenting a solution based on one small segment. The proposition has been identified by different writers as the central idea, the statement, the big picture, and the controlling assertion.

22. Lloyd M. Perry, *Biblical Sermon Guide* (Grand Rapids: Baker, 1970), pp. 15-22.

The body of the sermon will include steps to be followed as one seeks a solution. The sermonizer surveys the biblical incident and asks himself, "How did this individual in Scripture discover a solution to the problem at hand?" Were there steps that the individual took or did God make special provisions? Those steps when arranged in logical order provide the framework for the body of the message. They are referred to homiletically as the main points of the message. They should be timeless in nature; therefore, they will not include proper names other than the name of God. The steps composing the solution should be so evident that each can be documented by chapter and verse within the passage. This documentation should be placed after each main point and given to listeners as the message is presented. There must be no question in the minds of the listeners as to the Scripture location of the solution.

Each of the steps that form the body of the message will need elaboration. That is called in homiletics *amplification*. The amplification takes the form of subpoints. The simplest way to amplify the steps is to apply interrogative adverbs and pronouns to the main point. What does the step involve? Why should the step be followed? When should it be carried out? How can it be developed? Where would be a good location to carry out the step?

One might develop the main points of the message by showing how each is related to the biblical incident, how each is related to modern counseling theory, and finally, how each can be applied to daily living.

Illustrations throw light on ideas and concepts. The sermonizer will find excellent illustrative material within the Scriptures. Scripture not only provides a wealth of material, but when illustrations are taken from it, the listeners get an additional exposure to biblical content.

The introduction for this kind of sermon will be longer than a normal introduction. Speech writers have stated that a normal introduction should not be more than 15 percent of the total sermon length. The introduction, however, must establish the logical, psychological, and biblical base for the sermon.

The *logical base* is established as one shows the prevalence of the problem in present society, which will emphasize the need for finding a solution to it. A quick survey of modern books, magazines, and television and radio programs will provide information at this point.

The *psychological base* will present in capsule form some of the proposed solutions that scientists have advocated. The preacher should not offer a solution to a problem until he has become acquainted with some of the secular solutions.

The *biblical base* for the sermon will be established as the context of the scriptural passage is delineated. The scriptural surroundings give validity to the use of a particular text.

As those three bases are presented in the introduction of the message, the listener becomes aware that the problem for which he seeks counsel is one that others face. He notes in the development of the introduction that secular sources have advanced possible solutions. He becomes acclimated to the biblical setting so that he can appreciate the biblical solution.

The best and most comprehensive solution to a problem will have little effect until it is put into real-life experience. The conclusion of the message will challenge the listener to carry out the steps outlined in the body of the message.

We have, to this point, surveyed in simple form that which is developed more minutely and technically in *Biblical Preaching for Today's World.*[23]

THE ILLUSTRATIONAL SERMON

An illustrational kind of message might be used to set forth a solution or series of solutions to a problem. More than one individual in scriptural accounts may have experienced the same problem, and their solutions may have been similar. Each individual's experience would become the basis for a main segment of the body of the message. Homiletically speaking, we would refer to it as the basis for each of the main points of the message. This delineation of a series of incidents would have popular appeal for several kinds of audiences. The preacher must bear in mind that he is preaching to people. The message must be presented in a form that the listeners can grasp. The test of a message is what happens to the listener. Nothing will happen, humanly speaking, unless the message is clear.

There may also be situations in which several individuals faced a similar problem, but the solutions differed. Those different solutions could form the outline of the body of the message. The series of solutions blended together within one message would provide more comprehensive help for a listener facing the same problem, but in varied circumstances.

Preaching should stimulate thinking and discussion. Many sermons attempt to give pat answers without challenging the listeners to use their own logical thought processes and biblical knowledge.

23. Lloyd M. Perry, *Biblical Preaching*, pp. 25-80.

THE DISCUSSION METHOD

Preachers have found that the kind of sermon used must be varied if dialogical preaching is to be effective. Responses on the part of the listener can be stimulated when the preacher discusses a problem in the pulpit by using the problematical kind of message. The discussion method is a problem-solving process based on John Dewey's five-step thinking process.

Ilion Jones saw Dewey's thinking process as the basis for an outline of a life-situation sermon, as suggested at the 1955 meeting of the Association of Seminary Professors in the Practical Fields.[24] Halford E. Luccock[25] and Ronald E. Sleeth[26] see a similar relationship to Dewey's pattern of reflective thinking.

John Dewey identified five steps necessary for a complete act of thought. He made his analysis of reflective thinking in his book *How We Think*.[27] Reflective thinking begins with the recognition of a felt difficulty. The second step is its location and definition. Then come suggestions of possible solutions. Each of the suggested solutions is rationally considered. Finally, further observation and exploration will lead to the acceptance or rejection of the solution.

There are two limits within which all reflection falls. At the beginning is "a perplexed, troubled, or confused situation," and at the close is "a cleared up, unified, resolved situation."[28] Falling between those two limits are the five phases or aspects of reflective thought. Dewey technically calls those: *suggestion, intellectualization, hypothesis, reasoning* (in the narrower sense), and *testing of the hypothesis* by action. The sequence of the five phases is not fixed, and more time may be spent with one than with the others, depending on the problem and the persons involved. Dewey defines reflective thinking as "the kind of thinking that consists in turning a subject over in the mind and giving it serious and consecutive consideration."[29] The function of reflective thought then is "to transform a situation in which there is experienced obscurity, doubt, conflict, disturbance of some sort, into a situation that is clear, coherent, settled, harmonious."[30]

---

24. Jones, p. 107, n. 15.
25. Halford E. Luccock, *In the Minister's Workshop* (New York: Abingdon-Cokesbury, 1944), p. 56.
26. Sleeth, p. 91.
27. John Dewey, *How We Think*, 2d ed. (Boston: D. C. Heath, 1933), pp. 102-18.
28. Ibid., p. 106.
29. Ibid., p. 3.
30. Ibid., p. 101.

James H. McBurney and Kenneth G. Hance have written a textbook that is based on the premise that the five steps in reflective thinking are useful in discussion.[31] Discussion is defined by the authors as "the cooperative deliberation of problems by persons thinking and considering together in face-to-face or coacting groups under the direction of a leader for purposes of understanding and action."[32] They see three kinds of problems: 1) problems of fact dealing with what is true in a given situation; 2) problems of value dealing with what is good, best, or great; and 3) questions of policy, dealing with what should be done in a given situation.[33]

The authors make the following adaptation of Dewey's analysis of the thinking process: *defining and delimiting the problem; analyzing the problem; the suggestion of solutions; reasoned development of the proposed solutions;* and *further verification.*[34] The authors also suggest questions with which those five steps can be developed.[35]

Definition and delimitation of the problem is realized as satisfactory answers are given to such questions as these: What is the problem? What are its limits? What is the meaning of the terms used to state the problem?

Once the problem has been located, the second step in the discussion method is analysis of the problem. The difficulty can be diagnosed with such questions as these: What are the symptoms of the problem? What are its causes? What is the status quo with respect to it? Also at this stage there must be a determination of what is expected of any proposed solution. The authors call that determination "discovery of criteria" or "standards of value." The following questions would help here: What are the purposes, motives, or desires of the persons attempting to solve the problem? What are the criteria by which the hypotheses or solutions are to be measured? What are the values that are operating? What is the priority of those values or criteria? What is the relative weight attached to those values or criteria?

The third step, suggesting hypotheses or solutions, must answer such questions as these: What are the possible hypotheses or solutions to the problem? What is the exact nature of each hypothesis or solution?

Fourth, there is a development or appraisal of the hypotheses or

31. James H. McBurney and Kenneth G. Hance, *Discussion in Human Affairs* (New York: Harper & Brothers, 1950), pp. 65-68.
32. Ibid., p. 10.
33. Ibid., pp. 19-24.
34. Ibid., pp. 10-12.
35. Ibid., pp. 65-83.

solutions. They must be weighed and compared as to their relative merits. That can best be done by asking questions such as these: What will be the consequences of the adoption of each hypothesis or solution? To what extent will each answer the basic question or solve the problem? What is the relation of each hypothesis or solution to the criteria or values? What are the advantages and disadvantages of each? What are their relative merits?

The last step is further verification, answering such questions as the following: What can be done to test the hypothesis or solution concluded to be the best? What practice situation can be devised to test it? In the case of a question of policy, what steps would need to be taken to put the hypothesis or solution into operation?

Those five steps in reflective thinking are said to constitute the logical pattern of discussion from two points of view: as the overall pattern of discussion, and as independent acts of thought within that overall pattern.[36] The authors point out that the sequence of steps is not necessarily to be the same in every instance, nor are they always to be distinct and separate entities in group thought.[37] And so, in discussion as a necessary form of social inquiry, the authors make an adaptation of Dewey's thought process to the solution of problems. It is important in the discussion process for each speaker to give others an idea of what he believes, and why and how he reached his conclusion. McBurney and Hance call this method the empirical method.[38]

Alan H. Monroe also presents a method for deliberative groups based on Dewey's analysis of how we think reflectively when we are confronted with a problem.[39] He acknowledges that this is only one of several possible ways of discussing a problem, and suggests five steps: defining the problem, analyzing the problem, suggesting solutions, evaluating the solutions, and putting the desired solution into effect.

Debate is an ancient form of speech in which persons attempt to speak formally to an issue or proposition in such a way that they are able to win their case by their language, logic, and delivery. A standard debate textbook[40] suggests four principal ways of finding

36. Ibid., p. 68.
37. Ibid., pp. 69-70.
38. Ibid., pp. 205-06.
39. Alan H. Monroe, *Principles and Types of Speech*, 5th ed. (Chicago: Scott, Foresman, 1962), pp. 560-64.
40. Donald H. Ecroyd, "Analyzing the Proposition," in *Argumentation and Debate: Principles and Practices*, David Potter, ed. (New York: Henry Holt, 1954), p. 35.

issues or "bones of contention" that need to be proved or disproved if a debate is to take place. They are: "(1) Define your terms clearly and carefully; (2) Analyze the history of the problem at hand; (3) Examine the motivating forces behind the proposal; (4) Consider what would be the likely results if the proposal were to be enacted." Appropriating these suggestions will enable one to engage efficiently in argumentation and subject development.

In the same textbook various kinds of debate are discussed and outlined. One kind is the problem-solving debate, which is really a combination of discussion and traditional debate. It is an intellectual, cooperative effort to solve a problem as opposed to "winning at all costs."[41] It is not as competitive as other kinds of debate and puts a priority on a scientific approach requiring logical procedure and educationally sound objectives in solving a problem. Analysis of the problem is to be unbiased, and criteria are to be the best possible ones for the problem at hand.

THE MOTIVATED SEQUENCE

One of the speech structures suggested by Alan Monroe is what he calls "the motivated sequence."[42] He sees it as a way of adapting speech organization to the audience's thinking process. He identifies five steps in the motivated sequence: attention, need, satisfaction, visualization, and action.[43] There are striking similarities between his deliberative plan for group discussion and his motivated sequence for individual speeches.

He applies all five steps of the motivated sequence to persuasive speeches with an end to stimulate, convince, or move to action. The function of the first step is to get attention that is favorable and leads toward the main ideas of the speech. The function of the second step is to show the need or describe the problem. That can best be done by statement, illustration, or ramification to make the need convincing and impressive to one's audience. The function of the third step is to satisfy the need by presenting the solution. That can be done by statement, explanation, theoretical demonstration, examples from practical experience, or by anticipating objections. Fourth, the results must be visualized to intensify desire. That may best be done by projecting the audience into future conditions. The last step is to

41. Gifford Blyton, "The Problem-Solving Debate," *Argumentation and Debate*, pp. 251-55.
42. Ibid., pp. 280-329.
43. Ibid., p. 283.

request action or approval. That involves translating the desire into an attitude, belief, or action. Those steps correspond to the natural process of thinking.

Monroe claims that "this normal process of human thinking is sufficiently uniform that, in spite of variations in individuals, we can outline a form of speech structure that will conform to it rather closely on nearly all occasions."[44] He believes this sequence should serve as the backbone for all kinds of speeches, "needing only to be modified by omitting or lengthening certain parts according to the particular situation. . . . Speeches constructed on this basis are not sure of success, but they are more likely to be successful than those put together without considering their psychological effect upon the listener."[45]

The following methods of analyzing a problem are helpful in preparation for life-situation preaching. A life-situation sermon might be constructed after the Hegelian method. This would involve three steps. The first should be the statement of the thesis. In this step, the speaker sets up the truth or ideal; the way things ought to be. He then proceeds to the antithesis in which he states the facts of the situation as they appear. The third step is the synthesis in which he gives the process and prospects of transformation. In a sermon this would tell how the truth of God transforms the problem situation into one of promise.

Ilion Jones, in his book *Principles and Practices of Preaching*, has a preaching pattern that might have possibilities for a life-situation sermon. He suggests that the preacher answer four questions: Where are we? How did we get here? Where do we want to go? How do we get there?

Clarence S. Roddy, in his article entitled "The Classification of Sermons," from *Baker's Dictionary of Practical Theology*, suggests some ideas on methodology in life-situation preaching.

> The sermon grows out of a life-situation known to the pastor. It presents an existential problem that calls for a solution from the Word of God. . . . It must always be kept in mind that the solution is not found in the characters involved, but in their "God or Christ." A sample outline might follow this order: (1) Problem or situation; (2) Principle—base of solution; (3) Program—way of doing it. Or we could treat it thus: (1) Where are we? (2) How did we get this way? (3) Where do we go from

44. Ibid., p. 281.
45. Ibid., pp. 282, 301.

here? (4) How do we go? These presented are in principle only, various forms are possible.[46]

The examination of a problem homiletically involves five steps. The first is the definition of the problem. In defining the problem we should establish its limits, discover the meaning of each term, put it in its proper classification, and illustrate it to explain its nature more clearly. The second step involves the analysis of the problem. The difficulty can be diagnosed by noting the symptoms, status, and causes of the problem. This step also includes the discovery of the standards of value at work. What are the motives of those trying to solve the problem? What values are operating in this search for a solution? The third step outlines some of the possible modern solutions for the problem. The fourth step includes reasoned development and appraisal of the suggested solution, and it will include a consideration of the consequences that would result if the hypotheses were followed. The final step involves setting up a practice situation for testing the hypothesis.

Our task at this point is to formulate a sermon structure that will stimulate a consideration of a problem along those five steps and yet will lead toward a scriptural solution. Various portions of Scripture might be combined to provide a possible solution to the problem. The danger with that kind of approach, however, centers in the possibility of taking texts out of their contexts. It may lead one to mere prooftexting. To avoid such temptations, locate one passage that provides help toward the problem's solution.

Biblical preaching has several unique purposes that distinguish it from the general discussion of a problem in secular terms. The discussion process has, therefore, been adjusted to meet the needs of the biblical sermon. The outstanding feature of change is the special emphasis placed on the biblical solution to the problem.

THE INVESTIGATION SERMON

There are eight steps to follow in the process of forming an investigation sermon.

Step One: Determine the subject
Step Two: Select a theme
Step Three: Formulate a proposition

---

46. Ralph G. Turnbull, ed., *Baker's Dictionary of Practical Theology* (Grand Rapids: Baker, 1967), p. 61.

Step Four: Establish a transitional sentence
Step Five: Develop main divisions
Step Six: Amplify main divisions into subdivisions
Step Seven: Formulate an introduction
Step Eight: Formulate a conclusion.

We now proceed to identify and exemplify each of these steps.

DETERMINE THE SUBJECT

The *subject* is the broad or general problem area. In an outline based on 1 Kings 19, the subject would be "discouragement."

SELECT A THEME

The *theme* combines with the subject a limitation that indicates the particular emphasis of the sermon. The theme will always be a phrase. In our present illustration, the theme would be "overcoming discouragement."

FORMULATE A PROPOSITION

The *proposition* is interrogative in form because it states the problem for which a solution, cure, or answer is sought. This interrogative sentence should be concise and clear. It is the core of the entire sermon. The proposition for the example that we are developing might be, "How can a Christian overcome discouragement?" The proposition appears on the sermon outline as Roman numeral IV (see investigation sermon outline).

ESTABLISH A TRANSITIONAL SENTENCE

The fourth step in the process of construction is the establishment of a *transitional sentence*. The transitional sentence will transform the interrogative proposition into a declarative statement. The sentence will also include an interrogative or interrogative substitute and a key word. That means the transitional sentence for an investigation sermon will include the same elements as any transitional sentence used in the modification sermon discussed earlier in this chapter. It emphasizes that the fourth segment of the investigation outline is a modification sermon in miniature. An example of a transitional sentence that might be used in a sermon based on 1 Kings 19 is "A Christian can overcome discouragement by following the steps outlined in 1 Kings 19:1-18." The transitional sentence appears in the final sermon outline immediately after the proposition and explanation.

Before going further let us view the first four steps of sermon construction and their relationship to one another.

Subject: Discouragement
Theme: Overcoming Discouragement
Proposition: How can a Christian overcome discouragement?
Transitional Sentence: A Christian can overcome discouragement by following the steps outlined in 1 Kings 19:1-18.

DEVELOP MAIN DIVISIONS

We turn now to the second group of steps. Step five involves the formulation of the main points. Because this investigation procedure has been patterned after the discussion method employed in secular speech work, we have designated the number and nature of the points to be included in this outline. There will always be four main points and each of those will be given in the form of a question.

   I.   What is the problem?
  II. How prevalent is the problem?
 III. What have been some of the proposed solutions to the problem?
 IV. The interrogative proposition.

AMPLIFY MAIN DIVISIONS INTO SUBDIVISIONS

The sixth step in sermon construction involves the amplification of the main points, and thereby, determining the subpoints (arabic numerals).

What is the problem? The first main point can be developed by defining, limiting, and diagnosing the problem. The definition of the problem might be by negation, classification, etymology, context, illustration, or by giving synonyms. The limitation of the problem might come because of the character of the audience, the occasion, or the possible area of its application. The problem might be diagnosed by giving symptoms, causes, and effects. As part of this point, the sermonizer must be certain that there is a concise statement of the problem given.

How prevalent is the problem? As the sermonizer expands and develops this point, he will note the prevalence of the problem in reading, listening, and in the working experiences of the preacher and his people. The development will then show the occurrence of the problem in Scripture as a whole and in specific sections of Scripture. By giving specifics, the sermonizer is attempting to establish an evident need for dealing with the problem.

What have been some of the proposed solutions to the problem? This can be developed by giving at least two solutions advanced by extrabiblical sources. The source, nature, and sponsor of each proposal should be noted. That will enable the listener to study more at a later date if he so desires. It will also show the listener that the preacher has done some research on the problem. A fair evaluation of each extrabiblical solution and proposal will be given by the sermonizer. The sermonizer should seek to formulate an identifying label for each proposal.

The interrogative proposition. This presents the problem in interrogative form, which sets the stage for seeking a solution within the Scriptures. The sermonic explanation should appear in the outline between the proposition and the transitional sentence. That explanation serves to orient the listener to the relationship of the passage to the problem. The transitional sentence, as described previously, appears after the explanation. Each of the subdivisions within that main point should be characterized by the key word that appears in the transitional sentence. The amount of development listed under each subdivision will depend on the amount of time at the disposal of the preacher.

FORMULATE AN INTRODUCTION

The seventh step to be developed in the process of preparation is the *introduction*. There will be a strong emphasis on the presence of the problem in the daily experience of the listeners and the preacher. What prompted the preacher to give consideration to that particular problem as the basis for the sermon? Is the problem receiving national attention? Have magazines and newspapers been dealing with it recently? The introduction should be concise and specific. A visual aid may be used at this point by bringing an actual news item into the pulpit for reading. In this kind of sermon, the introduction could be formulated earlier in the sermonic process.

FORMULATE A CONCLUSION

The eighth step is the formulation of the *conclusion*. It will emphasize the applications and general development of the fourth main point of the message, which includes the biblical approach and proposals for a solution, cure, or answer to the problem. The listener should face a decision at this point. He should be challenged to put the biblical solution, cure, or answer into practice. Arthur L. Teikmanis has suggested that authentic preaching is a celebration of God-given victory over the crises of life.[47] The victory is always from God. The preacher should make certain that God gets the glory for providing the cure.

SERMON OUTLINES

Two sample sermon outlines have been included. The first sermon is based on the modification process. This kind of sermon would be especially suited to the traditional, biblically oriented congregation. The second sermon makes use of the investigation process. It will be especially useful when facing a university audience or professionally oriented audience or congregation, for they have been conditioned to consider a discussion approach to problems. Please note that the body of the modification sermon in condensed form is the substance of the fourth main point of the investigation sermon.

MODIFICATION SERMON OUTLINE

Subject: A Guilty Conscience
Preaching Portion: Genesis 32:24-32
Theme: Curing a Guilty Conscience
Sermonic Process: Modification

GOD'S CURE FOR A GUILTY CONSCIENCE

Introduction: "There is no worse suffering than a guilty conscience and certainly none more harmful" (Paul Tournier).

1. "Conscience makes cowards of us all" (William Shakespeare, *Macbeth*).
2. "Most of the cases of mental derangement of a functional type are due to a sense of guilt" (a physician quoted by Harry Emerson Fosdick in *The Secret of Christian Living*).

---

47. Arthur L. Teikmanis, *Preaching and Pastoral Care* (Englewood Cliffs, N.J.: Prentice-Hall, 1964), p. 17.

Scriptural Setting:

1. Genesis orientation and a guilty conscience
2. Guilty conscience and general scriptural context

Proposition: We can appropriate God's cure for a guilty conscience.
Transitional Sentence: We can appropriate God's cure for a guilty conscience by following these four steps.

I. RECOGNIZE THE LIMITATIONS OF THE PHYSICAL
(Genesis 32:25: "And when he saw that he had not prevailed against him, he touched the socket of his thigh; so the socket of Jacob's thigh was dislocated while he wrestled with him.")
1.
(Illustration)
2.
3. (Application)

II. REFUSE TO LEAVE WITHOUT THE BLESSING
(Genesis 32:26: "Then he said, 'Let me go, for the dawn is breaking.' But he said, 'I will not let you go unless you bless me.'")
1.
2.
(Illustration)
3.
4. (Application)

III. RECOGNIZE YOUR TRUE CONDITION
(Genesis 32:27: "So he said unto him, 'What is your name?' And he said, 'Jacob.'")
1.
(Illustration)
2. (Application)

IV. RECEIVE YOUR EVIDENCE OF TRANSFORMATION
(Genesis 32:28: "And he said, 'Your name shall no longer be Jacob, but Israel; for you have striven with God and with men and have prevailed.'")
1.
2.
3. (Application)
(Illustration)

Conclusion: We should appropriate God's cure for a guilty conscience. (Gen. 32:31: "Now the sun rose upon him just as he crossed over and Penuel, and he was limping on his thigh.")

INVESTIGATION SERMON OUTLINE

The investigation outline gives three-fourths of its coverage to the secular nature, background, and development of the problem. Only about one-fourth of the coverage pertains to solutions as found in the particular Bible passage. The investigation sermon structure presents the same biblical solution as the modification process, but in a more condensed fashion.

Subject: A Guilty Conscience
Preaching Portion: Genesis 32:24-32
Theme: Curing a Guilty Conscience
Sermonic Process: Investigation

GOD'S CURE FOR A GUILTY CONSCIENCE

Introduction: "There is no worse suffering than a guilty conscience and certainly none more harmful" (Paul Tournier).

   1.
   2.

I. WHAT IS THE PROBLEM?
   1. Guilt is the dread of the past—anxiety is dread of the future.
   2. Kinds of guilt
      a. Legal guilt
      b. Theological guilt
      c. Psychological guilt
   3. What are its limits, effects and possible causes?
II. HOW PREVALENT IS THE PROBLEM?
   1. In present-day living
   2. In history
   3. In Scripture
III. WHAT HAVE BEEN SOME OF THE PROPOSED CURES FOR THE PROBLEM? List two or three cures from other than Scripture and give the source, proponent, nature, and evaluation of each.
IV. HOW CAN A CHRISTIAN APPROPRIATE GOD'S CURE FOR A GUILTY CONSCIENCE?

Scriptural Setting: Genesis 25:24; 27:22; 32:6-8; 32:11-13, and 32:24.

Transitional Sentence: A Christian can appropriate God's cure for a guilty conscience by following these four steps in Genesis 32:24-32.

1. Recognize the limitations of the physical. "And when he saw that he had not prevailed against him, he touched the socket of his thigh; so the socket of Jacob's thigh was dislocated while he wrestled with him" (Gen. 32:25).
   (Insert subpoints)
2. Refuse to leave without the blessing."Then he said, 'Let me go, for the dawn is breaking.' But he said, 'I will not let you go unless you bless me'" (Gen. 32:26).
   (Insert subpoints)
3. Recognize your true condition. "So he said to him, 'What is your name?' And he said, 'Jacob'" (Gen. 32:27).
   (Insert subpoints)
4. Receive your evidence of transformation. "And he said, 'Your name shall no longer be Jacob, but Israel; for you have striven with God and with men and have prevailed'" (Gen. 32:28).
   (Insert subpoints)

Conclusion: We should appropriate God's cure for a guilty conscience. (Gen. 32:31: "Now the sun rose upon him just as he crossed over Penuel, and he was limping on his thigh.")

Part 2

A Counseling Perspective

There are fewer than 40,000 credentialed therapists in the nation. Mental health professionals are increasingly aware of the fact that local clergymen can be valuable allies in facing the tremendous counseling challenge. Family physicians also assist in carrying a large portion of the counseling load. Spiritual health and mental health are inseparably related.

Churches have always been major contributors to personality health. Karl Menninger observed, "Religion has been the world's psychiatrist throughout the centuries." John H. Jowett, in his book *The Preacher: His Life and Work*, recommended a "ministry of sympathetic listening."[1] He observed that ministers are word-oriented. Jowett felt, however, that more people need our ears than our voices. The counseling pastor should listen while involved in the ministry of visitation so that he can constructively provide help through his ministry of preaching.

There is a tendency to bypass the needs of parishioners who are wrestling with personal problems by either applying some sugary syrup or offering some sour comments. Theodore Heimarck, in his book *Preaching for Tethered Man*, lists some of the unfortunate attitudes of preachers that are discovered by parishioners who come to them for help. Some of the comments offered to those who come with problems are:

1. You should know better.
2. If you had stayed away from the wrong crowd, you wouldn't be in trouble.

---

1. John H. Jowett, *The Preacher: His Life and Work* (New York: George H. Doran, Co., 1912), p. 188.

3. Common sense would have prevented this trouble.
4. The right kind of discipline would have straightened you out.
5. You got what you deserved.
6. You were weak and easily led.
7. You're only trying to get sympathy.
8. Why don't you snap out of it?
9. You must have had a lack of good spiritual training.
10. A good lecture will straighten you out . . . this happened to me . . . let me tell you.
11. Why didn't someone help you long ago?[2]

Such comments as those merely compound the problem rather than guide toward a solution.

In his book *Pastoral Care: A Thematic Approach*, Donald Capps suggests that there are four elements in a counseling session. They include:

1. Identification of the counselee's problem.
2. Reconstruction of the problem. In this stage, various facets of the problem are explored.
3. Diagnostic interpretation. In this step, the counselor discusses with the counselee the negative and positive features. This does not need to be highly complex or technical.
4. Pastoral intervention. At this point, a plan or strategy is developed to deal with the problem.[3]

This particular section provides help in identifying personal problems by noting the various facets of a problem and some of the negative and positive aspects of it.

2. Theodore Heimarck, *Preaching for Tethered Man* (Minneapolis: Augsburg, 1962).
3. Donald Capps, *Pastoral Care: A Thematic Approach* (Philadelphia: Westminster, 1979), chap. 3.

It is significant, if not sinister, to note how the number of problems increase as the range of interest narrows from God to society, to family, and then to self. . . . Truly it would seem that we human beings are like tethered animals grazing around the stake of self and shortening our range by wrapping the tether more repeatedly around the ego. ("In order to prevent an introspective self-centeredness and preserve the full orb of the Christian message, life-situation preaching should be blended with biblical exposition and doctrinal teaching. . . . Yet instead of reducing the 'power from on high' to the scale of petty concerns, it leads us to the 'secret place of the Most High' where we abide 'under the shadow of the Almighty.' From the vantage point of spiritual altitude we look down on many an anxiety which had been attacking us. In the company of Christ we are lifted out of our littleness and emptied of our egoism.")[1]

1. Ralph W. Sockman, *The Highway of God* (New York: Macmillan, 1942), pp. 121ff.

5

Anxiety

All morning I have been in an emotional slump. On a scale of 1 to 10, my power of concentration would deserve a 2. I can't seem to keep my mind in one place long enough to get anything done. Thoughts travel on the surface of my mind like a monster meandering haplessly across a video game screen that I am unable to control. My mental condition infiltrates my body. On impulse, I rise from my desk and rush into the kitchen. I am almost surprised to find myself there, pouring another cup of coffee. A book on the kitchen table catches my wandering eye. I open it and find myself reading, even though the command center in my brain is telling me to get back to the typewriter. It is as if that ruler inside my head has lost his power. He cannot seem to give his orders with sufficient authority to make me respond. All of this is happening because I am tired and anxious. Deadlines threaten me. I have to prepare several courses for the next quarter; there are administrative projects, speaking engagements to prepare for, and on and on.

Anxiety is a typical human problem. It has been called the official emotion of our age, and the basis of all neuroses.[2] It gnaws at all of us, chewing up energies and destroying good feelings. It distracts us, dividing our minds so that concentration flits from place to place like a parakeet let loose in a house.

Sometimes it comes over us in an uncontrollable way, making us freeze in our tracks. For some, anxiety lasts for days, weeks, and even years, incapacitating them in their retreat from life itself. Something so pervasive needs a lot of study and attention. Yet, there is no solid agreement about what causes anxiety. And there is even some uncertainty about what it really is.

2. Gary Collins, *Christian Counseling* (Waco, Tex.: Word Bks., 1980), p. 59.

DESCRIBING ANXIETY

Anxiety is an emotion, like fear. In fact, some psychologists do not distinguish fear from anxiety. John Altrocchi describes anxiety as a "painful emotional state marked by disquiet, alarm, or dread and accompanied by some degree of autonomic nervous system arousal." That is the same definition he offers for fear. He maintains that the physical effects of the two are not distinguishable. Those effects are: rapid and unusually strong heartbeat, rapid or shallow breathing, trembling, sweating, muscular tension, dryness of the mouth, changes in voice quality, and faintness. The anxious person may suffer other changes that he cannot even perceive: heightened blood pressure, increased or decreased gastric secretion, and changes in the electrical resistance of the skin.[3] It sometimes creates paralysis and intense headaches.

A high degree of anxiety can shorten one's attention span, make concentration difficult, adversely affect memory, hinder performance skills, interfere with problem solving, block effective communication, and arouse panic.[4]

Although fear and anxiety are alike, psychologists usually distinguish between the two. The term *fear* is used when a person is in the presence of or has the anticipation of some real, often physical, danger. Whenever fear exists without any apparent danger, it is described as anxiety. That and other differences make it profitable to maintain a distinction.

KINDS OF ANXIETY

Anxiety is not easily classified into different kinds. But it does seem to show up in our lives in different ways, making a classification of anxieties useful.

ACUTE ANXIETY

Sometimes anxiety can be acute; it comes quickly and intensely. Its physical and emotional results make it a psychological problem.

CHRONIC ANXIETY

Chronic anxiety, in contrast to acute, is persistent and longlasting, but less intense. Individuals suffering from this kind of anxiety worry much of the time and are especially fearful of any threatening

---

3. John Altrocchi, *Abnormal Behavior* (New York: Harcourt Brace Jovanovich, 1980), pp. 42-44.
4. Collins, p. 60.

situation. The perpetual worrier will often be distracted from his or her obligations and experience other anxiety characteristics, possibly including physical ailments.

Both chronic and acute anxiety are considered abnormal. These conditions involve intense, exaggerated feelings of helplessness and dread, even when the danger is mild or nonexistent. Individuals in those states cannot handle their worry rationally.

GENERAL ANXIETY

We are using the term *general anxiety* to describe the anxious feelings all human beings have simply because they are human. Both psychologists and theologians acknowledge this universal condition. Wallace Kennedy, a psychologist, turns to philosophy to fully explain anxiety when he writes: "Kierkegaard has said that anxiety is the price of being in the world, a natural outcome of being fully conscious of the nature of things."[5] Gordon Jackson calls this "theological anxiety." He describes it almost poetically: "We are not completely comfortable with the stuff of our lives: things, jobs, relationships. We know that rust consumes, thieves break through and steal, the bell tolls. It may toll for a friend, a spouse, for me. I am . . . tomorrow I may not be."[6]

General anxiety is caused by the human state of being helpless. Life consists of one step after another. Each step is filled with threat. Around the corner may be danger, even death. We are always being propelled into the future. Growing old is itself threatening. A woman who no longer counts her birthdays is trying to handle that threat by denial. Seen in this way general anxiety is caused by the act of living itself, since life must continually go on. Its continuance is filled with threat to self and existence. For that reason some call it "existential anxiety."

We might expect that something so pervasive as anxiety might be basic to psychology's view of mankind and central to a theological understanding of the human condition. If so, the concept of anxiety may provide the organizing principle in a biblical psychology. Anxiety could then be seen as the basic dilemma and disorder of all people. Both psychologists and theologians have made anxiety central to their system of thought. Although this approach may not be the final system

5. Wallace Kennedy, "Anxiety in Childhood," *International Encyclopedia of Psychiatry, Psychology, Psychoanalysis, and Neurology*, 12 vols., ed. Benjamin B. Wolman (New York: Aesculapius, 1977), 2:71.
6. Gordon Jackson, "Anxiety and the Church's Role," *Journal of Religion and Health* 14, no. 4 (1975): 231.

for relating biblical and theological truth, it is commendable. It also offers insight for dealing with anxiety as a human problem.

General anxiety is basic to some schools of psychology. Anxiety was a basic ingredient of Freud's thinking. He maintained that it resulted from the built-in, inner conflict in all humans. His view of anxiety was rooted in his portrait of the person. The human personality has three parts: the *id*, which consists of the instincts which yearn for gratification, the *ego*, which is the self in its awareness of the external world, keeping us in touch with reality, and the *superego*, which is the moral sense of right or wrong. Those are always in conflict with one another, producing anxiety, sometimes in a very severe form. When the id gets too powerful, it may threaten to overwhelm the ego and cause a person to act in socially unacceptable ways. For example, a man may suddenly feel homosexual impulses that cause an unexplained anxiety. Unconsciously, he fears he will commit some act that will destroy him. Or, the superego gets so powerful that a person is overwhelmed by guilt and anxiety occurs. In that case, the man with homosexual tendencies may have an unconscious guilt that produces a terrible dread of the future.

Most psychiatrists have departed from Freud's view of anxiety, but they still maintain that anxiety is rooted in the inner rooms of a person's self. Human development, they affirm, is confronting individuals with threatening situations at every turn. Anxiety is a natural reaction to danger, as Freud himself said, and the existence and stability of the ego is constantly being threatened. Psychoanalytic theory attempts to explain the source of that threat. Gordon Jackson says:

> Birth is the first [threat], as the infant separates from the warm security of the womb. This experience is prototype of all separation-anxiety. Life is characterized by myriad experiences of loss, but they come the hardest when the nascent ego is struggling for survival and is least equipped to handle shock. The very first year of life, following upon its rude and abrupt entry into the world through the trauma of birth, is a series of losses or threatened losses. We cannot know what a shock to the baby it is that day when he glides his hands over the one surface of his body and his mother's and discovers the rent of the subject-object. Mother is separate from him. Until that day she was continuous with him.[7]

---

7. Ibid., pp. 235-36.

Jackson continues to explain that the further separation of mother and child through early childhood produces a feeling of being left alone, of being empty. Thus, the child is nurtured in anxiety.

Seen in that way, anxiety is a part of life from the very beginning. In fact, psychology affirms wholeheartedly that anxiety is an instinct. It is genetically determined. "That a child comes into the world equipped with instinctive anxieties has been noticed from antiquity," claims Wallace Kennedy.[8]

> Any healthy infant demonstrates a characteristic response associated with anxiety when exposed to loss of support, unexpected loud noises, restriction of movement, or sharp pain. Since these characteristic responses are present at birth, long before they could have any rational or cognitive component, they must be considered anxiety rather than fear.[9]

What we have seen is that some psychologists see anxiety as natural to life. "A child can never be without anxiety so long as he is fully functioning; for to be without anxiety is to be somewhat less than human."[10]

General anxiety is also basic to a theological viewpoint. Psychologists only partially explain man's anxious condition. They link it to the fear of being hurt or killed. However, anxiety takes on greater proportions when it is joined to a theological picture of man. Since men and women are created to have a relationship with God, they are insufficient in themselves. They are in a dependent relationship, unable to stand alone, even with the support of others. Therefore, if we try to live without dependence upon God we will be anxious. Apart from God, there is nothing to give us assurance that there is any ultimate good for us around the corner.

Theological anxiety also includes the feeling of meaninglessness and emptiness. Cut off from a relationship to God, man is devoid of a real reason to live. The ultimate answer to that dread is found in God. The deep-seated anxiety about the future and the meaning of existence must be treated by faith in the One who is in control. Faith amounts to the admission that we are creatures who must depend on the Creator.

But not all turn to the Creator. It is characteristic of mankind to try to fill the void and calm the anxious thoughts by depending on

8. Kennedy, 2:71.
9. Ibid.
10. Ibid.

something other than God. Pagan idols, money, things, philosophies, and human relationships are used to cure the anxiety. Jesus explained: "Do not be anxious then, saying, 'What shall we eat?' or 'What shall we drink?' or 'With what shall we clothe ourselves?' For all these things the Gentiles eagerly seek" (Matt. 6:31).

Once men turn from faith in God to trust in substitutes, the anxiety problem is compounded. They experience what Gordon Jackson calls "guilt anxiety."[11] When we turn our backs to God to find the solution for anxiety in business, human relationships, and good causes, we estrange ourselves from God. We make idolatrous commitments. A spouse, a job, or a pleasure becomes our god. We seek meaning and security in those things that cannot offer complete satisfaction or certainty.

That produces guilt. Men go about their lives denying both the guilt and the anxiety. The anxiety that should lead us to God leads us instead to substitutes that cannot deal with our actual condition. Existential and guilt anxiety combine to give an underlying sense of dread, a panicky sense of catastrophe.[12]

What Gordon Jackson has presented sounds much like the view of Lawrence Crabb, a conservative Christian psychologist. Crabb has integrated psychology and theology around the basic view that man seeks satisfaction from sources other than God. He calls this illegitimate search for contentment "foolishness," based on the assertion of the fool that there is no God. Considering the attempts that have been made to relate psychology and theology, the anxiety approach is a very promising one. Both psychology and theology have led us to observe a deep-seated ontological anxiety common to the human condition.

It is also possible to go further and relate this general anxiety to the more neurotic forms psychologists treat. *General anxiety is related to neurotic problems.* This brief discussion of anxiety does not permit extensive technical discussion of the relationship of abnormal (neurotic) problems and general anxiety. But noting that relationship is very crucial for the minister's approach to preaching and counseling.

First, it is strategic to see that this general anxiety can be behind the development of neurotic forms. The child demonstrates anxiety from the moment of birth. His environment will immediately act on that to formulate his inner psychological world. If parents are present and loving, the child learns a basic form of human trust. If there is a long

11. Jackson, p. 233.
12. Ibid., p. 237.

separation from parents and others, the baby faces tremendous threats. There is clinical evidence to show that the damage done to normal development can cause severe problems later.

Behavioral psychologists will explain the abnormal behavior in terms of learning. For them, anxiety is an unwanted human emotion. A person is conditioned to fear or be anxious. Thus, a child who has no natural fear of mice will become afraid whenever his parents react strongly to the presence of one in the house. Later, that may even produce anxiety in the child whenever the thought of mice is entertained. Thus, the child may have a deep feeling of anxiety without knowing what causes it.

Behavioristic explanations of neurotic anxieties are not completely incompatible with the theological view of anxiety presented here. It is possible to see how certain anxieties can be explained as having been learned. That does not deny that there may be a basic anxiety of the human condition explained by our need to relate to God.

Psychoanalysts relate general anxiety to abnormal conditions in terms of defense reactions. A defense mechanism, in psychological language, is the ego's response to danger. A child who is deserted by a parent is in a severely threatening situation. To compensate for the loss, to defend his ego, he might resort to a number of reactions. Some of those are maladaptive, thus resulting in abnormal behavior. For example, a rejected lover might repress his feelings, trying to convince himself that he was never really in love. Since this forgetting and denying is unconscious, it can lead to a denial of feelings of love in general, making him grow old thinking he cannot really love anyone. Or, the deserted child might react in a manner that is termed *projection*. Unable to face the hatred he may feel for the parent who left him, he might project that emotion on the parent. For the rest of his life he might firmly believe that the parent left because of intense hatred for his child, though that may have been the case. It might cause other adjustment problems since the child must live with the thought of having been so severely hated and rejected.

There are other defense mechanisms, but the description of those is not essential to the present discussion. It is sufficient enough now to see that the theological notion that anxiety is basic to human life is also involved in an explanation of neurotic development.

Also, it is essential to see that specific reactions to anxiety may be related to one's ability to handle general anxiety. Our general dread of life makes us trust or fall back on something. Yet, the anxiety is always present, creating the need to exercise daily trust. It is normal to live with that fear. Specific happenings constantly arouse it, even when the threat is not actual. A telephone call at 3:00 A.M. rouses us from sleep and immediately stirs the deep dread within us. Inwardly, we say to ourselves, *Something is wrong.* The few seconds before we pick up the receiver we resort to our method of handling anxiety. We remember God and His promises, if we are Christians. If not, we might fall back on luck, or our concepts of fate, or some other means of assurance.

Facing anxiety, then, is a daily occurrence. We are not called on to handle it only when it occurs in abnormal proportions. Therefore, how we handle general anxiety will provide a basis for reacting to concrete circumstances that are anxiety-producing: being wheeled into surgery; seeing a daughter off to her first year at college; facing a financial setback; or facing the death of a terminally ill spouse. If person has an adequate way of handling general anxiety, it is probable that he or she will face those specific circumstances that arise without generating abnormal anxiety reactions.

Treating Anxiety

Having viewed the relationship between general and specific abnormal manifestations of anxiety, it is possible now to state two general principles for dealing with anxiety.

First, it will become evident that the major ministry of God's servant will be in helping people deal with general anxiety. Preaching and teaching of constant trust in God is the most effective medicine for both general and abnormal anxieties.

Second, it will be important to see that treating general anxiety will not always be effective whenever the anxious condition is abnormal. Neurotic psychological conditions can sometimes hinder the person's ability to trust in God. Removal of the disorder might be part of the task of bringing the person to faith. Gordon Jackson offers examples of this.

> A young man's anxiety over repressed hostility before authority figures may have to be dealt with before he can in any meaningful way face up to confronting God. A woman's feelings of being rejected, stemming from childhood, when her father made it clear to her that he preferred boys, may have to be worked through before she can trust God, who is almost always portrayed in masculine terms.[13]

13. Ibid., p. 239.

Thus, the healing of neurotic anxiety can open a person for a deeper healing.

With those two generalizations in mind, we can now proceed to a discussion of how the church and its leaders can face anxiety in themselves and others.

DEALING WITH ANXIETY

First, we can treat anxiety by proclaiming God and His good news. The minister and Bible teacher have an advantage over the secular psychologist. We know the depth of man's predicament. We are not merely treating superficial, learned psychological problems with human solutions. We are not merely sharing principles and practical suggestions as mental health experts. Situational preaching is not merely the offering of suggestions.

It can become therapeutic when it proclaims God's gracious activity of bringing anxious individuals into a relationship with Himself. Preaching must not be reduced to simple teaching about the steps to solving life's problems. It is the proclaiming of the gospel, of the good news that God exists, that it is in Him we find what fills our emptiness and gives life to our meaninglessness. Situation preaching calls people away from the trust in empty cisterns to which they turn to the living fountain of water.

Preaching speaks to the deepest levels of our predicament: assurance of eternal life in the face of death; God's plan in working out the confusion and seeming purposelessness of our lives; and the grace of forgiveness overcoming our anxious guilt. Those who suffer from normal anxiety will need this assurance. Anxiety will never go away to stay; it is a normal condition of life. God commands us not to be anxious because He knows it is in our nature to be so. Instead, He urges us to trust in Him. "Be anxious for nothing, but in everything by prayer and supplication with thanksgiving let your requests be made known to God. And the peace of God, which surpasses all comprehension, shall guard your hearts and your minds in Christ Jesus" (Phil. 4:6-7).

Our anxiety will constantly drive us to Him. And when we come to Him, He does not remove our worrying once and for all. Rather, when we trust, the peace of God keeps our hearts and minds. The Greek word for *keep* is used of placing a lid on a boiling pot. And so it is with the treatment of anxiety. Once we turn from trust in Him, the internal water boils. It is only constant faith that keeps the Christian in a state of peace. The boiling, the churning, is always potentially there. God will put the lid on it.

Even those with abnormal anxieties will benefit from this message. Sunday after Sunday they will come to hear from God's Word the assurance they need to keep from being destroyed. In the meantime, they will need to memorize and concentrate on verses of Scripture that tell of His care and presence.

It is not surprising to find that Romans 8 is among the best-known and loved passages of Scripture, for it offers the ultimate cure for our universal plight of anxiety.

> For I am convinced that neither death, nor life, nor angels, nor principalities, nor things present, nor things to come, nor powers, nor height, nor depth, nor any other created thing, shall be able to separate us from the love of God, which is in Christ Jesus our Lord. [Rom. 8:38-39]

DISTINGUISH BETWEEN ANXIETIES AND CONCERN

Anxiety is really not always bad. In the New Testament, the term usually translated "anxiety" has several meanings. Sometimes it means undue concern, what we normally think of as anxiety. At other times, it merely describes a concern. Paul said that members of the Body of Christ are to be anxious for one another (1 Cor. 12:25). Yet, he also said that we were to be anxious for nothing.

Distinguishing between normal concern and worry is not always easy for us to do. We say to each other: "You worry too much." Yet, all the while we thought we were showing due concern. We even say to ourselves, "Stop worrying." We are never sure when we are mentally and spiritually healthy. When we feel anxious or concerned, we often condemn ourselves for it. That doubles our problem. We begin to worry about our worrying. Our anxieties have anxieties.

The Christian who wants to help others with anxiety can help them understand that it may be a normal reaction to certain kinds of situations. It is proper to have a "realistic concern" writes Christian counselor Gary Collins. "Although Paul could write that he was not anxious (that is, worried) about the possibility of being beaten, cold, hungry, or in danger, he said that he was anxious (that is, concerned) about the welfare of the churches."[14]

---

14. Collins, p. 60.

RECOGNIZE AND TREAT NEUROTIC ANXIETIES

There are times when individuals are overcome by an intense condition of anxiety that lacks an identifiable cause. The exaggerated feelings of helplessness do not respond to the sufferer's rational and spiritual attempts to manage them. Inner conflicts combine with outer circumstances to produce neurotic anxieties. Sufferers identify that what is causing their anxious condition is a major part of treating it.

Gary Collins categorizes the causes into five types.[15]

Threat. Danger can be in the form of violent weather, crime, illness, and so on. But it can be more subtle. Experiences may make us fear the loss of self-esteem. Something in our future may be provoking our fears without our being fully aware of its effect: a possible failure in a job we are doing; an exam we have to take; or an appointment we have scheduled.

Sometimes the threat may be related to our reputation or spiritual welfare. Collins mentions the young man who was seized with intense anxiety one evening while watching a ballet. He felt better upon leaving the theater, but subsequently went for counseling. The counselor concluded that he had strong unconscious homosexual tendencies that he was struggling to keep from becoming conscious. During the performance, he was attracted unconsciously to the male dancers. The anxiety was thought to be a reaction to the threat that he might give way to his homosexual impulses and be discovered.

Conflict. Being forced to make a difficult decision occasions anxiety. Sometimes it is a no-win decision. We might have to choose between two painful alternatives: choosing, for example, to have surgery or continuing to suffer pain for a time with the hope it will go away.

Fear. Anytime we are close to a failure, rejection, or challenge, we build up anxiety. If the fear is known and imminent, it should be understood and treated according to the information included in the later section on fear. However, if the object of the anxiety is not immediately evident, the counselor should explore with the counselee his or her inner world and total circumstances. The person's values and past experiences will converge to bring about severe worrying. Unconsciously, he or she may fear success because of a sense of unworthiness. Or else, too great an attraction to things may make a wealthy

15. Ibid., pp. 62-64.

person become extremely anxious about losing his money. Perhaps numerous fear objects produce a build up of fear, creating extreme anxiety.

Unmet needs. People get "up-in-the-air" whenever basic needs such as food, security, and even sexual fulfillment are left unmet. Life seems to be incomplete.

Individual differences. "It is well known," explains Collins, "that people respond differently to anxiety-producing situations. Some people are almost never anxious, some seem highly anxious most of the time, many are in between."[16] The counselor can look for personality traits, personal values, and past experiences in diagnosing individual cases of anxiety. It seems clear, for example, that parents can produce anxious children by their own pattern of reaction to world and family events. Even a person's physical condition should be considered. Since illness, chemical imbalance, and other physical problems can stimulate anxiety, the counselor may send his counselee to a physician for a physical examination.

Collins recommends several methods for identifying anxiety. First, the counselor should recognize his own anxieties. When talking to his client, he should be asking himself, "What in this situation is making me anxious?" It is possible for the counselor to use the answer to that question to learn about himself as well as the anxieties of the person he is trying to help. Second, observe. Watch for evidences of anxiety (shifting position, deep breathing, perspiration) whenever various topics are discussed. They may offer clues as to what is bothering the person. Third, reflect upon the situation. Ask such questions as "When are you most anxious?" "When was the last time you felt really anxious?" "What was happening in your life then?" Fourth, contemplate. As a counselor, think through the possible causes of anxiety just discussed. Raise some of those issues and, as the counselee talks about them, watch for signs of anxiety. Discuss your hunches.

While searching for a cause, Collins asks us to remember the need for patience and understanding.

> By its very nature, anxiety often arises in response to threats which are vague and difficult to identify. By pushing the counselee to "snap out of

16. Ibid., p. 64.

it" or to "hurry and tell me what is wrong," we increase the anxiety, create more confusion, and risk losing or alienating the anxious person.[17]

BUILD A SHARING RELATIONSHIP AND A SUPPORTING COMMUNITY

Talking about one's anxieties, fears, hope, and faith is one of the most effective forms of perpetual therapy. Thus, the church not only offers a treatment for anxiety through its message, it also offers help within its life. As a community of accepting people, the church has a built-in means for helping with anxiety. The anxious person needs those around who can understand his condition and support his faith and hope. No human pain needs an accepting and affirming community more than anxiety.

The church should promote open and honest group-sharing about the circumstances of life. The anxious person needs to know that he is not alone—that others, too, are anxious. For that reason, it is always uplifting to read the writings of Paul Tournier. He so often shares himself with the reader. He does not merely scoop things off the surface of his mind, dishing out mere intellectual opinions. He shares the bottom half of himself, the larger submerged part of the iceberg, by describing honestly his insecure feelings, his worries, and his worrying. His genuineness makes his readers feel real and normal and prompts them to surface their own dreads and commit them to God.

Drawing near others who, like us, are anxious is part of the cure for anxiety. Loneliness only accents our human condition. Discussing a matter of burnout, which is closely related to anxiety, D. G. Kehl observes that we Christians have a tendency to withdraw from one another.

> Just as distancing, detachment, and withdrawal are allies of burnout, so fellowship, closeness and mutual edification are foes of burnout. The evangelical loner, so proudly private that he is reluctant to reveal himself or permit anyone to invade his personal spaces, is all too common. Experiencing both rewards and setbacks in a vacuum, he is ripe for burnout. Conversely, it is hard to imagine a believer experiencing burnout who enjoys a close sharing fellowship with other believers who both give and receives edification.[18]

17. Ibid., p. 68.
18. D. G. Kehl, "Burnout: The Risk of Reaching Too High," *Christianity Today*, 20 November 1981, p. 28.

Becoming a warm, caring community of believers is not beyond the reach of churches that give it priority. Assuring concern for one another can be fostered in small groups formed for that purpose. The pastor and other church leaders can create a climate of honesty by their own example of openness. The situational preacher will need to include himself in the human situations he addresses. He will share his struggles as well as his successes, and urge others to do the same. In that way, we can best minister to the anxious, which includes us all.

6

Conflict

HANDLING OUR DIFFERENCES

Prominent on the contemporary national scene are sociologists who study institutional conflicts. One of those experts recently did a study of congregational disputes. In an article in *Newsweek* magazine entitled "Why Pastors Are Fired," Speed Leas, a "crisis manager," stated flatly that churches in general do not know how to deal with conflict. Their unwillingness to handle it showed up in the fact that 83 percent of the congregations refused even to discuss with him why their ministers were dismissed.

The American ineptitude at handling differences within the church seems to be matched only by our inability to do so in the home. The two out of every five marriages that end in divorce show us that one of the major ways of managing conflict is separation. The need to cultivate the art of harmonious living is not merely serious, it's urgent!

RECOGNIZE THE INEVITABLE

We must first recognize that conflict is healthy. The inability in handling conflict usually comes from refusing to accept it. Speed Leas, the human explosion expert, says that Christians portray an unwillingness to accept conflict. They think that because they should love one another it is wrong to have differences. That keeps them from facing conflict properly when it comes, as it inevitably will. That tendency to deny conflict may not be exclusively a Christian reaction. Prominent psychiatrist Eric Fromm observed that "man would rather flee than fight." As in other psychological or interpersonal relationship problems, our first reaction is one of denial.

That Christians should be ready for combat ought to be obvious. Not only should we be prepared for warfare with our enemies, we should also be prepared to differ with our friends. In his book *The Intimate Enemy*, George Bach reminds us that our most terrible enemies are the ones closest to us. The fiercest, most deadly combat is close combat. So, he says, "The family that fights together stays together."

Before we march George Bach up an appropriate scaffold for that remark, we need to understand what he and other conflict experts are saying. They have formulated some helpful distinctions. We should separate, they maintain, the idea of conflict from the results of that conflict. We should expect conflict. But that should not necessarily foster arguing, fighting, slandering, and abuse of one another. Having differences with each other is not necessarily wrong or sinful. Even the apostle Paul anticipated that we would have differences when he urged us to "put up with one another in love." Put in that way, conflict is defined as happening whenever one person becomes an obstacle to another person.

Conflict of values. Conflict can happen over differences of value. For example, one person in the church may like fast, joyful gospel songs and another may like solemn, stately hymns.

Conflict in perspective. Conflict can occur when there is a difference in perspective. One person may see remodeling the church sanctuary as a way to win others to Christ, while another person may view it as selfish catering to the congregation's wants.

Conflict of limited resources. Conflict usually comes because of limited resources. Church members can clash over getting their piece of the church budget like children over a bigger piece of Mom's chocolate pie. Imagine, too, the family conflict that inevitably comes from the question of which TV show to watch. One television set is a limited resource; we are bound to have different opinions about how it should be used within a given hour.

Viewing conflict from that perspective makes us see how normal it is to life. We have "conflicts," rightly defined, not because we are necessarily sinful, but because we are alive and different. Simply, we have differences because we are different.

Henry Brandt humorously shows us that any room of the house can provide the scene for conflict.

Start with the living room. What do you do with the newspaper? Fold it neatly on the coffee table? Or leave it strewn around the room, a section here, a section there?

When you come home from work, do you change clothes before you sit down in the living room? Or lounge around with your grubby clothes on? Let's move into the bedroom. How cool do you set the air conditioner? How high do you open the window? Do you undress with the blinds down and the lights on? Or leave the blinds up and undress in the dark?

Take the bathroom: What do you do with wet towels? Drape them over the shower curtain? Over the bathtub? Put them in the clothes hamper? Or hang them neatly on the rack? Do you start on a new tube of toothpaste before you've squeezed the old tube flat? How do you squeeze the tube?

Move into the dining room: Do you keep the different foods separated on your plate or mix them together? How do you serve the mustard and catsup? In bottles . . . or in pretty little dishes? How do you appear for breakfast? All dressed? Or in your bathrobe?[1]

In the Bible are numerous examples of that kind of contention. Although Sarah is credited for being submissive and calling Abraham "Lord," she had two severe encounters with him (Gen. 16:1-7; 21:8-14). Although Paul and Barnabas were intimately linked together in ministry, they clashed over their viewpoints of John Mark (Acts 15:36-41).

Conflict is not always wrong. It is not something we should be ashamed or afraid of, cowering from it like scared campers fleeing from a forest fire. If we see conflict from the correct viewpoint, we can even welcome it rather than fear it.

SEE THE VALUE OF CONFLICT

Conflict is not only inevitable, it is *invaluable*. It is valuable because it shows that we have a relationship going. Closeness magnifies our differences and increases our dissension. Marriage is like two porcupines sleeping together; the closer you get, the greater the chance you will hurt one another. The same is true in the church. A close friend of one of the authors, who said that he did not go to church because "all they do down on that corner is scrap with one another," had a solution to harmonious living that was quite simple and effective. He stayed away. Withdrawing from conflicts is essentially withdrawing from relationships. The withdrawal can actually take the form of physical

1. Henry Brandt, *I Want My Marriage to Be Better* (Grand Rapids: Zondervan, 1976), p. 39.

separation, as avoiding each other in the church hallway. More often, the withdrawal is emotional; we refuse to get close, withdrawing into our own solitude. Some couples and even churches have "peace at all costs." The cost is sometimes the relationship.

In addition to showing that we have a close relationship, conflict can also help bring us closer. Jesus expressed that idea when He spoke of rebuking our brother who sins against us: "If he listens to you, you have won your brother." The intimate words He uses here suggest what we all know about resolving conflict. Whenever we work through our differences it always brings us closer. Avoiding important contentions usually will only separate us further.

Conflict also leads to self-improvement. People with whom we differ become "God's sandpaper" to round off the rough edges of our personalities. When you face conflict in a healthy Christian way, it will add to your Christian maturity.

RECOGNIZE THE CAUSE OF CONFLICT

After examining the advantages of conflict, we would do well to observe the dark side of conflicts as well. Although not all conflicts are the result of sin, some are. A quick survey of the Scriptures reveals numerous, ungainly human qualities behind our strife.

Without cause—Proverbs 3:30
Pride—Proverbs 13:10
Selfishness—Philippians 2:3; 2 Corinthians 12:20
A negative personal life-style—1 Timothy 6:4-5
Characteristic of the flesh—James 4:1; Proverbs 17:18
Foolishness—Proverbs 18:6.

The Scriptures instruct us to make sure that we have a "just" cause before making an issue of a conflict. If pride or selfishness is motivating us, we had better back off. "Love covers a multitude of sins" (1 Pet. 4:8). But that does not mean that we reject legitimate rights and differences, always backing out of a potential contest. We cannot be effective in our interpersonal relationships if our pattern is always one of withdrawal and submission. You cannot be a good parent, for example, if you are not willing to face conflict. David never "crossed" his son, Adonijah, and the results were disastrous (1 Kings 1:6). Having conflict is not wrong; but the way we handle it often is.

RECOGNIZE THE WRONG RESPONSES TO CONFLICT

Much of what the Bible has to say about conflict has to do with the results. Biblical words translated "quarreling," "strife," "slander," and "fighting" are describing how people clash. Our human emotions are greatly agitated whenever someone becomes an obstacle to us. Aroused anger, resentment, and bitterness give birth to all kinds of dysfunctional behaviors. Anger makes us blame the other person. Professor Higgins of the Broadway play *My Fair Lady* became upset with the young girl Eliza because she made him angry, something he claimed he rarely experienced. When we blame other persons in that way, we are blaming them for their very existence. By blaming them, we deny them the right to have opinions and rights. Our anger leads us to "slander." Sometimes it is overt: we call each other names. More often it is less direct: we get sarcastic. A wife who differs with her husband about evenings away from home says: "If I ever get taken out, it will be feet first, when they carry me out."

Our reactions to differences sometimes lead to physical abuse. In an unusual church squabble, a deacon rushes onto the church platform to strike the pastor. A parent reaches out to strike his child. Experts estimate there are more than one million child beatings a year. Those are caused more by the child's differences than his disobedience. Even parents are objects of abuse in family fights. One out of every ten children under eighteen years old assaults his parents.

In less harmful ways, we may handle the conflict by bitterly complaining to others. Instead of discussing his differences with his wife, a husband pours out his feelings and describes her faults to his secretary. Instead of sharing his feelings and viewpoints in the board meeting, a church leader stands in the parking lot verbally cutting to pieces those who oppose him.

That there are more functional and positive ways of handling conflict is the obvious message of Scripture. Conflict management technique is consistent with biblical truth whenever it designs to teach us how to handle conflict in a constructive way.

RESOLVE CONFLICT IN A VARIETY OF WAYS

Foremost among the biblical and contemporary suggestions for dealing with the conflict is the practice of confrontations. "Whenever your brother sins against you," Jesus instructed, "go and speak to him in private" (Matt. 18:15). We have the right and obligation to face conflict head-on. David Augsburger calls this "care-fronting," maintaining that it is the creative way through conflict.[2] Confrontation should be done in private and lovingly. Venting your feelings is not what Jesus had in mind. He intended that you restore the person and the relationship.

That is not to say that every little difference must be aired. Sometimes we ignore differences and forbear in patience. Long-suffering and gentleness are the fruit of the Spirit. Paul exhorted: "Be kind to one another, tender-hearted, forgiving each other, just as God in Christ also has forgiven you" (Eph. 4:32).

Kindness and forgiveness do not require that we always back off and ignore the differences. We sometimes, in the process, swallow negative feelings that will harm us or our relationships. Whenever it is necessary for our own emotional health, the well-being of the relationship, or the cause for which we stand, we need to lovingly confront the other person about the difference that exists.

Discussing the issue with another is just the first step in resolving it. After that, there has to be some means of effectively handling the differences. The following options are open.

Toleration. Sometimes we have to live with the difference, knowing that the circumstances may never change. Sometimes that is easy because we benefit so much from the relationship. "Harold won't pick up his socks," said one housewife, "but he is such a wonderful husband in other ways." In such cases the toleration is easier because the trade-off is worth it. In all relationships there will always be these two opposing tensions: the pull of attraction that makes the relationship fulfilling and meaningful; and the repelling features that make you want to retreat. Building positive bonds will make it easier to tolerate the areas of difference.

Accommodation. Conflict can be resolved when one person is willing to change to accommodate the other. But sometimes that change is difficult to make. Change does not come easy in the area of habits. Some people like a ten o'clock Sunday morning worship service, while others are accustomed to the eleven o'clock hour. The attitudes and feelings that accompany that kind of conflict are not changed in one week. Consider a marriage in which one mate is a night person and the other is an early riser. (Why does the night owl always

2. David Augsburger, *Caring Enough to Confront* (Ventura, Calif.: Regal, 1974).

seem to marry the morning dove?) Learning to live with late nights is not so easy, even if done in the name of love. Even if a wife believes strongly in submitting to her husband, she may have a terrible struggle trying to accommodate him. For him to blame her for not submitting— or worse, not loving him—is one of the usual follies in a conflict of this kind.

Perhaps, in a loving relationship, the one to change is the one for whom it will be easier. Recently, a student said that because he must use a lot of hours studying at home, he had to either study late into the night or during the early morning hours. He asked his wife to make a choice: would she rather he go to bed with her at night or be there in the morning when she awakens. She chose his being with her in the evening. Although he is actually more comfortable studying at night, he rises early in the morning to do his homework, lovingly accommodating himself to his wife's needs.

Compromise. Whenever toleration and accommodation are not feasible or advisable in a conflict, we must resort to compromise. For persons who see everything in terms of right or wrong, black or white, sin or righteousness, compromise is a naughty word. "After all," they may say, "Christians should be of the same mind." Certainly, the more we conform to God's will, as revealed in His Word, the more alike we will become, and the less conflict we will experience. But single-mindedness does not mean that we always think the same. It means that we try to live harmoniously. Therefore, harmony can sometimes be fostered through compromises. As various factions of the church express what they believe to be the will of God, our compromises eventually become His will for us. Thus, we compromise on the budget issues. Instances of compromise are found in Scripture. The decision of the Jerusalem Council in Acts 15 seems to contain a compromise to those Jews who were still holding to some of the vestiges of the Old Testament way of life. Paul seemed to compromise when he agreed to purify himself for the sake of appeasing the Jews (Acts 21:17-26).

Observers of the church today are almost in unanimous agreement that our greatest need is for closer relationships. Demonstrating love for one another is our basic task. But love does not prelude conflict. Close relationships of love will only be possible when we learn to properly face conflict, rather than improperly avoiding it.

7
Contentment

Read the biblical texts that deal with contentment and then observe how a current psychology text handles the same subject. There appears to be a contradiction. On one hand, the Bible commands Christ's followers to be content. "Godliness actually is a means of great gain, when accompanied by contentment. . . . And if we have food and covering, with these we shall be content" (1 Tim. 6:6, 8). On the other hand, psychologists tell us that discontentment is the fuel that fires the human engine. We humans are never content. When one need is satisfied, we turn to another. That is what keeps us going; it is the stuff of life. Douglas McGregor speaks for many other psychologists when he says, "Man is a wanting animal. . . . As soon as one of his needs is satisfied, another appears in its place. This process is unending. It continues from birth to death."[1] One of today's most popular psychologists, Abraham Maslow, builds his whole system of motivation on discontentment—man's desire to fulfill his needs.

Can the biblical and psychological viewpoints be combined without compromising biblical truth? We must first determine precisely what each is saying.

BIBLICAL VIEW OF CONTENTMENT

There is no doubt that the Scriptures urge us to be content. The statement of Hebrews 13:5 is quite clear: "Let your character [way of life] be free from the love of money, being content with what you have; for He Himself has said, 'I WILL NEVER DESERT YOU, NOR WILL I EVER FORSAKE YOU.' " Summarizing all that the Scriptures have to say, this idea of contentment includes the following.

---

1. Douglas McGregor, as quoted in B. V. Gilmer, *Psychology*, 2d ed. (New York: Harper & Row, 1973), p. 283.

1. The Christian should be satisfied when his minimal needs are met because he knows that God is the provider. This type of contentment is primarily external; it is marked by a lack of complaining, by joyfulness, and by the absence of a frantic seeking after riches.
2. The Christian should be satisfied with the meeting of his minimal needs because he does not place value in the accumulation of riches. In this case, contentment is linked to values. "But those who want to get rich fall into temptation and a snare and many foolish and harmful desires which plunge men into ruin and destruction. For the love of money is a root of all sorts of evil" (1 Tim. 6:9-10). Contentment is equal to a lack of covetousness, which refers to a strong desire for those things that matter less than eternal matters. "For we have brought nothing into the world, so we cannot take anything out of it either" (1 Tim. 6:7). It is also pointed out that this desire for riches can be harmful. Understood in that way, contentment is a matter of choice.
3. The Christian must be content in order to accomplish the mission of God in the world. In this case, the Christian is encouraged to be content with dissatisfaction. Certain needs may not be satisfied. But God's servant is willing to suffer deprivation to accomplish the greater purposes of God. That is Paul's spirit in Philippians 4:11-12:

> I have learned to be content in whatever circumstances I am. I know how to get along with humble means, and I also know how to live in prosperity; in any and every circumstance I have learned the secret of being filled and going hungry, both of having abundance and suffering need.

A person on a mission is satisfied with less than one who is seeking his own welfare.

Contentment in Scripture is linked to (1) values: choosing what you want; (2) external actions and internal attitude: a person does not gripe, complain, and hedonistically scramble after that which he really does not need for happiness and satisfaction; and (3) one's mission in life: being content to suffer a need.

Contentment in Scripture, therefore, does not mean that a person is to be satisfied about all things, living without discontent. Martin Lloyd-Jones makes that clear when writing about depression.[2] Con-

---

2. Martyn Lloyd-Jones, *Spiritual Depression: Its Causes and Cure* (Grand Rapids: Eerdmans, 1965), pp. 279-80.

tentment, in his definition, means that the Christian does not allow himself to be controlled by circumstances; he makes a choice about what will motivate him to action.

There are two things that contentment does not mean. First, it is not equal to submission to poverty. The command to be content is not to be used as an excuse for laziness and inactivity. The Bible never teaches that man should never endeavor to better himself. The apostle Paul's command to be content was not an unconditional one. One must have food and shelter. Nor does contentment dictate indifference to circumstances. Lloyd-Jones calls this indifference a "negative resignation of a pagan stoicism."[3] A Christian should not be mastered or controlled by his circumstances. But that does not imply indifference toward those circumstances. By all means, the Christian should improve his situation if possible. However, if he is not able to do so, he is not to let negative conditions determine his misery or joy.

PSYCHOLOGICAL UNDERSTANDING OF CONTENTMENT

Since our task is to compare the biblical concept of contentment with modern psychology, we will now examine what psychologists say about human need and contentment. Abraham Maslow will provide us with a view that is representative of psychologists who make need fulfillment the central part of their thinking.

Maslow has presented a model of man's needs in terms of a hierarchy of priority, which includes lower and higher needs. The lowest needs are *physiological*: food, drink, and shelter. The second level, *safety needs*, refers to protection against danger, threat, deprivation, and the need for a "fair break." The *social needs* are described as belonging, association, acceptance, and the giving and receiving of friendship and love. Two kinds of needs are described as *ego needs*: those that concern self-esteem, involving self-confident feelings of authority and independence, knowledge, and achievement; and the needs for status, recognition, and respect from one's fellow men.[4]

Self-actualization, or self-fulfillment, is at the top of the need hierarchy scheme. At this level the person tries to realize his own potential. He shows tolerance for ambiguity and uncertainty, can accept himself and others, and is discriminating in the influence to

---

3. Ibid., p. 279.
4. A. H. Maslow, *Motivation and Personality* (New York: Harper & Brothers, 1954), p. 82.

which he yields. Being problem-centered rather than ego-centered, he is relatively independent while not flaunting convention and shows a fair measure of objectivity. Considered mentally healthy, this kind of person has a social interest and is effective in personal relationships. A sense of humor and creativity helps to establish his or her individual style. Such a person succeeds in a search for privacy without becoming a recluse.[5]

Several characteristics of Maslow's description of needs are basic to his psychology. First, the lower-level needs have to be met before a person turns to the higher needs. Social needs, for example, will only take on an importance to a person who has his physiological and safety needs met.

Second, man's needs are primarily positive. Maslow regards man's inborn nature as basically good; therefore, antisocial needs, such as aggression, are not included in man's basic needs. A need to be aggressive comes from the fact that man is weak and can be influenced by outside pressures.

Third, when a person's needs are not met, negative responses often occur. When a social need is not met, a person may become antagonistic, resistant, and uncooperative. The behavior is a consequence of need failure, not a cause of it.

Fourth, some needs are never satisfied. Man's ego need, for example, is rarely satisfied, for when a person seeks status, achievement, and recognition, he is never quite sure when he has had enough of it. That is somewhat of a cultural problem because contemporary culture does not always clearly tell us when we are fully appreciated or fully accepted.

Fifth, relatively few people fulfill the need for self-actualization. Self-fulfillment seems to involve a rising above the meeting of one's own needs, a transcendence of the need orientation to life. Achievements that are only compensations for unsatisfied needs do not bring true self-fulfillment.

Sixth, man is motivated primarily by this quest for fulfilled needs, for we humans are primarily motivated by what we do not have.

COMPARING MASLOW AND SCRIPTURE

Enumerating the points of agreement will be the first half of the process of comparing Maslow's ideas with the Scriptures. First, the

5. Ibid., pp. 203-34.

emphasis on human need is certainly a legitimate one. Scripture clearly affirms that man was created with needs. The Christian is not to be put into a position of constantly denying his needs. We find that God recognizes man's needs. Paul presents Him as the One who "shall supply all your needs" (Phil. 4:19). In 1 Corinthians 7 Paul recognizes the sexual needs of the Christian married person. Both husbands and wives are urged to meet the needs of their spouses. The idea that the Christian life is one of self-denial, as if human needs are improper and ungodly, is not acceptable. Paul clearly condemned asceticism in Colossians 2:20-23.

Second, it may even be possible to confirm the particular needs Maslow mentions. The need for physical and safety needs are obviously confirmed by Scripture. The same is true with man's social needs. Scripture declares: "It is not good for man to be alone" (Gen. 2:18). Apparently, Adam's fellowship with God in the garden did not satisfy his need for interaction with others.

It is at the highest levels, the needs of the ego and the need for self-fulfillment, that Maslow becomes more controversial. A case can be made that each of us needs a certain self-esteem, self-confidence, and a feeling of status in his relationship to others. In his book *Hide or Seek*, James Dobson defends the child's right to the satisfaction of those needs, urging parents to provide opportunities for their children to achieve and gain recognition.

Self-fulfillment, too, may not be out of keeping with what the Bible says about the Christian life. If we look at self-fulfillment in terms of fulfilling one's self in the will of God, Maslow's concept does not appear to be as selfish as some might claim. Every Christian is endowed with abilities and spiritual gifts to be expressed as part of the Body of Christ, the church. If we speak of fulfillment as the opportunity to express oneself and service as ordained by God, it can be equated with Maslow's idea that a person has a need to realize his own potential.

The apostle Paul often expressed the great desire and need he had to complete the task given to him, to finish his course. He had a sense of vocation, of calling, that was central to his motivation.

Martin Luther spoke of every Christian's vocation as something given to him from God. Luther expanded the idea of calling to include jobs other than those directly related to church ministry. It was Luther who gave some dignity and Christian calling to secular work.

But Maslow's view of man's needs is insufficient in itself, and may even contain a kernel of error that can be especially dysfunctional for the Christian. The first obvious insufficiency of Maslow's hierarchy of needs is the omission of the spiritual world. That man is made for fellowship with God is central to Christian theology. Many theologians see it as the essence of being created in the image of God. Also lacking is the fact that God can meet certain needs. While it is true that God is not a proper substitute for food, He can function at the other levels of our needs. He can offer a sense of safety, even in times of trouble. Our belonging needs are partially met in our belonging to Him and His kingdom. Even the ego need of status may be resolved in the fact that we are held in esteem by God. Our self-esteem and confidence will come, not merely from our achievement, but from our being accepted by God.

That has a very practical application in our struggle to meet our needs and attain a level of satisfaction. Maslow indicates that the ego needs may never be satisfied since a person can never really get enough prestige to be satisfied. However, the Christian can seek to practice contentment, knowing that God is with him. It is not that he is denying the need for achievement and acceptance; rather, it is that those needs are met through his relationship to God.

Most problematic about Maslow's scheme may be how others have interpreted and applied it in the modern world. Sociologist Daniel Yankelovich has strongly attacked Maslow's emphasis on self-fulfillment. He describes and criticizes that viewpoint, showing how it is inadequate for modern living.[6] First, he recognizes some of the truth in Maslow's scheme.

> There is obviously, some sense in which human priorities do function according to hierarchy. When we are sick, all that counts is getting well. When our survival, physical or economic, is threatened, it powerfully concentrates the mind (as Samuel Johnson observed about the prospect of being hanged).[7]

In "Maslowism," the self-actualized person who steps off at the top of the escalator is a particular personality type. He or she is assumed to be creative, autonomous, and virtually independent of culture. The problem with Maslow's need-centered approach is that it puts too

6. Daniel Yankelovich, "New Rules in American Life: Searching for Self-Fulfillment in a World Turned Upside Down," *Psychology Today*, April 1981, pp. 35-91.
7. Ibid., p. 47.

much emphasis on self. Yankelovich is severe in his criticism and analysis:

> By now, millions of Americans have garnered extensive—and painful—experience in personal struggles with the new, Maslow-inspired duty-to-self ethic. It has, to be sure, some benefits to offer the individual, but the core idea is a moral and social absurdity. It gives moral sanction to desires that do not contribute to society's well-being. It contains no principle for synchronizing the requirements of the society with the goals of the individual. It fails to discriminate between socially valuable desires and socially destructive ones, and often works perversely against the real goals of both individuals and society. It provides no principle other than hedonism for interpreting the meaning of the changes and sacrifices we must make to adapt to new economic-political conditions.[8]

If Maslow's view is taken in that way, as a selfish pursuit of one's own needs, it is evidently contrary to Scripture. Contentment for the Christian is to be found within the framework of self-sacrifice, not selfish fulfillment. Serving God and others will play a prominent role in his life, not because it is self-fulfilling, but because it is ordained by God.

But Yankelovich's criticism may be too severe. Maslow's idea of self-fulfillment need not be equated with selfishness. Rather, it can be seen as a driving force in man to fulfill his potential in the will of God. As we have already seen, it can be looked upon as the desire to be what one was created for. It can be part of what it means to be created in the image of God. No doubt, the non-Christian will not fulfill that potential. His sinful nature will dominate, and he will turn his opportunity to be what God designed for him into what he wants for himself. Yet, the Christian, by the power of the Spirit, has a nature that now seeks to conform to God's image. Built into him is that drive to fulfill the potential given to him. Therefore, the drive to fulfill needs will be a basis of motivation. Discontent becomes a legitimate propelling force. The Christian, therefore, cannot always be completely content, but will be in a process of seeking contentment.

We must conclude that for the Christian contentment means several different things. If we are talking about contentment as a state of control over circumstances, a satisfaction with what God provides, there is no question that the Christian should learn to be content. If, on the other hand, we mean by contentment the complete absence of

8. Ibid.

drive toward fulfillment, we cannot expect that of any man. By our very nature, we are driven to meet our needs and reach our potential. The Holy Spirit is also given to guide us to that fulfillment within the will of God.

To help others find contentment our task is twofold: to warn them of the illegitimate discontentment of being needlessly unthankful and dissatisfied; and to encourage believers to seek legitimate contentment by aggressively approaching life to satisfy legitimate needs. There are several ways those concerns can be dealt with.

DEALING WITH DISSATISFACTION OVER THINGS

Dissatisfaction over what we do not possess can snatch away our contentment more than anything else. It is a problem for those who have much as well as those who have little. When one of the Rockefellers was asked how much money was enough, he replied, "Just a little bit more."

Preaching and teaching biblical principles relating to contentment will be a perennial need. But we can offer some other practical suggestions for handling this problem. First, we can help people recognize that this dissatisfaction really exists. Too often we go through life with a vague feeling of discontent that we have not really pinpointed. Careful thought may establish the fact that the discontentment is related to a desire for a better house, a newer car, or a better wardrobe. In such cases a person needs to come to grips with the dimension of his dissatisfaction. The thing he desires is not worth his loss of joy over the lack of it; such malcontentment will prove to be unreasonable.

Second, we can help people understand the inner forces that cause dissatisfaction related to things. Underlying psychological needs or problems can make us yearn for something we do not have. A woman, for example, may want to buy furniture and clothes to satisfy her desire to be loved. Not having a close relationship with her husband and others, she might unconsciously fill that need with the thrill of new purchases and new things. Sometimes that results in a pile of debts that hinders her relationship with loved ones, compounding her problem. A struggle for self-esteem might also make a person abnormally yearn for material possessions. In our society cars, homes, and clothes are status symbols. When those are acquired, we feel better about ourselves.

A discontented person needs to realize that there are other ways within his or her reach to gain self-esteem, and that doing it solely through material things is a superficial, unbiblical way. There are numerous other psychological conditions that make us yearn for things. We need to provoke ourselves and others to ask: "Just why do I want this so much?"

Third, make others aware of the outer factors that cause discontentment. All of us need to be warned that there are people whose major vocation is to make us feel dissatisfied and insecure. Some advertisers will use any means to make us feel discontent if we do not have their products. Our Western world is plagued by "consumerism." We are made to think that we are not socially acceptable if we do not have the right label on our jeans or sneakers. We are even made to feel unloving and unconcerned if we do not have a garage door opener, for example.

In the church we will do well to preach against materialism. But we will do better to explain the forces that lie behind it and help one another deal with them. We will be far along in handling it if we can recognize those inner and outer forces that work upon us, breeding our discontentment.

HANDLING JOB DISSATISFACTION

Christian authors Jerry and Mary White were prompted to write a book on job satisfaction because they found so few people who were satisfied with their jobs. Their book, *Your Job: Survival or Satisfaction*, contains biblical and practical suggestions that could easily become the basis for a series of sermons or lessons on this topic. Their answers do not merely include adapting to one's present work; they recommend considering another kind of employment or moving to another place that brings fulfillment.

SEEKING MARITAL HAPPINESS

Like a vocation, a person's marital situation is too important to be neglected or merely left to fate. The biblical commands to be content should not keep us from trying to get more fulfillment and happiness out of our job and family life. In fact, surveys seem to show that marriage is the most important source of satisfaction in the modern world. Reporting on a recent extensive study, the researchers concluded: "The estimated contribution of marital happiness is far greater than the estimated contribution of any of the kinds of satisfaction, including satisfaction with work."[9] The study showed that women as

---

9. Norval D. Glenn and Charles N. Weaver, "The Contribution of Marital Happiness to Global Happiness," *Journal of Marriage and the Family*, February 1981, p. 161.

well as men depend very heavily on their marriages for psychological
well-being.

That being the case, it is important for the church to address matters
related to marital adjustment and growth. Efforts should be made to
provide sermons, classes, conferences, books, and cassettes that help
people overcome the problems that keep them from marital happiness.

ADJUSTING PERSONAL GOALS

The biblical perspective of discontentment indicates that it is not
related merely to what we need, but to what we want. At times, we are
discontent because we have adopted goals that are inconsistent with
our abilities, and thus out of the will of God. Psychologists today relate
discontentment, stress, and burnout to the individual goals a person
sets for himself. Don Osgood explains how that was true in his life:

> The first step is one of reexamining our egos. Dr. Harry Levinson, the
> noted psychologist, talks about something called an ego ideal—a bright
> shiny notion we have of who we might ultimately become. We'll do almost
> anything to see how big or how good we are, because we want to be able
> to like ourselves. But there is often a gap between what we are and what
> we'd like to be, and this gap can cause stress disease—or I'll call it ego
> stress—because our egos are what cause the underlying problem. That's
> why, even though you may be a committed Christian, you need to
> reexamine your way of life.
>
> My own experience with this kind of stress taught me a powerful lesson.
> I was asked by my company if I would consider an assignment in Japan. It
> was a great ego builder, but I knew that I might create family problems if I
> accepted. I had already moved my family to four different cities, and after
> one of these moves, my oldest son, then 15, ran away for several days. I
> should have known that I had no business considering another such move
> now that another son had reached the critical age of 15. But I let
> management consider me along with others for six long weeks. All the
> while I kept saying in my prayers, "I won't try to sell myself, God. I'll just
> let them decide." My wife, Joan, said, "I'm praying for direction for us,
> Don." And I knew the way she said it that she didn't want to go. My
> 15-year-old son said flatly, "I don't want to go, Dad!"
>
> At the end of the sixth week the announcement was made that an-
> other person had been selected. "It's all right," I said. But it was just
> two days later that I developed an intestinal disorder that wouldn't go
> away, and only then did I begin to realize how deep the struggle had been.
> After four days of discomfort I was awakened in the middle of the night
> by the same trouble, and with the honesty that exhaustion brings I
> prayed softly, "I understand now how deeply I have struggled, Lord.

Heal me of my sin of preoccupation with my wants. Heal my relationship with my family . . . and please heal me of my physical discomfort, too."

I never had to get out of bed that night because my sin was forgiven, and my difficulty instantly vanished along with the tension. I had finally learned a powerful lesson. A person can get so busy gaining a place in life that he risks losing his own family and spiritual relationships.[10]

Some people reach too high. Discontent with their abilities, achievements, and circumstances they are feverishly driven into endless activity. When they do not measure up to their expectations, they end up disillusioned and sometimes "burned out." Fatigued and depleted instead of energetic, they give up and continue to live without any mission. "Christians are particularly susceptible to burnout," claims one writer, "because of our typically idealistic/perfectionistic aspirations and high expectations."[11]

The major cause of burnout is discontentment over the dichotomy between expectation and actuality. Thus, Kehl advises, "Prevention and cure lie in seeking realistic goals, in reassessing and readjusting when necessary, in accepting our limitations."[12]

Applying that understanding to the pulpit, the preacher will be cautious about causing too much discontentment. Fired up about the mission to win the world and to make an impact, the minister may foster an intense disappointment. As a result, members of the congregation may drop out of the life of the church, if the challenge becomes too much for them. We must help ourselves and others to make sure our vision of Christian service squares with the reality of God's will and our human circumstances.

10. Don Osgood, "That Uncomfortable Feeling Called Stress," *Bridge Leader* 21 (Spring 1981): 4.
11. D. G. Kehl, "Burnout: The Risk of Reaching Too High," *Christianity Today*, 20 November 1981, p. 26.
12. Ibid., p. 28.

8

Depression

Depression is in. Popular terms like "being down" and "the pits" show how preoccupied we are with our "blue" moods. A clinical counselor says that half of all his patients come because they are depressed. "It is the most common kind of abnormal behavior," according to the experts.[1] As a result, the study of depression is one of the most active research areas in the field of abnormal psychology.[2]

In a lifetime, a person has a one-out-of-ten chance he will become clinically depressed. If for no other reason than its frequency of occurrence, a pastor should be acquainted with this human ailment. But there is another reason: depressed people are the most likely to commit suicide. How a pastor counsels and preaches about the loss of joy could be a life and death matter.

DEFINITION OF DEPRESSION

"It was horror and hell. I was at the bottom of the deepest pit there ever was. I was worthless and unforgivable. I was as good as—no, worse than—dead."[3]

That statement by a severely depressed person shows why suicide is such an attractive option to the depressed. The features of depression tend to make life seem worthless. First, there are the inner feelings: a sense of helplessness, a feeling of worthlessness, a loss of self-esteem, feelings of pessimism about the future, and an intense sadness.

Manifestations of certain behaviors are related to these feelings: a

---

1. John Altrocchi, *Abnormal Behavior* (New York: Harcourt Brace Jovanovich, 1980), p. 56.
2. Ibid., p. 438.
3. Ibid., p. 436.

loss of interest in the ordinary events of life, a tendency for withdrawal from activities, a downcast expression, and a slump in posture. The person may complain that simple daily tasks seem mountainous, that food tastes peculiar, and that the appetite has seemed to vanish. Loss of sleep, sluggish flow of thought, poor concentration, and even physical symptoms like headaches, chest pains, muscular aches, and lack of sex drive can occur.[4]

Psychologists consider depression to be the oldest kind of psychological abnormality, even noting how the oldest biblical book, Job, is an account of a man in depression. Job had these symptoms.

Extreme sadness. "Why is light given to him who suffers, and life to the bitter of soul" (3:20).

Desire for death. "Who long for death, but there is none, and dig for it more than for hidden treasures" (3:21).

Sleep disturbance. "When I lie down I say, 'When shall I arise?' But the night continues, and I am continually tossing unto dawn" (7:4).

Pessimism about life. "Man, who is born of woman, is short-lived and full of turmoil" (14:1).

Helplessness. "I am not at ease, nor am I quiet, and I am not at rest, but turmoil comes" (3:26).

Life seemed worthless. Although Job believed he was innocent before God, life seemed worthless to him. "I am guiltless; I do not take notice of myself; I despise my life" (9:21).

Physical signs of sadness. "My eye has also grown dim because of grief, and all my members are as a shadow" (17:7).

KINDS OF DEPRESSION

If we were to cast a net over the entire history of psychological thinking about depression, we would pull in numerous systems of classification of the kinds of depression. Most of those are technical classifications for purposes of extensive scientific research. The modern tendency is to avoid extensive labeling and see most depression along a single dimension.[5] For a general understanding of depression we can classify it according to cause and severity. Depression can be

4. Paul E. Huston, "Depression: Psychotherapy," *International Encyclopedia of Psychiatry, Psychoanalysis and Neurology* (New York: Aesculapius, 1977), 4:59.
5. Altrocchi, p. 438.

categorized in two ways based upon cause. First, depression can occur because of an illness or a tumor. Second, primary depression is considered to be the major problem with a person. The depression is not an accompanying illness or some mental problem, such as schizophrenia, but the depression itself is the "primary" mental health problem.

Once that distinction is made, we can classify primary depressions according to their severity. Severity includes both the duration and the intensity. A person suffers grief and depression at the loss of a spouse; that is expected. But if that depression continues beyond three or four months and keeps that person from social contact and his daily work, it is then considered to be a different kind of depression.

We can distinguish three kinds of depression according to severity.

NORMAL DEPRESSION

From time to time we have all felt a lack of energy, a negative self-image, or a sense of hopelessness. All of those characteristics are the same as the more severe forms of depression, but there is a difference.

We can usually point to a clear cause; recovery from an illness, exhaustion from speaking five times in one weekend; or getting over the loss of a close friend or relative. And such a depression does not linger for months and actually incapacitate us. A woman knows she may be depressed during certain days in the month, her mood altered by her menstrual cycle. She knows what causes the depression and expects it to pass. A man who has lost a girl friend and feels worthless and lonely will overcome that, given time and a few special dates. Depression becomes abnormal when it lingers and nothing seems to help.

NEUROTIC DEPRESSIVE REACTIONS

A more intense, longer-lasting sadness distinguishes this kind of depression. "The person feels sad, depressed, blue, and often guilty, deserted, lost, and empty. The more severe the depressed mood is, the more likely are feelings of helplessness, hopelessness, and despair, and associated thoughts of death or suicide."[6] When a person is in this state, the idea of rejoicing seems impossible. He or she may seem to have lost the normal capacity for pleasure and mirth.

6. Ibid., p. 58.

SEVERE DEPRESSION

Although psychologists note that such a neurotic depression is very serious, some maintain that there is an even more serious form. Psychologist John Altrocchi calls it "severe depressive behavior." In such cases, it is not possible for the person to function without institutional care. That is primarily because the great agony the person experiences becomes extremely disturbing to others.

N. S. Kline cites a classic description:

> He walked the streets, in madness of melancholy, with his lips moving in indistinct curses, or with his eyes upturned in passionate prayers (never for himself, for he felt, or professed to feel, that he was already damned) . . . with his glance introverted to a heart gnawed with anguish and with a face shrouded in gloom, he would brave the wildest storms and at night, with drenched garments and arms wildly beating the wind and rain, he would speak as if to spirits. (A friend's description of Edgar Allen Poe as Poe entered his last days of depressive self-destruction by means of alcohol and opium.)[7]

CAUSES OF DEPRESSION

Although there has been extensive study of depression, its causes are not yet thoroughly understood. Causes of normal depression are not so evasive as those of the more severe forms. And while the causes of all levels of depression are similar, they will be more clearly understood if they are classified separately.

CAUSES OF NORMAL DEPRESSION

To label depression as normal may be a mistake according to some Christians. Since God commands us to rejoice and provides the Holy Spirit, whose fruit is joy, it might seem obvious that all depression is sinful. When we do look at the murky depths we sometimes experience, we are more likely to call it by a more acceptable name, such as loneliness or bereavement.

That depression can be a normal Christian experience should not surprise us if we would concentrate on but a few statements of Scripture related to the Christian's inner state. Jesus, in Gethesemane, was free to admit that His soul was exceedingly sorrowful, even to the point of death. The author of the book of Hebrews reminded his

7. N. S. Kline, *From Sad to Glad* (New York: Putnam, 1974), p. 36.

readers that the chastening of the Lord would be grievous, not pleasant (Heb. 12:11). And Peter did not scold the suffering Christians to whom he wrote for being "grievous." Commenting on that passage, John Calvin was most understanding of the temporary depression that Christians suffer:

> But it seems somewhat inconsistent, when he says that the faithful, who exulted with joy, were at the same time sorrowful, for these are contrary feelings. But the faithful know by experience, how these things can exist together, much better than can be expressed in words. However, to explain the matter in a few words, we may say that the faithful are not logs of wood, nor have they so divested themselves of human feelings, but that they are affected with sorrow, fear danger, and feel poverty as an evil, and persecutions as hard and difficult to be borne. Hence they experience sorrow from evils; but it is so mitigated by faith, that they cease not at the same time to rejoice.[8]

Many Christians do not think that way. I remember being surprised as a young Christian when my theology professor said: "Sometimes when you feel down, you don't need to pray more, you need a good night's sleep." His statement relieved me from feelings of guilt I was experiencing at that time, apparently from the unrealistic view I had had of the Christian life.

When there is adequate cause for feelings of depression we should not feel an urgent need to get right with God or to restore the joy of salvation. Surely, a woman can accept a recurring monthly mood, waiting for it to pass, without resorting to self-blame and confession. The sadness, sense of helplessness, and loss of love for life that attacks us when we lose a loved one should be considered a normal, Christian condition. More serious forms of depressive behavior—neurotic and severe—probably have causes beyond the "normal," although such causes can also contribute to normal depression as well.

ILLNESS OR INJURY

Depression and illness go together in a variety of ways. Sometimes the depression is a direct result of illness. Diabetes and Cushing's syndrome are two diseases that sometimes produce it. Usually, there is

8. John Calvin, *Commentaries on the Catholic Epistles*, trans. John Owens (Grand Rapids: Eerdmans, 1948), p. 32.

some depression accompanying any injury or illness. It is the most common emotional response to illness or injury for both children and adults, often coming a few days after the injury or the onset of illness. When healing or recovery is slow or delayed, depression may set in. These feelings come as a result of the individual becoming aware of what is really happening to him.

BIOLOGICAL PROBLEMS

Throughout medical history it has been quite evident that strokes, brain injuries, and tumors can cause depression. It is not so evident that depression can be caused by other physical ailments. Yet, there is growing evidence from research that some people experience depression because of some chemical problem within their system. Christian counselor Wayne Oates is one who maintains that such depression, termed "endogenous depression," is both constitutionally and biochemically based and can be modified by medical intervention.[9]

Up to this point it seems evident that the minister, when preaching on Christian joy, should not be unrealistic. Christians who are suffering from depression because of physical or other justifiable causes are experiencing some loss of self-esteem in addition to their loss of joy. Making them feel guilty or ashamed over their lack of joy will drive them further into depression. Our emotions cannot be changed by command. "Don't feel depressed" is an impossible demand.

There are psychological causes for depression, especially in the more severe forms. For many years, psychologists have noted that people who become depressed often are those who have had significant losses in their childhood. The study of Rene Spitz is significant here. It shows us the importance of parental affection during the early years of life. In a documentary film, he tells the pitiful story of ninety-seven babies, ages 3 months to 3 years:

> [They] sickened and died for lack of love. . . . The orphanage in which they had been placed was equipped to give normal routine care. The children were adequately fed, clothed, and given proper medical attention. . . . Only one element was lacking. . . . They had no time to play with their charges; they could give them no comfort or emotional exchange of any kind. . . . At the end of five months, deterioration had

9. Wayne E. Oates and Herbert Wagemaker, "The Professional Evaluation of Depression," *Pastoral Psychology*, vol. 25, no. 2, Winter 1976, p. 88.

set in with accelerated swiftness. Most of the babies became shrunken beyond recognition. . . . Twenty-seven of those children died in their first year of life. Seven more died in the second year. Another twenty-one . . . managed to survive, but they were so altered by the experience that they had to be classified as hopeless neurotics, or worse.[10]

Stress is another cause of depression. While all of us may experience the symptoms of depression when under unusual stress, stress may actually precipitate a long period of severe depression. A change in jobs, the loss of a spouse or a friend, a move to a new community, and even the changes that come from success can be stressful. That a person does not "get over" such a stressful experience does not mean that the circumstance is the actual cause of the depression. Most people are able to handle stress. It is believed that the circumstance triggers the severe depression. The evidence of numerous studies suggests that there must be some predisposition to depression at the time that the environmental stress occurs.

What makes a person predisposed to depression is not fully understood. Klerman notes that "it is widely believed that persons prone to depression are characterized by low self-esteem, strong superego, clinging and dependent interpersonal relations, and limited capacity for mature and enduring object relations."[11]

PREVENTION AND TREATMENT OF DEPRESSION

The pastor as a counselor and an educator is in the position to help others face and overcome depression. There are some important areas in the prevention and treatment of depression that the pastor needs to be mindful of when dealing with depression and the depressed.

THE NORMALCY OF DEPRESSION

The pastor can help others understand the normalcy of depression. The victorious Christian life does not come without a struggle. Teaching that it is normal to face periods of depression will prepare people for them. There are some reasons why it is important to accept depression as a part of life. First, one of the least effective ways of fighting depression is through denying it or telling it to go away. The more you fight depression, the more you lose. Of course, that does not

---

10. Smiley Blanton, *Love or Perish* (New York: Simon and Schuster, 1956), pp. 39, 49.
11. Armond M. Nicholi, Jr., ed., "Depression," *The Harvard Guide to Modern Psychiatry* (Cambridge, Mass.: Harvard U., 1978), p. 272.

mean that one should give in to depression. There are ways of treating it. But merely resolving not to be depressed is not one of the ways. Sometimes depression must be allowed to run its course.

Martin Luther had markedly severe periods of depression that were not abated by anything that he tried. Even spiritual success, such as translating the Bible into German, did not cause those attacks to end. Luther describes the extremity of his emotional state: "For more than a week I was close to the gates of death and hell. I trembled in all my members. Christ was wholly lost. I was shaken by desperation and blasphemy of God." Luther even saw those moods as beneficial to his understanding the Christian life. "For without them," he wrote, "no man can understand Scripture, faith, the fear or the love of God."[12]

Second, depression may be worsened by too high ideals. There is evidence that persons prone to depression have a low self-esteem and a very strong consciousness about right and wrong. If we tend to suggest that depression is not part of the normal Christian life, we will make them even more prone to depression. They will take our words more seriously than others. When they have the normal moods of sadness, they may feel guilty, lowering their self-esteem even more. Such people need to know that struggling with the slough of despondency does not make them abnormal or of less worth to God.

John Bunyon explained that in his *Pilgrim's Progress*. "Pilgrim's episode in the Slough of Despond," Virginia Owens reminds us, "shows that the frantically sought for 'cause' of depression is nothing less than the total experience of being human."[13]

THE SYMPTOMS OF DEPRESSION

The pastor can teach others the symptoms of neurotic and severe depression, and urge those needing it to get professional help.

DEALING WITH ANGER

He can teach others to deal with their anger. It is possible that a predisposition to depression is caused by a person's fear of his own anger and assertiveness. Whenever a teenager, for example, has hostile feelings toward a stern, unloving father, he may repress such feelings. He may actually fear hating or being angry with that parent. He may unconsciously deny what he is feeling, and act submissively to make the father react with kindness and love. However, his anger will

12. Roland Bainton, *Here I Stand* (New York: Abingdon, 1950), p. 36.
13. Virginia Owens, "Naming the Darkness," *Christianity Today*, 19 January 1979, p. 22.

continue, perhaps inwardly leading him to bad feelings about himself and his life. Turned inward, anger causes a reaction of depression.

NEED FOR CLOSENESS WITH OTHERS

The pastor can urge others to be close to someone, to be able to speak their feelings openly and intimately with another. Research indicates that during a stressful experience, women who report having a close companion were less likely to become depressed than were women who did not have a close and intimate confidant.

TREATING DEPRESSION

The pastor can help people focus on treating depression through environmental changes. Milder bouts of depression can be helped by Bible reading and prayer. But more practical measures might also be necessary. It might be best for the depressed to ignore his heavy heart and seek the company of others. Manual labor can offer some relief. "A good way," counseled Luther, "to exorcise the Devil was to harness the horse and spread manure on the fields."[14]

GETTING CONTROL

The pastor can urge the depressed person to get control of his or her life. One of the marks of depression is the morbid sense of fear of what is happening. The future is dreary; in the present, there seems to be little the person can do to help himself. That kind of attitude needs to be changed. The counselor and preacher can help the person see that there is hope, that he or she still has a will and an ability to maintain control.

Doing something that makes the person feel as if he is in charge will be very helpful. The counselor should ask what the counselee would like to undertake, and encourage him to do it. For example, if the person wants to do something about his weight, he can be encouraged to begin a diet. Often, a depressed person has a weight problem, caused by eating as a means of bringing some enjoyment. If he begins to do something about the problem, it will be a step toward regaining the mastery that seems to have been lost.

By all means, we should treat depression in a spiritual way and with recognition of its spiritual causes. But we also should become increasingly aware of practical treatments of a psychological order that stems from many and varied causes.

14. Bainton, p. 364.

9
Fear

Fear is sometimes clearly sinful. Take the case of the generation of Jews who had come out of Egypt and were a short distance from the land they had been promised. The spies had made a reconnaissance to prepare for the seizure of the land. But the majority report caused the people to respond in fear: "We are not able to go up against the people, for they are too strong for us" (Num. 13:31). For that reaction, God made them wander in the wilderness and die without ever seeing the land of promise. God's judgment seems quite severe to us. Robert E. Morosco explains: "From a purely psychological perspective, it seems almost unfair that God should so react to the fear of man. After all, were not the circumstances such that anyone with any sense would have been afraid to enter the territory of the powerful Canaanites?"[1]

But the people clearly disobeyed. God had told them repeatedly, "Do not fear the people of the land" (Num. 14:9), and, "Do not fear or be dismayed" (Deut. 1:21). Yet, fear had made them reject God's will.

Think of how fear, at one time or another, pushes all of us into retreat and into making unsound and unbiblical decisions. Afraid another man might not come along, a Christian girl marries a non-Christian man. Fearful of what people might say, a Christian businessman fails to ever share Christ with others. Fear may be more closely associated with our sinfulness than we might realize. Paul Tournier has speculated that perhaps one of the most basic of all sins is "cowardice."

But God addresses our timidity: "God has not given us a spirit of timidity [fear]" (2 Tim. 1:7). Fear should not guide or motivate us. Therefore, we need to understand fear and deal with it.

---

1. Robert E. Morosco, "Theological Implications of Fear, the Grasshopper Complex," *Journal of Psychology and Theology* 1, no. 2 (April 1973): 47.

Definition of Fear

A definition of fear clearly emerges from psychological literature. "Fear is an emotion one experiences in the presence of or anticipation of real, often physical danger."[2] Usually, it is distinguished from anxiety where there is an absence of definable external danger. Thus, anxiety is a reaction to unrealistic internal (psychological) dangers. A person who is in the midst of a flu epidemic might fret about getting sick—that is fear. Another person might fret every day of his life about getting sick—that is anxiety.

However, fear and anxiety seem to produce the same physiological response. The autonomic nervous system is aroused in either case. Arousal can produce a rapid and unusually strong heartbeat, rapid or shallow breathing, trembling, sweating, muscular tension, dryness of the mouth, and changes in voice quality and faintness.[3] Fear clearly produces an increase of adrenaline in the bloodstream.

Defining fear as an emotion seems to make calling it a sin unfair. Can a person in the face of danger control his emotions? What does it mean when God tells us not to be afraid?

Distinguishing Various Facets of Fear

FEAR UNDER CONTROL

Biblical passages that touch on fear describe it as something that can be regulated by the human will. That helps us understand why God, at times, treats human fear as an affront. In the Scriptures, fear is generally not seen as merely an emotion.

Robert Morosco explains: "Though the Scriptures sometimes speak of fear in the emotional sense, the most significant texts are concerned with the volitionally controlled or theological fear."[4]

To understand how fear has both emotional and willful aspects, we need to distinguish clearly various facets of our reaction to danger. There are three of these: (1) Our perception of danger. We might see something as a threat and having the power to harm us. It might be an engulfing danger, such as a thunderstorm. Or the danger might pose less of a problem, but one that, nonetheless, can render a person helpless, such as the sudden appearance of a bumblebee. (2) There is the emotion itself. We can feel something and even experience physical

---

2. John Altrocchi, *Abnormal Behavior* (New York: Harcourt Brace Jovanovich, 1980), p. 41.
3. Ibid., pp. 42-43.
4. Morosco, p. 44.

changes. (3) There is also the response to the fear. We might think or do something as a reaction to the impending danger. If there is a rattlesnake in our path, our fear will cause us to stop, back off, and carefully make a wide circle around it. Normally, we might not think of this part of the process as "fear." But the Bible seems to indicate that it is.

Morosco shows how true fear can sometimes be dealt with by one's actions of surrender or acceptance. Whenever a person truly fears something, he may acknowledge the object's mastery over him. We sometimes use the term "respect" to cover that aspect of fear. A hiker who carefully backs away from the coiled rattler is saying by that action, "I respect rattlesnakes." We would regard that person as wise; his fears are legitimate and his actions proper. We would consider it abnormal to continue walking into its path.

By looking at those three aspects of fear we can begin to understand why fear can be sinful. One can sin by failing to perceive actual danger. A person can ignore the warnings of others about alcohol, and as a result, have little respect for the effects of excessive drinking. The Bible, in particular, warns against ignoring God as the One who ultimately poses the greatest danger to humans. Thus, Jesus said, "Fear Him who is able to destroy both soul and body in hell" (Matt. 10:28).

In commands like that (and there are many), people are asked to acknowledge the overwhelming power God has over us and to surrender to Him. Thus, we are to surrender to Him and acquiesce to His power over us.

This perception is similar to the perception of an object of danger, such as the poisonous snake. It is not merely dread or repulsion. Rather, it is a surrender to the authority of that object. When a hiker avoids a rattlesnake, he is admitting the snake's authority over him.

Man's greatest sin is, therefore, his failure to fully respect God and to fear Him above all. Failing to do that is a failure to perceive a danger that really exists: His wrath.

Another form of human failure is to fear something that is really not dangerous to us. The Bible deals with this: "The LORD is with us; do not fear them [the people of the land]" (Num. 14:9). With that in view, we can clearly see that we are responsible for our fears. If we give God His rightful place as the one Creator and ruler, He alone should be respected. If we surrender to realities that do not really constitute danger for us, we are giving them the place reserved for God. Thus, to fear those things He has told us not to fear dethrones God. For that reason, the Jews were always being told not to "fear other gods" (2 Kings 17:35). Fearing the wrong object can amount to idolatry.

Morosco explains well this moral aspect of fear:

> Since God Himself, in accordance with the reality of His nature, demands to be the highest fear-object in the thinking of His creatures, the possibility of moral error is present whenever someone or something is selected to be revered above Him. When the Exodus generation exhibited their fear of the Canaanites by accepting their will over Jehovah's, they, in essence had elevated the power and impendency of the Canaanites over the omnipotence and imminence of God, who was with Israel.[5]

That, of course, involves fear-objects other than pagan gods. We can put anything into God's place and revere it above Him. A person who is afraid of losing his wealth is acting like a person who worships another god. The same can be said for those with excessive fear about loss of health, friends, or career.

But the biblical commands about fear have much to do with the third aspect of fear: the response to it. The spies who returned to the people of Israel, waiting on the border of the land, were obviously afraid. They characterized themselves as grasshoppers in contrast to the land's giants. It is probable that God was not impatient with their emotion of fear. After all, their enemies were very big and powerful. However, God did command that they not act on those fears. Their sin lay in both their perceptions and their actions. They perceived their enemies to be more than they could handle, and even more than their God could deal with. They acted on those viewpoints by retreating from God's command to go in and conquer. When God told them not to fear, He meant that they should not act on fear. They should not give such respect to their enemies. In doing so, they were not respecting God; they were surrendering to their enemies instead of surrendering to God.

In the New Testament, the apostle Peter provides an example of that. He refused to eat with the Gentiles, "fearing the circumcision party." Because of that fear, he failed to dine or act in a manner that was consistent with the gospel.

Many biblical passages urge us to fear God above all. The preacher of Ecclesiastes says that it is the whole duty of man to fear God

---

5. Ibid., p. 48.

(Eccles. 12:13). Fear is commanded in the many passages that equate it with worship (Pss. 19:9; 34:11; 96:9; Jer. 2:19; Heb. 12:28). The Proverbs explain that the fear of the Lord is the beginning of wisdom (Prov. 1:7).

But this fear of God is not equated with feelings of dread. The effects are positive: happiness (Prov. 28:14); prolonged life (Prov. 10:27); and righteousness (Prov. 16:6). In addition, the Bible teaches that only the fear of the Lord can alleviate one's captivity to human fears (Rom. 13:1-14), such as the fear of death, which the devil is said to use to keep man in slavery (Heb. 2:15). And in 1 John 4:18, we find that "perfect love casts out fear [in its destructive form]."

As ministers of Christ, it will be our duty to show the connections fear has with sin and faith. But in doing so, we need to be careful to explain all that the Bible and psychology teach about fear. Otherwise, our teaching might appear to condemn those who struggle with fear on a daily basis, especially those who have unusually destructive forebodings and dreads.

Our teaching and preaching can profitably include the following.

FEAR AS AN EMOTION IS NOT NECESSARILY WRONG

"Fear, in and of itself, is not morally evil or wrong; fear is neutral."[6] As an emotional response to danger, fear is like pain; it is necessary and useful. It warns us of danger. A snowstorm should arouse enough fear to make us drive cautiously. Thus, it is obvious that a Christian should not expect to live a fearless life.

A Christian should learn to fear those things that are harmful to him. Fear of the occult, sin, and other dangers will be normal reactions to life. Paul the apostle told Christians to fear the government:

> Let every person be in subjection to the governing authorities. For there is no authority except from God, and those which exist are established by God. Therefore he who resists authority has opposed the authority of God; and they who have opposed will receive condemnation upon themselves. For rulers are not a cause of fear for good behavior, but for evil. Do you want to have no fear of authority? Do what is good, and you will have praise from the same; for it is a minister of God to you for good. But if you do what is evil, be afraid. [Rom. 13:1-5]

It is quite normal, then, while driving, to cringe in fear when a police cruiser's lights flash behind you.

6. Ibid., p. 45.

FEAR CAN BE A DAILY STRUGGLE

Dealing with fear is a continual struggle. Even when fear is illegitimate, we should help others understand that it might not easily go away. In spite of the numerous passages in the Bible commanding us not to be afraid, we should recognize that struggle with fear can be prolonged and difficult. In some respects, it is the essence of the Christian's struggle. The answer to our human fears is trust in God. David said, "When I am afraid, I will put my trust in Thee" (Ps. 56:3). But trust is always our greatest challenge. "Fight the good fight of faith" (1 Tim. 6:12), said Paul, who often referred to the Christian life as warfare.

FEAR CAN BE RELATED TO AGE

Fears can be related to a person's age. Childhood is a time of fear. When asked, the great majority of adults report that they hold fewer fears than they did when they were children. Younger children usually hold more fears with greater intensity than do older children, adolescents, and adults. Even a child's place in the family can make a difference. Youngest and oldest children in families indicate they have more fears than do middle-born children.[7]

Children under four years of age are most afraid of the unfamiliar: noise, objects, and persons. Boys, aged four through six, are most concerned for personal safety, whereas girls are more concerned with noise and conditions associated with noise. Around the age of eight, children become more aware of their total environment and potential dangers. Both boys and girls report, most commonly and intensely, fears of natural phenomena, such as tornados, hurricanes, and even polluted water and air. They also fear getting sick and dying from taking drugs.[8]

At about the age of eleven, the concern for ecological and natural phenomena continue, but there is now greater concern for political items, such as the occurrence of war and being overrun by our enemies.

Adolescents show an increasing concern for political fears to the point that those fears overshadow all other categories of fear. This anxiety over personal safety accounts for a lot of the adolescent problems. The use of drugs, excesses in rock music, and the newer

---

7. James W. Croake, "Fears: Development Perspective," *International Encyclopedia of Psychiatry, Psychology, Psychoanalysis, and Neurology*, 5:21.
8. Ibid.

destructive forms of punk rock (where harm is inflicted on oneself) may be associated with fear of this kind. Adolescents also show an increase in fear related to personal relations with family and friends.

Adult fears cover a whole range of matters, but they are related to adult development. Thus, the middle-adult man fears being replaced by younger people at his job, losing his sexual ability, and so on. Older adults fight the fear of being left alone, the fear of sickness and pain, and the fear of dying.

FEAR MAY BE A SIGN OF MAJOR PROBLEMS

Excessive, prolonged, or unusual fears can be signs of major psychological and spiritual disorders. Schools of psychology have different approaches to the analysis of fears. They all agree that a fear is an abnormal problem whenever it results in making life uncomfortable or destructive for the individual. An individual who cannot handle responsibilities and makes life uncomfortable for others, because of fear, is in need of treatment. A person who is constantly late for work because he is so afraid of leaving the house is an example of abnormal fear.

There are different kinds of problem fears. (1) Fearing when there is nothing to fear. It is normal to fear being bitten by a poisonous snake. But a person who allows that fear to keep him confined indoors obviously has a problem fear. (2). Excessive reactions. It is normal to fear sickness-causing germs and to take appropriate precautions to avoid them. But spending countless hours doing unnecessary things to keep one's surroundings clean is indicative of a problem. I know of a woman who, once a week, takes down all the curtains in her bedroom, washes them and the windows and windowsills; she turns over the mattresses weekly and vacuums them. Through the years, she has had little social life because so much of her time is spent in housecleaning; she has tried to force those same habits on her children, creating fears and conflicts in them.

It is most important that we recognize when such persons need special therapy and recommend that they get it. We must be careful not to treat their condition lightly and suppose that a Scripture verse will cure them.

It is also crucial to recognize that fear, such as depression, can be the result of other psychological problems. A person may have great fear that something dreadful is about to happen (often termed anxiety). It could be caused by some deep-seated guilt resulting from disobedience in his life. Some psychologists maintain that some fears are a result of pent-up anger. Thus, a child who may have unusual fears may be harboring some anger against a father who divorced his mother.

Past experiences can provoke fear reactions. A woman's fear of men could have been caused by her father's mistreatment of her. A general state of fear can be caused by a situation unknown to others; a man with homosexual tendencies may have a perpetual fear of being discovered.

Thus fear, in some cases, can be seen as a symptom of a greater or unconscious problem. In those situations, the removal of the cause is necessary to the removal of the symptom. Treating only the symptom might only cause greater complications for the individual.

FEAR CAN BE DEALT WITH IN A VARIETY OF WAYS

Trust in God is the most obvious remedy. For those who have abnormal fears, counseling may be necessary to uncover the cause. For those with more normal struggles with fear, there are some practical suggestions that can be followed.

Face the fear object. It seems clear that running from what is feared increases the fear. Becoming more familiar with what scares us is one of the most basic ways of dealing with it. That is because there is a relationship between fear and closeness to the cause. "It has been shown that there is some relationship between holding fear more frequently and intensely when there is little justification; whereas, there is a tendency toward lessening of fear when one has closer contact with the menacing stimulus."[9] The anticipation of going to a dentist seems almost always to be more frightening than the treatment itself.

Contact with the fear object can be had through study of it. We should encourage adolescents, for example, to study what is happening internationally. Children can be encouraged to read Christian literature about ghosts, demons, and other menacing monsters to understand them more accurately.

Deal with fears through association with other people. Children's fears, for example, seem to be handled best through exposure to adult's reactions. Whenever adults make too much of a child's fears, fussing over them and trying to explain them away, the child's fears increase. Acting calmly and confidently without a lot of assuring talk

9. Ibid.

seems to calm the child more. "The calm assurance by the parent's behavior, not words, tells the child that he need not react so fearfully to the situation." As one child said, "When my parents explain a lot why I should not be afraid, I know they are worried, and I really do have something to be afraid of."[10]

That confirms our knowledge of how people handle fears. We often do so by identification; we try to associate ourselves with people who do not fear what we do. Thus, a Christian who fears demons will be helped by associating with a congregation of believers who do not.

Avoid fear-producing stimulation. Children exhibit fears whenever they have been exposed to movies and books that communicate matters that frighten. Certain books or TV programs can cause overstimulation and lead to nightmares.

Even adults can use caution here. A woman recently told us that she has avoided seeing a certain popular movie that has a major scene involving thousands of snakes, of which she has a morbid fear. Her decision was a wise way of dealing with her fears.

Discuss fears with others. Like other human emotions, fear needs to be exposed. It can, like anger, be repressed and pushed under the surface of our awareness and do a lot of damage. When we discuss our fears with others not only do we get a better grasp of the fear object, but also a better understanding of our fear and what it is doing to us.

Resolve not to act on fear. One of the most difficult things about fear is distinguishing between what is legitimate and what is excessive. Fear can torment us, debilitate us, and push us to constant panic, making us unable to move and act. It can send us into a rage of overreaction. For example, it is proper to fear addiction to alcohol. But think of what it can do to a father who smells beer on his teenage son's breath for the first time. His fear might provoke excessive rebuke, outrage, and even panic. What, then, is the problem? Is the fear too great, or is the reaction to the fear excessive? It is sometimes hard to distinguish between the two.

Perhaps it is a good rule for us not to be led by our fears as well as dominated by them. "God has not given us a spirit of timidity [fear]" (2 Tim. 1:7), said Paul. Should a father out of fear rebuke his son who

10. Ibid., p. 22.

is experimenting with alcohol? Should he not control his fearful reaction and speak to him out of love?

What about fear that causes a husband to jealously guard his wife's activities? Fear of her unfaithfulness may prompt him to ask suspicious questions and cast distrustful glances in her direction. A husband should resist that response to fear.

But another voice tells us that we should respect and fear the fruits of the flesh, the world, and the devil. When is a fear a warning that something might be wrong? When should we respect it, examine it, and determine what response we should make?

It seems that as Christians we should respect the reality of fear as a regulatory part of life. But, on the other hand, we should not let that control us and dominate us or lead us to excessive actions or emotions. We should remember that, above all, we are only to fear Him.

10

Grief

A woman had an unusual grief reaction about a film on childbirth I showed to my classes. After viewing half the film, she got up and left. Later she came to me to express how surprised and confused she was over her response. She had been overcome with extreme sadness and an uncontrollable urge to cry, which she did for more than an hour after leaving the film showing. She asked if it might be related to events four years previously. At that time two very serious events occurred. Within a matter of weeks, she had suffered a miscarriage and her husband suddenly died. As we talked, she wondered whether her reaction to the film about babies was a delayed grief experience. She remembered that she had spent little time "working through" the loss of her baby because her husband's death solely occupied her thoughts and emotions during that period.

It is quite conceivable that that woman's experience is a classic example of what can happen whenever the grief process is hindered. Psychologists today are unanimous in their belief that grief is a normal and necessary process. If it is not "worked through" properly, it can show up later as "delayed grief" and even produce serious emotional or physical problems.

When speaking of grief, one of our first objectives should be to help others accept it. That is especially necessary for evangelicals since, in contrast to those in biblical times, we tend to view grief as a weakness. Ancients were not ashamed to display grief during times of personal crisis. The great generals Cyrus and Alexander are known for their public weeping. Even the apostle Paul acknowledged the legitimacy of such displays.

Paul told the Philippians that he was capable of great sorrow. Speaking of God's healing of Epaphroditus he wrote: "God had mercy on him; and not on him only, but on me also, lest I should have sorrow upon sorrow" (Phil. 2:27). The expression "sorrow upon sorrow" is based on a Hebrew idiom that pictures intense wailing and weeping. And Paul did not criticize the Christian leaders from Ephesus who wept and sorrowed greatly because of his departure from them (Acts 20:36-37). When he said we were to "sorrow not, even as others which have no hope," he was referring to the manner of sorrowing, not the fact (1 Thess. 4:13). There is no doubt that Paul did not forbid sorrow in the Christian's experience.

Accepting instead of resisting grief will help in a number of ways. First, the acceptance of grief will begin to prepare a person for it when it happens. As with other human experiences, being around people who have seen their spouse or child die is not the same as having it happen to you. That creates the usual lament: "I was never prepared for this." In a sense, a person can never fully activate what emotional reactions he will have at such a time. But if a person believes he should not sorrow or "break down," he will be less prepared than someone who accepts such reactions. Such a person's grief experience will be compounded by guilt and be repressed, possibly causing problems later. Second, if a person accepts grief as a legitimate experience, he will be open to understanding it and studying it. A great deal of research has provided some helpful insights into this universal experience. Although not a replacement for Christian faith, such an understanding will contribute to a person's success in dealing with a loss.

Our resistance to grief and sorrow is no doubt more cultural than biblical. Its source may be Anglo-Saxon heritage, which tended to disdain emotions in favor of willful behavior. Our country was built upon rational ingenuity. As certain emotions tended to get in the way of progress, we suppressed them.

Grief as an Emotion

To properly understand grief, we must see that it is an emotion. Outward behaviors like sobbing or even dressing in mourning clothes are part of grief. But grief is not really a behavior; it is an emotion. Thus, it is not something one causes to happen, but something that naturally happens. Grief can be defined as the complex emotional response to loss.

Grief is a complex response, not merely sadness. Although grief is a universal experience, one psychologist reminds us, the task of defining it is not an easy one. That is because grief varies "widely with the unique individuals involved."[1] Sex, age, religious belief, personality structure, and duration and intensity of the relationship with the lost object will make each person's loss uniquely his own. Also, Sullender reminds us, grief reactions vary with the kind of loss. The grief one experiences over the death of one's parents is not exactly the same as the grief experienced over the loss of a job. Grief reactions vary within different cultural contexts. Varying subcultures and family systems will mold the social expressions of grief.

One of the authors recalls his embarrassment at a Filipino funeral. As an American, he tried to console a wailing, screaming woman, but she easily gained her composure for a moment to glance at him with the nonverbal message: *Leave me alone!* She then immediately went back to her "show" of emotion, apparently certain that the surrounding relatives would expect her to behave in that way. She knew that her love for the lost one would be measured by the outward display of grief.

CAUSE OF GRIEF

Psychologists have different theories about the cause of grief. One theory, originating with Freud, argues that grief is an instinctive reaction. It occurs whenever there is a conflict between reality and what we want to exist. Whenever a person or thing is lost to us, it sets up a conflict within us. The reality of the loss forces us to detach ourselves from the person or thing. But since through the months and years we have built up a loving relationship, we want that relationship to continue. Thus, there is a conflict over the need to sever the contact and the desire to continue it. Therefore, some psychologists view grief as a reclaiming of emotional capital. The person must disengage himself from the relationship that once existed and reinvest it in a new and productive direction for the health of his or her future.

The need to reinvest causes tremendous inner conflict, which results in anxiety and sadness. For example, when a person loses his job he must move in two directions. He must sever his attachment from the past job and then enter another one. In the case of a spouse's death, however, that does not mean that a person must reinvest his love in another for the grief process to be complete. But it does mean that the bereaved must continue to build healthy relationships with others

---

1. R. Scott Sullender, "Three Theoretical Approaches to Grief," *The Journal of Pastoral Care*, December 1979, vol. 23, no. 4, p. 243.

around him and not allow a continued emotional attachment to his dead spouse to interfere with those relationships.

One of the most helpful psychological ways of understanding grief is to see it as a reaction to loss. Whenever we lose something, we are emotionally stirred to search for it. That is part of being human. Our emotions support what is a logical human behavior. Were we not to care about the loss of food or other valuable items, we would not be able to survive. Thus, whenever there is a loss there are the accompanying actions. Colin Parkes has argued that this "urge to search" characterizes all grief. It is particularly present in the early stages of bereavement. According to Parkes, "Typical searching behaviors include anxiety, restlessness, preoccupation with the lost person, . . . focus of attention toward those parts of the environment in which the lost person is likely to be, and even 'calling for the lost person.' "[2]

We have all experienced degrees of those feelings and behaviors whenever we thought we lost something. Have you ever misplaced your car keys or your wallet before attending a meeting? You had to give up your search until the meeting was over. Remember how difficult it was for you to forget about the loss while you waited for the meeting to end? Anxiety and restlessness robbed you of concentration. Mentally, you were retracing your past steps, making a search for the lost object.

GRIEF IS A REACTION TO ANY LOSS

Viewed as a reaction to loss, we can see that grief is not a response unique to the loss of a friend or loved one. Life's infinite variety of losses produces grief. That explains why even less significant losses bother us so much. Some people may have a very difficult time "living down" the loss of a ten dollar bill. It may take days for them to get the loss out of their mind. It also explains why some experiences, although short of death, are terribly disastrous.

Looking at grief as loss will also help us understand the terminally ill and their families. We now know that the terminally ill person goes through a grief process. He or she is suffering extreme loss, as well as expectation of further loss. Illness cuts the seriously ill from his job, his ministry, and even severs his relationship from many people. The losses are overwhelming. The grief is sometimes complicated by an additional reaction known as *anticipatory grief*. The terminally ill person, knowing that he or she is about to die, may begin to work

2. Sullender, p. 244.

through the emotions of losing loved ones with whom he or she still has contact. That complicates the relationship; the sick person becomes more distant from the loved ones, and the relationships become confusing and strained.

Those close to the terminally ill may also experience grief over their loss, since their loved one is out of his normal routine of life. They, too, are subject to the experience of anticipatory grief. Over a period of weeks or months they may begin to emotionally separate themselves from the dying person. That is caused by the unconscious working through of the expected loss. Loved ones withdraw before the actual separation. It is often quite difficult for those involved to understand what is happening to them. They should resist the tendency to withdraw and instead, seek to stay emotionally close, even though that closeness will make the eventual separation even more painful to the surviving loved ones. If that closeness is not maintained, it makes prolonged dying a tragically lonely experience.

High on the list of losses is the loss of a greatly loved person through deliberate separation. Whenever a person is "jilted" it often occasions severe grief responses. Most young adult suicides are prompted by this "loss of a love." Divorce also ranks high as a grief-producer. It is even more complex than a spouse's death, since a divorce involves rejection as well as separation. Death, unless it is suicide, is inevitable and uncontrollable. Divorce is someone's choice, and may be more difficult to work through than loss through death.

The concept of grief as a response to loss also helps us justify the Christian's grief experience. When a loved one dies, the Christian does not experience eternal, hopeless loss, but he does experience loss. A young mother whose husband dies must continue to live without him. The hope of future resurrection is comforting, but it does not remove entirely the pain of separation and deprivation. It will be normal for her (as with others in loss situations) to expect some emotional reactions to all that is happening.

GRIEF AS A PROCESS

What we have said so far about grief has implied that grief is a process. In other words, the emotional response to loss runs a course. For many years, mental health experts have studied this process. We now have substantial research data to construct the "stages of grief." A number of books have been written to explain those stages to the average person. Granger Westberg's *Good Grief* is the briefest, simplest explanation. Although reading it will not remove the pain of grief, it may help remove the accompanying mystery, confusion, and guilt for those suffering from grief. Also, knowing what happens at each stage will assist all of us who are in a position to help someone going through grief. The following is a brief description of each stage, including suggested means of handling them for the person who is grieving and for those who are supporting him.

STAGE ONE

This is the shock stage. Lasting for hours or even days, this response involves denial and disbelief. Emotional and physical shock will occur, sometimes preceded by initial anger. Sufferers will sometimes be unwilling to believe the loss has happened. "I can't believe it," they may repeat over and over.

Guidelines for the Griever. Eventually, the griever must accept the reality of the loss. Whatever actions can be taken to respond to the loss, such as telephoning relatives and reaching out for help will make it more difficult for the person to deny what has happened.

Guidelines for Helping. Encourage the griever to face reality. Do not be afraid of using the word "dead." Help make phone calls and eventually the funeral arrangements. If you protect the person from those "hard" activities, you may prolong the denial stage. Allow the person to take the lead in conversation, and listen without blame to statements of bitterness or anger. Urge the griever to look for eternal hope and to rest in God's will. Although he needs to face the fact that the loss has actually occurred, do not try to force him to fully accept it at once. Acceptance may take time. Encourage "grief work" immediately. Encourage proper responses by telling them it's acceptable to cry or to feel badly. That will help them deal with the shock as well as the truth of what has occurred.

STAGE TWO

This is a controlled stage, which in cases of death ends after the funeral and the departure of loved ones. At this phase, the person is controlled by grief and by others. Characteristics include: passiveness, lack of reaction, feelings of emptiness, difficulty in making decisions, panic, fear, anxiety, and a lack of connection to self (depersonalization).

Guidelines for the Griever. At this stage there may be nothing to prevent those feelings. But in spite of them, the griever must continue life's activities. He must go to work, though he may not feel emotionally involved. He must be with other people, though his thoughts may be elsewhere. It will take time for those feelings to fade. In the meantime, it is important to continue one's life.

Guidelines for Helping. Continue to encourage "grief work." The person may complain of attacks of weeping and wonder if he or she is abnormal. Anxiety and fear may make the griever uncertain about his mental stability or even his Christian faith. Give assurance that all is normal.

Be present to help. Although the person may need some time alone, it is important for him to maintain contact with others. The best pain reliever for the agony of separation is a community of supporting individuals. Be an understanding, empathetic friend.

STAGE THREE

This is a regressive stage (three months). During this stage, the person becomes more active in an attempt to cope with the loss. But coping is more selfish and may even seem to be a regression from stage two. Characteristics include: expending a great deal of energy on maintaining control, being apathetic and helpless, and experiencing considerable tension. There is a tendency to simplify complex matters: "If only we had gotten another doctor's opinion," is a sample statement of that kind of thinking. There is also a preoccupation with the deceased. C. S. Lewis told of his dominating urge to try to recall everything he could about his wife.

Diminishing self-respect results. Shame over lack of control may be the cause. Or, the griever may see the death as something brought on by his unworthiness. His religious behavior may become simplified. He may give simple answers or solutions to what happened. "If I give some money to the church, I'll feel better." At this stage, communion with God sometimes is difficult. Doubt is evident as well as an increased interest in religious questions. Guilt, anxiety, and depression may still be lingering. Anger at God, the doctors, or even the person who died may crop up at this stage as well as at an earlier stage.

Guidelines for the Griever. The griever needs to deal with all of the things that come up at this stage. As in the book of Job, he may need to try to explain rationally what has happened and express his displeasure toward God. He may need to understand that the thinking that goes on at this stage may not be normal for him. But he will accept this thinking as part of the process. C. S. Lewis told of dwelling on the concept of God as some cruel heavenly monster at one point in his grief experience.

Guidelines for Helping. Continue to encourage "grief work." Crying and other emotional behaviors are still quite normal.

1. **Listen.** Allow the person to direct the conversation, and hear him out, even if what he say things may not sound very reasonable.
2. **Be alert to questions**. When the griever asks, he is reaching out for help. The grieving person may not always seem willing to agree with you, but he needs to hear some answer. Giving biblical insights and reading biblical passages is important whenever the person asks for answers.
3. **Ask questions**. Even gently challenge what the griever says. You are a link to reality. The person will recognize that his thinking is distorted by feeling.
4. **Be patient.** Do not rebuke the griever for his feelings or irrational thinking. It is best not to argue. However, if the person is still denying the death, or is failing to behave in ways that are helpful, a loving rebuke may be necessary. To say, "You must realize your husband is dead," is not cruel. Urge the person to "get out of the house" more often.

STAGE FOUR

This stage involves adaptation. The regressive forms of the previous stage are given up and a number of things occur.

1. The person is liberated from the self-image of mourner. Sometimes, the emotion of happiness suddenly occurs. Or, perhaps more slowly, the person regains his emotional composure when the more negative emotions are balanced with the joy of being alive.
2. The griever has a new perspective of the lost one. That person's memory will be respected and held in a normal way. There is still attachment, but it is entirely different.
3. The griever has regained a true focus on reality. The earlier distorted and simplistic thinking has given way to rational argu-

ments. Or perhaps, the griever is willing to live without complete rational explanation, just as he does in other areas of life.

Guidelines for the Griever. The griever will come to this stage if the prior stages have been handled properly. If he has not done his "grief work" by denying his loss or the emotions that resulted, he or she may end up with physical ailments or even delayed grief reactions. Unresolved anger, bitterness, or guilt may prevent the person from normal relationships, normal thinking, and normal living. Sometimes, for example, the loss of a child will cause damage to the parents' relationship because one of them did not go through the grief process.

Guidelines for Helping. In addition to what you may have offered to the griever before, he may need more. He may need someone to watch for symptoms of failure to adequately deal with the loss. These are common symptoms to watch for.

Inhibited grief

If, during the months following the death, little emotion has been shown or discussed, the person may not have allowed the healing experience following grief. That may reveal itself in certain problems: alcoholism, loss of sexual drive, or physical illness may occur. In those situations, the person will need counsel to see the link between his loss and his problem.

Delayed grief

If, after a long period of time, the person has an unusually severe emotional reaction to the loss, you may help him understand how that can be a delayed grief. Perhaps it was caused by stoic efforts to control emotions to be a "good testimony," or not to "disturb the children."

Elongated grief

It is not easy to determine exactly how long an individual's grief experience should last. Noting the stages should help us determine if a person is headed for unusual trouble. If, for example, after three weeks a wife is still not willing to admit her husband has died (in spite of the funeral and all other evidence) she is no doubt in need of some counseling. Sometimes people fail to enter stage four. In such cases, they may enter a new relationship with the lost one. A Chicago man, for example, never adjusted to the death of his young son. Years later, he still keeps his son's room as it always was, visiting it frequently each day. He has substituted the objects in that room for his departed son, never fully accepting the fact that his son is dead.

Even if we did not have scientific research on this subject, there is plenty of evidence for the stages of grief. C. S. Lewis's *A Grief Observed* is one of the finest literary accounts of the inner emotions and struggles of the process. The book of Job confirms that grief is a normal experience, even for the believer. That the oldest book of Scripture deals with the human reaction to loss is itself a testimony to the prominence of this experience in human life. When preaching on this subject we will greatly help people to realize that it is normal to go through it, as did Job, but also that it is normal to survive it, as did he.

11

Guilt

A wife of a young attorney was making a name for herself in the community. Her life consisted of a round of social events and community activities. Suddenly, she lost her vitality and began to drop out of those activities. She was deeply depressed, unable to sleep, and without an appetite. What was wrong?[1]

A man with two teenaged children and married for more than eighteen years was put into the hospital for tests. On three occasions, while at work, he had found himself gasping for air, unable to catch his breath. The third time he was forced to leave work. After a week of tests, the doctor dismissed him from the hospital, because tests showed that there was nothing physically wrong with him.[2]

The attorney's wife was suffering from an emotional problem: *guilt.* Her doctor believed her depression was caused by chemical problems and treated her accordingly. However, a Christian psychologist discovered that her problem stemmed from an affair she was having with a friend of her husband's. The psychologist reported: "Guilt and bad feelings about herself had caught up with her. The deceit with her husband, the lies, the attempts to cover up, her own lack of sexual response to her husband—all these came to a head in emotional exhaustion and depression."[3]

The respiratory problems of the teenagers' father were caused by guilt. For ten years he had been involved homosexually with the same person. Again and again he had tried to call it off, only to return compulsively. He was constantly deceiving his wife about the many

---

1. Roger Barrett, *Depression: What It Is and What to Do About It* (Elgin, Ill.: David C. Cook, 1977), pp. 154-55.
2. Ibid., p. 161.
3. Ibid., p. 155.

evenings he had been gone from home. "The massive deceit and a great deal of self-revulsion had caught up with him," Barrett concluded.

Guilt is a powerful human emotion. It turns people into bundles of nerves and sends them to the hospital for diagnoses of physical complaints. Sometimes they end up in psychiatric hospitals and receive shock treatments and drugs. Guilt awakens people in the middle of the night and makes them fearful and fretful about what the morning will bring.

Guilt may be what many alcoholics are trying to numb by their drinking. It prompts millions of Americans to gulp down pills and capsules to tranquilize their anxiety. It also creates critical monsters of some of us. We lash out at others to make ourselves feel better. Feeling so badly about ourselves, we deal harshly with others in an attempt to improve our self-image.

NATURE OF GUILT

Guilt is an agitation. Whenever we do not live up to our standards, expectations, and values we feel guilty. Barrett describes it as "the cutting edge of conscience that is called into action by the dissonance that exists between one's behavior and one's values."[4]

Psychological guilt, such as love and anxiety, is a human emotion. What we commonly call "guilt," is an abbreviated phrase meaning "feelings of guilt," according to the *International Encyclopedia of Psychiatry and Psychology, Psychoanalysis, and Neurology*.[5]

Those guilt feelings vary and have many faces. Each of the following manifestations can be a root of personality and emotional disorders.

DEPRESSION

When a person feels guilty, he feels unworthy. Because he fails to meet his standards, he becomes disappointed in what he has done and looks down on himself. He feels God and others are angry with him; that may then make him feel angry with himself. The anger and discouragement may cause a depressed, unhappy state.

David experienced that kind of depression whenever he sinned. In Psalm 51 he expressed his lack of joy by praying for restoration:

4. Ibid., p. 180.
5. *International Encyclopedia of Psychiatry, Psychology, Psychoanalysis, and Neurology*, 5:294.

"Make me to hear joy and gladness, let the bones which Thou hast broken rejoice. . . . Restore to me the joy of Thy salvation" (vv. 8, 12).

The depressed person may turn the anger in on himself so violently that he takes his own life, as happened in an incident in Chicago. When a small plane plummeted into Lake Michigan near the Chicago shoreline, the pilot tried unsuccessfully to help the passengers cling to the aircraft. He managed to stay afloat, but the others drowned. He was emotionally devastated. One by one, he had seen his wife and children sink into the waters to their deaths. He blamed himself for causing the accident. Several days later, the distraught pilot was discovered dead. Although he had survived the crash, he did not survive the memory of it; he committed suicide.

REJECTION

Guilt feelings often include feelings of rejection. Some psychologists claim that this is a reaction to childhood experiences. A child who is late for dinner may be sent to his room. Thus, he links the breaking of standards with separation from others.

Behind the sense of rejection is a feeling of unworthiness. Unconsciously, the person says to himself, "I am not worthy of the companionship of others." If that person believes in God, he transfers that to his relationship with Him.

FEAR

The guilty person may think he deserves punishment and be overcome by fear of what will happen to him. That fear may be an immediate reaction, as when a child is caught stealing something at the local drug store. Or, it may be a long-term, deep anxiety about the future, which awakens a person in the middle of the night and makes him wonder what awful thing is about to happen.

BASIC CHARACTER OF GUILT

It becomes immediately evident from the preceding examples that guilt could be the number one cause of psychological and emotional disorders. It could easily be linked to a man's inability to have intercourse with his wife. For example, he may feel unworthy of sexual pleasure because of his wild behavior before marriage. Or, guilt could be linked to a person's chronic unhappiness. He or she may spend a huge amount of money to go to an amusement park, only to find that it did not turn out to be much fun. That lack of joy could be explained by a deep down unworthiness. Inwardly, the person is saying to himself, *I don't deserve to have any fun.* Fear may be dominant and cause such worry about some possible catastrophe that the good time is bleached out.

Because all people sin, it is obvious from a biblical viewpoint that guilt will always be a major problem with the human race. Some psychologists also maintain that fact. They see that guilt is built into the nature of man. It is biologically rooted.

"Since it is related to the need of being cared for by a mother and raised within a family, it is one of the essential devices for survival itself." Thus, guilt is seen as a social thing. It is related to our failure to live up to the expectations of others. A child needs to feel that internal feeling if he or she is to conform to a parent's wishes. Guilt is socially useful.

Herbert Mower of the University of Illinois claimed that guilt feelings are basic to a person's psychological problems. An individual becomes guilt-ridden because of his behavior. By choosing to do something that is deliberately wrong, he creates an emotional disturbance within himself. Misconduct produces guilt, and guilt manifests itself in numerous emotional and even physical disorders. The nationally known psychiatrist Karl Menninger also endorses that viewpoint. In a recent book, *Whatever Became of Sin*, he maintains that psychologists must do more to treat the condition of guilt. Pastors, he claimed, are in a good position to help people with psychological disorders, because wrongdoing lurks behind so many of the problems of man.

But not all psychiatrists and psychologists agree with Mower and Menninger. Although they recognize that guilt is prevalent in the human condition, they do not recognize that it is caused by misbehavior.

Freud taught that we should help people get rid of the feeling of guilt rather than its cause. "The disease of the neurotic is his guilt. This guilt is, in itself, an evil and its removal is good." A popular novel propagated that view. In one scene the central character, a divorced woman, consults her analyst about the sexual temptations she is having. The psychologist suggests that she find some men to satisfy her needs. When the divorcee explains her moral objections to that, the psychologist coolly explains: "Guilt is an unnecessary human emotion." She is to solve her guilt by discarding her morals. That is a contemporary trend.

NORMALCY OF GUILT

In the face of those secular views of guilt, the Christian must maintain that guilt is a normal and proper human emotion. Like pain, it is a sign that something is wrong.

CIVIL GUILT

Guilt is proper when there is an objective reason for it. *Civil guilt* is proper when laws are broken. Whenever a person breaks a social law, he may feel rejected, depressed, and fearful. All of those emotions may converge to make him feel very sorrowful for what he has done. Such emotional reactions are legitimate and necessary to an orderly society. Sometimes, persons called psychopaths have no such feelings and create tremendous havoc. They have no emotional reactions to deter them from breaking laws.

THEOLOGICAL GUILT

Theological guilt is also proper. Breaking God's laws makes a person guilty before Him. The biblical word *condemn* conveys that idea. Although all men have sinned and are condemned, there is a way for the removal of guilt. There is no condemnation to them who are in Christ Jesus because He died to pay the penalty for sin. Thus, Christ removes theological guilt for those who are Christians.

FALSE GUILT

Having noted that guilt is sometimes proper, we must immediately see that it is sometimes a problem. Thus, Christian psychologists distinguish between real and false guilt. Reactions called *guilty reactions* sometimes occur when there is no immediate reason for them. Every time a person is depressed, feeling unworthy, and experiencing other manifestations of guilt, we need not assume he is guilty of something.

False guilt does have a cause, however. But it is not legitimate, nor is it always clearly apparent. Barrett lists some causes of false guilt.

PERFECTIONISM

Some persons feel depressed and unworthy if they do not attain perfection. They may have been made to feel that way by parents who pressed them to achieve overly high standards. Barrett explains:

> We may feel guilty for not measuring up to standards that are too high, inappropriate or perfectionistic. . . . Every therapist has seen this kind of

guilt with depression. The lady, motivated by guilt, gets up at five in the morning to clean an already spotless house for fear that it doesn't "measure up." The wealthy doctor who drives mercilessly because he hasn't achieved and exhausts himself in a guilt depression. There is the case of Amy, the straight *A* sophomore in high school who took her own life when she received her first *B* in a course at school.[6]

A perfectionist may blame himself for what is happening around him. Family quarrels, the death of a loved one, or the car breakdown can cause a person to be overwhelmed with self-blame.

NOT PLEASING OTHERS

Whenever those whose love we seek do not accept our feelings or behavior, we may feel guilty. A child may feel guilty for not pleasing an impossible father or nagging mother. In cases of adults, the connections between guilt and cause may be difficult to trace. A person can be gripped by fear of the future and have attacks of anxiety that prevent him or her from doing daily chores. Or those emotions may make the body break out in pain and disorder.

The cause might be a father who always pressured his child to measure up. Years later, he or she continues to try, harder and harder, to measure up to that built-in standard. But the result is regular failure, constant guilt, and continuing depression.

Paul Tournier makes the pressure to please others the basic criterion for distinguishing between false and real guilt. He maintains that true guilt comes from those things that are reproached by God in our inner heart. False guilt is a result of the judgment that comes from what men suggest. In that way Tournier makes the Bible very important to the Christian, for the revelation of God will enable him to distinguish between true and false guilt.[7]

HANDLING GUILT

TEACH GUILT AS NORMAL

First, reality demands that we inform people it is normal to have guilt feelings. That includes the assertion that guilt feelings are also good for us. "Guilt feelings are not always bad," writes the evangelical

---

6. Barrett, p. 121.
7. Paul Tournier, *Guilt and Grace* (New York: Harper & Row, 1962), p. 67.

psychologist Gary Collins. "They can stimulate us to change our behavior and seek forgiveness from God and others."[8]

Paul Tournier also embraces the viewpoint Gary Collins offers. But some differ from Collins. Bruce Narramore maintains that all psychological guilt is destructive, and therefore wrong for a Christian. Whether you agree with Collins or Narramore on that issue will depend on two foundational matters: the view of salvation and the definition of guilt. Narramore maintains that guilt feelings are not necessary to the Christian because all theological guilt is removed. There is no condemnation for believers. Therefore, because the objective basis of guilt is gone, the subjective experience should also be removed. Narramore's Calvinist position of the security of the believer is evident here. However, Collins and Tournier also seem to fall into the Calvinist camp; yet, they come to a different conclusion about guilt. That is because of their different stand on the second matter: the definition of guilt.

Narramore defines guilt feelings as fear of punishment, loss of self-esteem, and feelings of rejection. He insists that a Christian should not have such feelings, because God will not punish him or reject him. His self-esteem is to be based on the fact that God created him and loves him, not on whether or not he has been obedient. Narramore does not deny that a Christian might have some bad feelings if he sins or fails. However, he calls that feeling *constructive sorrow*, based on Paul's words to the Corinthians (2 Cor. 7:8-10).

The difference between Narramore, Collins, and Tournier becomes clear at this point. Neither Collins nor Tournier want to define feelings of guilt as narrowly as Narramore does. Tournier's description of guilt sounds very much like Narramore's concept of constructive sorrow. He explains that when he has a lecture to prepare or an article to write he continues to put it off, although inwardly he promises himself to take time and do it carefully. The desire to do it well makes it difficult for him to settle down and get to work. Thus he wastes time, which builds up a sense of guilt. He then finds that that sense of guilt gives him the drive to do the work. He compares it to having the power of an auxiliary motor that eventually gets him moving. Just before the lecture or manuscript is due, he feels so conscious-stricken at having prepared so badly that he rushes to the job just as one must jump into the water from a burning ship.[9]

8. Gary Collins, *Christian Counseling* (Waco, Tex.: Word, 1980), p. 117.
9. Tournier, p. 25.

What Tournier describes as guilt, Narramore would call "constructive sorrow," or a regret that one has failed to live up to certain expectations.

However, the controversy is not that easily resolved. It seems that Narramore goes too far in trying to rule out subjective guilt feelings for the Christian. Granted, he makes a good case for showing that a Christian should not have any fear of punishment. He distinguishes between judgment and chastisement as does the apostle Paul. The Christian will be disciplined by God but not eternally condemned.

However, Narramore goes beyond what Scripture affirms when he suggests that a Christian never experiences fear, loss of self-esteem, or a sense of isolation because of his behavior. That may create a rather unrealistic expectation on the part of the believer. Surely, a Christian who sins will experience feelings that we would normally call guilt feelings. Fear of being chastened by God is certainly a normal deterrent to sin, although it is not the highest motivation for obedience. That the apostle Paul considered fear of chastening valid is evident by his exhortation, "Those who continue in sin, rebuke in the the presence of all, so that the rest also may be fearful of sinning" (1 Tim. 5:20). Paul himself was motivated by an enormous dread of failure (1 Cor. 9:24-27).

Narramore's intention is good; he is aware that too many Christians base their self-esteem on how well they obey God and live up to their expectations. Because their behavior falls so short of God's standards, Christians tend to have an abnormally morbid dislike of themselves. Narramore's emphasis is good, but he goes too far in divorcing our behavior from the way we feel about ourselves. It seems unreasonable to suggest that when a Christian commits a serious sin he should not experience strong feelings of guilt, or that he should only expect to have a "constructive sorrow."

That notion might too easily make a Christian neglect to relate what he is doing to how he is feeling. While justification by faith should give us peace with God, cleaning up our act when necessary may contribute to peace within ourselves. Thus, the counselor who deals with a person with the symptoms of guilt should consider the possibility that some disobedience is generating those feelings. But because there is also the possibility that guilt feelings may not be related to an immediate sin, we must also consider the second step in our treatment.

IDENTIFY FALSE GUILT

Help others distinguish true guilt from false guilt. True guilt feelings result from behavior that is morally or socially wrong. The proper response to it is confession and resolve to obedience. False guilt is different from true guilt in both its reaction and its cause. The reaction can be wrong in itself; a person can hate himself for what he has done. Such a loss of self-esteem is unnecessary. The reaction can also be too intense; a person can have such an intense fear of failure that it immobilizes him. False guilt may also be identified if it is without proper cause. In that case, a person may have strong guilt feelings for something that is not from the point of view of God or others.

Getting others to see that their sense of guilt, their conscience, is not always accurate will be helpful to them. Paul Tournier takes issue with that. Although he spends a great deal of time distinguishing between false guilt and true guilt, he advises the counselor not to try to help the counselee make that distinction. His major reason seems to be a practical one: it is impossible to make a guilty person see the distinction. All subjective guilt is real in the sense that it is real to the guilty person. Therefore, trying to explain that it is not real will not work. Rather, counselees should be directed to confession and the grace of God.

Other Christian psychologists differ from Tournier in this matter. Biblically, real guilt and repentance involve a matter of wrongdoing, not what a person merely thinks is wrong. Therefore, the Bible is our guide for dealing with true guilt as well as getting rid of false guilt. That is based on the following.

Conscience is not a reliable guide. Our experiences with our parents and others have formed our consciences. Often we have a consciousness of wrongdoing, even when we do something God does not forbid. In the first century, Christians who ate meats offered to idols had that problem. Paul made it clear that such eating was not wrong for someone who had the proper understanding and attitude. Yet, some still felt wrong about doing so. Their consciences needed to be reeducated to be conformed to biblical truths. Christians need to understand that the conscience is not a proper guide. Therefore, we should not be governed or dominated by guilt feelings.

Deception by false teachers. There are others who want to make us feel guilty for doing something that is not wrong. Christ's apostles were quite aware of false prophets who sought to gain followers by preying on persons' guilt feelings. "Some will fall away from the faith, who forbid marriage and advocate abstaining from foods, which God has created to be gratefully shared in by those who believe and know the truth" (1 Tim. 4:1, 3). Those who do this are they who have their conscience "seared . . . with a branding iron" (v. 2). Although that expression could mean that the conscience is destroyed, it probably means that the conscience is "branded as with a hot iron," meaning that something is imprinted that should not be there.

Satan can cause guilt feelings. Paul links false prophets who forbid marriage and command abstinence from meats to those who give "attention to deceitful spirits and doctrines of demons" (1 Tim. 4:1). That fits the biblical notion that Satan is an accuser of the brethren (Rev. 12:10). Christians should be aware that self-condemnation and regret are not always caused by God's Spirit, who brings true conviction of sin. Satan, too, can be responsible for feelings of conviction and guilt.

Several questions can be asked to help distinguish false guilt from true.

1. Can I trace my feelings to some disobedience of scriptural truth?
2. Do my feelings relate in any way to my past experiences as a child?
3. Do my guilt feelings persist after I have made a confession of my sin, and after I have obeyed God by not continuing any known sin? If so, they are probably due to some internal psychological state that needs to be understood and handled.
4. Are my feelings related to some unrealistic standards I have set for myself? Collins identifies this problem:

> As they grow older, children take over parental and theological standards. They expect perfection in themselves, set up standards which never can be reached, and slice into feelings of guilt and self-blame following the inevitable failures. Guilt feelings are one of the ways in which we both punish ourselves and push ourselves to keep trying to do better.[10]

5. Do I fear giving up my feelings of guilt? Sometimes our behavior is prompted by the avoidance of guilt. If we fail to feel guilty, we fear

10. Collins, p. 120.

that we are failing to achieve our goals. But although guilt feelings may sometimes be a proper motivation, they are not the highest reason for obeying God and growing as Christians. As Collins says, "God expects us to be pressing on toward the goal of Christian maturity, but surely he does not want us to wallow in self condemnation and guilt feelings. Such an attitude has no biblical basis. Love should motivate us—not guilt."[11]

TEACH THE MESSAGE OF GRACE

Paul Tournier contends that guilt is one of mankind's greatest problems. He links it to theories of psychoanalysis and all forms of human experience. Because it is so persuasive, the gospel is the greatest psychological answer to the human predicament. But, for Tournier, the gospel must not be a moralistic message summoning us to obedience. It must be a message of grace that gives salvation despite our disobedience.

No man lives free of guilt, Tournier concludes. If that guilt is repressed, it leads to anger, rebellion, fear, and anxiety. A moralistic religion, a religion saturated with the idea of taboos and picturing God as a threatening being, will not help the human plight. Instead, he says it sets in motion a "sinister mechanism of revolt and wickedness." But grace can break into that vicious circle and lead to repentance and freedom from guilt, instead of repressed anger and rebellion.

COMMUNICATE ACCEPTANCE

The counselor's positive attitude and manner of acceptance is one of the major forces in treating a person's guilt. As a representative of Christ, the Christian mediates the acceptance of God to the sufferer.

The whole Body of Christ can also convey God's forgiveness. Every effort we make to create an atmosphere of love and acceptance in our worship services and fellowship gatherings will be part of our treatment of this human problem.

This warm acceptance is particularly needed by those who suffer from false guilt. Some people especially have a difficult time accepting God's favor. Although they need God's word of forgiveness, they also need the warm feeling of being loved by the Christian community. That acceptance was once communicated to a girl who was struggling with a severe consciousness of guilt. Before her conversion, she had

11. Ibid.

been heavily involved in drugs and immorality. Since coming to Christ she suffered from feelings of rejection and unworthiness. At a youth retreat with a group of college-aged Christians, she shared her inner hurt. The youth leader knew the seriousness of her problem and asked for a display of affection for her. He invited any of the girls of the group to go to that girl where she sat and put their arms around her. Soon the troubled young woman was surrounded by thirty or forty others. While they communicated through touch their warm expressions of love, several persons prayed for the depressed woman.

That youth leader understood how human love can be a conveyor of divine love. He used it as a treatment for healing those tormented by guilt. In contemporary society, there seems to be many who need such treatment.

12

Loneliness

One of the saddest contemporary songs is entitled, "Alone Again, Naturally." The verses tell of a man's life journey dominated by loneliness, and end by telling of his intended suicide. The song's ending is disastrous enough, but two other features of the song make the whole thing appear even more tragic: (1) a deep malady shows up in the title. "Alone Again, Naturally" suggests an inevitable surrender to the fate of loneliness, as if nothing more from contemporary life can be expected. (2) The contrast between melody and lyrics makes its message so pathetic. The lighthearted tune in which that awful tale is wrapped seems to be more fitting for lyrics about someone's pet collie or a spectacular mountain hike. The melody is as fit a companion to the words as is a yellow polka dot shroud for a rotting corpse. The mix of title, lyrics, and melody has one pessimistic message: expect nothing more in life than loneliness.

That loneliness should be so accepted as a human condition is not surprising in a society that has also given us other songs: "All by Myself," "Lonely Street," "Have You Ever Been Lonely," and "I Ain't Got Nobody." The isolation in our society is also documented in a number of books, whose titles embody the same theme: *The Lonely Crowd*; *We, the Lonely People*; and *A Nation of Strangers*.

Singing and writing about loneliness is just one sign of how it dominates so many people today. Twenty-six percent of the people questioned in one survey had felt very lonely at some point during the weeks preceding the survey.[1] Several psychiatrists have estimated that

---

1. Craig W. Ellison, "Loneliness: A Social-Developmental Analysis," *Journal of Psychology and Theology*, Winter 1978, p. 3.

between seventy and ninety percent of Americans are chronically lonely.[2]

Coping with loneliness requires a lot more than merely accepting it as a fact of life. One expert claims that loneliness is one of the most harrowing states of mind that an individual can experience.[3]

It is well established that loneliness plays a major role in suicides. That it also leads to murder is not fully documented, according to John Altrocchi, expert in abnormal psychology. But he notes that a number of individuals who have allegedly attempted to kill prominent Americans have been discovered to be "loners," such as Lee Harvey Oswald, Sirhan Sirhan, and James Earl Ray.[4] Many contemporary psychologists such as Erich Fromm and Erik Erikson see loneliness and alienation as a central psychological problem of our times.

The predominance of loneliness is reason enough for Christian leaders to be prepared to discuss it. That it is one of the most painful of all human experiences should arouse our compassion to do all we can to help people deal with it.

DEFINITION OF LONELINESS

Loneliness is distinct from aloneness. A person can be alone, but not feel lonely. Conversely, a person can be surrounded by people in a downtown crowd at lunch hour and be extremely lonely. For example, as I was writing these words in the basement of a seminary library, I was very much alone, cut off from any human contact and among stacks of books. Yet, I did not have the faintest sense of loneliness, because I was enjoying immensely the sabbatical the seminary had granted to me. However, after I had returned to the seminary for only a few hours, I had a sense of loneliness, even though I was surrounded by people. Having been on a sabbatical gave me the feeling of being left out, a spectator watching other people with whom I was not involved as before.

The nature of loneliness is precisely that left-out feeling. "Loneliness is living in a shell," writes psychiatric researcher Ina May Greer.[5] Loneliness is caused by the absence of intimacy with others. Pangs of loneliness occur whenever we are cut off from the support and

---

2. Keith Miller, *The Becomers* (Waco, Tex.: Word, 1973), p. 32.
3. Jeffrey G. Sobosan, "Loneliness and Faith," *Journal of Psychology and Theology*, Spring 1979, p. 104.
4. John Altrocchi, *Abnormal Behavior* (New York: Harcourt Brace Jovanovich, 1980), p. 252.
5. Ina May Greer, "Roots of Loneliness," *Pastoral Psychology*, June 1953, p. 27.

understanding of others. An acutely lonely person lacks two interpersonal experiences that most of us have on a regular basis. First, he lacks a sense of belonging. The lonely person feels isolated and unattached. Second, he or she lacks the feeling of being understood. "The lonely person has either lost or been unable to form a relationship in which he can share ultimate concerns with another person who is interested, sympathetic and accepting," writes Craig Ellison.[6]

Loneliness, then, is an emotional experience. It is feeling a loss of intimacy and a sense of belonging. Sometimes the loss is caused by a broken intimate relationship through death or separation. Thus, half of all widows over fifty living in one large metropolitan area said that loneliness was their worst problem.[7] Loneliness has a variety of causes and can be described in many ways.

STATES OF LONELINESS

Individual experiences of loneliness vary a great deal. All of us have moments of loneliness. Perhaps sitting in a crowded airport terminal or bus depot away from home, we have been overcome by a sense of loneliness, while others around us are talking and laughing. Loneliness becomes more serious when it is prolonged and severe. It seems that there are several varieties.

SOCIAL ISOLATION

Social isolation is marked by feelings of marginal existence and aimlessness. This deficiency is broader than lacking a close friend. The person lacks a whole network of accepting friends who regard him as part of the network. A teenager may feel this during the first months of his new college life. Or a man out of work may have a serious sense of being "out of it." Whenever it is prolonged and the rejection by society is more apparent, a person can become extremely alienated as Lee Harvey Oswald was purported to be. Perhaps by putting a bullet into a famous person he could make people aware of him and give himself a sense of belonging.

EMOTIONAL ISOLATION

Another form of loneliness, *emotional isolation*, is caused by a lack of close companionship. It is a sense of utter aloneness, whether or not others are near. The emotionally lonely person is in a condition of being unable to gain emotional satisfaction from relationships that are

6. Ellison, p. 6.
7. Ibid., p. 3.

important to him. Imagine the dismay of a teenager who wants to relate to a certain group at school that will not allow him to do so.

Whether emotional or social, whenever the state of loneliness is severe, it leads to feelings of depression and apathy; the person becomes very passive toward life. Physical symptoms sometimes occur, such as an empty feeling in the pit of the stomach or nausea.

Not all states of emotional loneliness lead to physical symptoms or even depression. Loneliness sometimes produces significant motivation to find interpersonal relationships.

The differences in reactions may help us diagnose the severity of the loneliness. There seems to be a clear distinction between situational and chronic loneliness. The person suffering situational loneliness feels all of the accompanying emotions. But there are two major differences between his condition and the one who has a chronic loneliness. Situationally lonely people, in a temporary state brought on by the loss of a loved one or a move to a new situation, are much more motivated and successful in communicating with others than the chronically lonely. The chronically lonely person is apathetic, passive, and poor at reaching out and communicating with others.[8]

In some cases, the chronically lonely person is in a shell and unable to get out of it successfully. Lonely individuals frequently have social-skills deficits. Studies show that the basic problem is an inability to self-disclose. Authentic self-revelation to another is the most important way of decreasing the interpersonal distance between individuals. But being willing to self-disclose is not enough. It appears that some people are unable to make social connections, because they are too self-disclosing. They lack the sense of timing in their sharing of intimate thoughts. Often impulsively going from the lung to the tongue, they do not discern when another person is ready and willing to listen to them disclose their personal feelings. Thus, self-disclosure, generally a positive means of building a relationship, can be inappropriate at times, generating withdrawal and rejection by others. Therefore, the chronically lonely person may lack disclosure flexibility, an ability to self-disclose and to know when to do so.[9]

Not all chronically lonely persons are merely socially inept. Long-term chronic loneliness is often a result of negative childhood experi-

8. Ann C. Gerson and Daniel Perlman, "Loneliness and Expressive Communication," *Journal of Abnormal Psychology* 88, no. 3 (1979): 258-61.
9. Gordon J. Chelune, Faye E. Sultan, and Carolyn L. Williams, "Loneliness, Self-Disclosure, and Interpersonal Effectiveness," *Journal of Counseling Psychology* 27, no. 4: 462.

ences. If a child is deprived of the satisfying experiences of being attached and accepted during the early years of life, he may suffer long-term effects. There is some evidence to suggest that adult psychological problems may arise from a mother's being too busy to hold and coddle her baby during the early months of infancy. A separation by death or divorce from one of the parents in early childhood may also lead to chronic feelings of loneliness.[10]

SPIRITUAL LONELINESS

Alienation from God is a central theme in Scripture, which makes loneliness one of the most serious of human problems. Not only are the wicked cut off from God, alone and without Him, but even the godly sometimes feel apart from God: "Why hast Thou forsaken me?" cried David (Ps. 22:1). Rebellion and sin cause isolation from Him: "Your iniquities have made a separation between you and your God" (Isa. 59:2).

Unanswered prayer may, at times, make the staunchest believer feel alone and without God. Communication may seem to have broken down. The believer may pray for the healing of a sick child who eventually dies. He may pray for success that does not come. It is as if God is not interested. We are tempted to doubt that we "belong" to Him and that He is the loving Father who is supposed to understand and care. Inwardly we may harbor a complaint against Him. "Camus feels isolated from God," Jeffrey Sobosan tells us, "because God seems continually to ignore or misapprehend the question of human suffering."[11]

Christians have ways of dealing with those feelings. They understand that God's acceptance does not depend on their righteousness, but on Christ's intercession. We know that God is there even when He does not comply with our prayers or inner wishes.

These three experiences of loneliness—social, emotional, and spiritual—must not be confused. Solving one's problem of spiritual loneliness and being reconciled to God may not reduce one's emotional loneliness. After all, Adam had intimate communication with God, but he was still "alone." A widow, an unmarried woman, or an elderly man should not expect his or her relationship to God to replace relationships with others. God can help us endure the pangs of loneliness whenever they occur. But social and emotional loneliness must

10. Craig W. Ellison, "The Roots of Loneliness," *Christianity Today*, 10 March 1978, p. 13.
11. Sobosan, p. 107.

be dealt with properly. The cures, as well as the causes, are not merely spiritual; they are also psychological and social.

THE CURE FOR LONELINESS

For the long-term chronically lonely person, a number of counseling sessions may be needed to enable him to cope with his condition. That is why we must preach on this subject with much sympathy and understanding. The feelings of loneliness will not go away by merely being told to do so. They are not demons to be expelled by sacred words. Feelings of loneliness are caused by what we lack: intimate friends.

Because loneliness, for some, is partially caused by interpersonal relationship problems, we can help by teaching and practicing good social relations. Urging a person to increase his social activity is not enough. Simply prompting the lonely person to "get out of the house" more or to "invite someone over for dinner" could do more harm then good. The lonely person often has as much social life as others.[12] Often, he is trying to drown his loneliness in a pool of social activity. But the problem is that he does not know how to make intimate friends; he does not know how to fit in and belong. He lacks quality, not quantity, in his social contacts. Thus, we can urge and provide for his finding some training in interpersonal relations building.

Another treatment for the lonely person is for all of us to build the community life of the church. Our relationships in the body also suffer most for quality rather than quantity. One of the reasons most of us suffer from loneliness is because we have lost the sense of "community." Numerous sociologists have observed that most Americans do not have a feeling of meaningful belonging or involvement in any sort of community. The relationships of local communities, churches, lodges, and so on, are often so superficial that individuals feel isolated from others. Yet, wholesome community life seems to be necessary for good mental health.

In his book *Abnormal Behavior*, John Altrocchi maintains that a sense of community actually diminishes deviant and abnormal behavior. "One aspect of what people seem to be looking for today is a psychological sense of community," he insists. "A sense that one is part of a readily available, dependable, mutually supportive network of relationships that minimizes the likelihood of experiencing the sustained feelings of loneliness and anguish, which often lead to

12. Chelune, p. 466.

desperate or destructive actions."[13] In these words has he not described the New Testament concept of the church? We can do more for the emotionally and socially lonely people (as well as spiritually lonely ones) in our midst by intensifying our efforts at developing the church as an open, accepting, and supporting group.

Such community life can be fostered in small groups as well as in the larger congregation. The widows, widowers, divorced, unmarried men and women, handicapped, seriously or chronically ill, and many other people who are feeling "shut out," can be best helped through a body of believers sensitive to their need for intimacy. Building such communities of love might be difficult, but it could well be the most important task we have.

13. Altrocchi, p. 662.

Part 3

A Devotional Perspective

I know a minister whose shoe latchet I am unworthy to unloose, whose preaching is often little better than sacred miniature painting—I might almost say holy trifling. He is great upon the ten toes of the beast, the four faces of the cherubim, the mystical meaning of badgers' skins, and the typical bearings of the staves of the ark, and the windows of Solomon's temple: but the sins of business men, the temptations of the times, and the needs of the age, he scarcely ever touches upon. Such preaching reminds me of a lion engaged in mousehunting.[1]

1. Charles H. Spurgeon, *Spurgeon's Lectures to His Students*, ed. David Otis Fuller (Grand Rapids: Zondervan, 1945), p. 66.

13

Selected Devotional Topics

There is a need to widen and deepen our understanding of human nature and the human situation. Such sources as art, literature, the behavioral sciences, and practical experience will assist in providing such understanding.

Preaching and counseling can help save parishioners from shipwreck on the hidden reefs of anxiety and guilt. These contacts can be both preventive and therapeutic. They can release strength within those who are struggling with personal crises, and support those whose spiritual foundations are weak.

This section contains quotations, poetry, illustrations from life, and sermonic sources. The lay person will find a clarification of concepts and some inspiration for the soul. A word or phrase may start a constructive thought process in the mind of the reader.

The preacher will find supporting material to use in the amplification of his message. This is an attempt to transfer psychological terms into understandable English and inspirational vocabulary.

Anxiety

There is a set of words used rather indiscriminately. We speak of fear, phobia, tension, and anxiety. In many ways, those terms fall into the same category; and yet, they are different.

Fear is a response to a threat that is specific and usually clearly defined. Fear is basically a healthy emotion, a God-given response to danger. It is a protection for man, since it gives him a driving force to get out of danger. The man who says that he has no fear has only learned to conquer some of his more basic fears.

A *phobia* is a fear that has become exaggerated and extreme. It is deep-set and hard to overcome. A fear of being shut up in a small place is quite normal, but when one develops claustrophobia and cannot be in a room with a door closed, he has an unreasonable and unhealthy fear.

Anxiety is more vague and diffuse. It is a condition in which we feel threatened at the very foundation of our existence. Rollow May defines anxiety as "a reaction to a threat to the existence of oneself as a human being, or to values that one has identified with his existence."[1]

ILLUSTRATIONS

> If the load of *tomorrow be added to that of* yesterday and carried today, it will make the strongest falter. Live in day-tight compartments. Don't let yesterday and tomorrow intrude on your life. Live one day at a time. You'll avoid the waste of energy, the mental distress, the nervous worries that dog the steps of the man who's anxious about the future.
>
> Sir William Osler, *A Way of Life*

> The foolish fears of what might happen,
> I cast them all away
> Among the clover-scented grass,
> Among the new-mown hay;
> Among the husking of the corn
> Where drowsy poppies nod,
> Where ill thoughts die and good are born—
> Out in the field with God!
>
> Elizabeth Barrett Browning,
> "The Little Cares that Fretted Me"

Nobody should ever look anxious except those who have no anxiety.

Earl of Beaconsfield

> Said the Robin to the Sparrow:
> "I should really like to know.
> Why these anxious human beings,
> Rush about and worry so!"

> Said the Sparrow to the Robin:
> "Friend, I think that it must be
> That they have no heavenly Father,
> Such as cares for you and me."
>
> Elizabeth Cheney, "Overheard in an Orchard"

1. Ralph Heynen, *The Art of Christian Living* (Grand Rapids: Baker, 1963), p. 125.

A well-known physician says there are three great killers in modern life: the telephone, the clock, and the calendar. They are the symbols of hurried, hectic living. The tyranny of the telephone is interruption, not only through a busy day, but often into the night. The tyranny of the clock is appointment, and that of the calendar is apprehension. Those are the things that keep us jumping and jumpy, the things that cause stress.[2]

Psychiatrists tell us to face anxiety. Actually, it would be easier to face a fear, for fear is specific, whereas anxiety is inchoate, as a clinging fog. But the counsel still holds: we can face anxiety to the measure of saying, "I am anxious. Why?" Certain fears might then shape themselves from the fog—fear of sickness or rejection or death; and the confrontation would, to some measure, grant us power.

Psychiatrists also tell us to take some action. There are perhaps times when any action in anxiety is better than acting like a bird mesmerized under the fang of a serpent. In anxiety regarding health, we can act by going to a doctor and confronting the worst or best. In vague misgiving, it would be better to do anything than to do nothing but moan. Face the anxiety and act, says the psychiatrist. That summary does no justice to his fine realm of healing, and less to our topic, but it does have some truth and value.[3]

Our modern anxiety is modern only in its form, for anxiety is as old as human nature. The nuclear age has not *caused* our anxiety; it has only *awakened* it to give it new occasion. Men have always been anxious, even though some generations seem to have been more anxious than others. Dread seems to have been extreme in Greece, just prior to the time of Plato and in Luther's day, just as it seems to be extreme in our century. But in every age there is anxiety. The "right" event—such as the Orson Welles broadcast of the arrival of men from Mars, which sent thousands running to the streets because they took the broadcast as factual—will drive a shaft to that hidden reservoir of anxiety-fear, and it will come boiling to the top.[4]

Then what is anxiety? Plato said: "Nothing in the world is worth anxiety." Jesus must have felt the same way, for he spoke about anxiety in His Sermon on the Mount. He understood how useless it is, how it destroys poise, wastes energy, saps vitality, ruins health, and shortens life. Dr. Charles Mayo once said that half of all the beds in

2. Lewis L. Dunnington, *Power to Become* (New York: Macmillan, 1956), p. 114.
3. George A. Buttrick, *Sermons Preached in a University Church* (Nashville: Abingdon, 1959), pp. 38-39.
4. Ibid., 39.

our hospitals are filled by people who worried themselves there. To live effectively we must learn how to conquer anxiety.[5]

Nothing significant would be performed in life without the aid of some healthy anxiety. Such an anxiety is a helpful emotional stimulus. Students who are striving for high academic achievements will be anxious. They have a strong drive to succeed and a concern that they might fail. It is good that ministers have some anxiety about the worship services of the coming Sunday. It serves as an incentive to go to the pulpit well prepared.[6]

People are always trying to find a fitting label for the age in which we live. One that is frequently heard and read is that this is an age of anxiety and insecurity. We need not look far to realize the truth of that description. Bill Mauldin, the cartoonist, in one of his picture interpretations, calls this a "scared-rabbit" generation. That does seem to describe the mad and restless quest for security.[7]

Sermonic Sources
"The Cure for Care" (Ps. 37:1)
  J. H. Jowett, *The Silver Lining*
"The Sin of Worry," "Why Be Distracted About Your Life . . . ?"
  Roy O. McClain, *If with All Your Heart*
"Win Over Worry" (Matt. 6:31)
  Daniel A. Poling, *Jesus Says to You*
"Living Without Strain"
  Lewis L. Dunnington, *Power to Become*
"Philip—The Conquest of Anxiety"
  Roy L. Laurin, *Meet Yourself in the Bible*

A CURE FOR ANXIETY
Matthew 6:19-34

> But seek first his kingdom and his righteousness, and all these things will be given to you as well. [v. 33, NIV*]

When we read Matthew 6:25, 31, and 34, we are a bit stunned to note that we should not be anxious. The King James Version has an unfortunate translation that reads, "Take no thought." The *American Standard Version* reads, "Therefore I say unto you, be not anxious."

5. Wesley H. Hager, *Conquering* (Grand Rapids: Eerdmans, 1965), p. 19.
6. Heynen, p. 125.
7. Ibid., p. 137.
New International Version.

That passage of Scripture does more than just give us an admonition to avoid anxiety. It gives directions that we can follow so that we can make verse 25 a reality in our daily living. The secret is to be found in putting God first. It is Henry Drummond who was reported to have said, "Don't touch Christianity unless you are willing to seek it first. I promise you a miserable existence if you seek it second." Bishop Cassels was one of the Cambridge Seven who went to China as a missionary. On each piece of his luggage he printed, "God First."

It is most important that we find an antidote for worry, a prescription for our anxiety, a way of escape from our tensions. Worry can undermine a person's health. The word *worry* literally means "to divide." Worry divides the mind between worthwhile interests and damaging thoughts. Besides that, worry is very contagious. A worrywart in a family can cause the whole family to be upset. People seldom worry alone; they tell others about their concern and others worry with them.

In verses 19-24 we are encouraged to put God first in the area of *savings*. This is the financial section of the constitution of the kingdom. One-tenth of the gospel of Matthew deals with money. We are commanded to avoid laying up treasures on earth. They should not be placed horizontally, thus being in a passive condition, but rather, perpendicularly so that they will be ready for service.

There is a human passion for possession. That in itself is not wrong. However, the abuse of this passion is wrong. Fortunes laid up for the present are perishing and passing. Those laid up for the future are lasting and eternal. In the East, wealth consisted of cloth and coin. The frail moth and the silent rust could destroy a person's savings. The Master has a note of urgency as He warns His listeners that where their treasure is, their heart will be also. We cannot serve God and Mammon, the Chaldean money God.

In verses 25-32 we are encouraged to put God first in the area of *supplies*. It is useless to fret over what we are going to eat, drink, or wear. God takes care of that which cannot sow or reap. The young ravens, which are among the most helpless of all birds, are provided for by God (Ps. 147:9). Certainly, God will provide for His own.

In verse 33 we are encouraged to put God first in the area of *service*. A successful life must have behind it a great compulsion. This verse says that our first duty or aim is to seek after the kingdom and His righteousness. We enter the kingdom by way of the new birth. Having entered, we should then put our heart experience into action. The object of our search involves putting God first in time, preference, and intensity. The reward of our search will involve all things being added to us.

A father helped his son button his coat. "Son," he said, "button the top button first and the others will line up correctly." That is what Jesus is telling us in principle concerning life.

The real victory over worry is the victory over ourselves—a victory that we will learn only at the feet of One who never worried, even though he was heavily burdened. He walked among the lilies of the field and said, "If God so arrays the grass of the field, . . . will He not much more do so for you, O men of little faith?" (v. 30).

There will be no place for anxiety in savings, supplies, or service when God is given priority.

CONFUSION

It is possible for a pessimist to become an optimist, but only when he learns to take a different view of life. Our viewpoint depends on the color of the lenses through which we see and interpret events. As Christians, we must learn to discard the dark-colored glasses, for there are great perils in pessimism.

We can do great damage to those about us by being disciples of gloom. For one thing, we greatly impair our Christian witness; we give the impression that religion is a gloomy thing. Actually, if there is anyone in this world who has a right to laugh, it is the Christian, for the laughter of the world is but hollow mockery.

That is not to suggest a Pollyanna view of life. We need to face life realistically and practically. But at the same time, we know that He who holds the world in His hand will cause all things to work for our good. Even the song that begins in a minor key ends with the song of hope.

ILLUSTRATIONS

In April 1854, one of the noblest of our modern American poets was born in Oregon. Many have been stirred by his spirit and moved by his verses. As a child he lived through the confusion and agony of the Civil War; as a young man he witnessed the colossal growth and development of the far West; just after his sixtieth birthday he saw World War I begin to wreck the modern world; and in his eightieth year he found America moving forward toward an essentially new social, political, and economic order. Can a human personality adapt itself to all those changes? Can a man, when he is past eighty, still make adjustments? Edwin Markham, a few years before he died, wrote of the years that lay ahead: "Come on! I am ready for you!"

Sermonic Sources
"Getting the Best of Doubt" (Matt. 28:17)
   Clarence Edward McCartney, *Facing Life and Getting the Best of It*
"Untangle Your Life"
   Lewis L. Dunnington, *Power to Become*
"Peter—The Conquest of Inconsistency"
   Roy L. Laurin, *Meet Yourself in the Bible*

CONFUSED? GET GOD'S POINT OF VIEW

Mark 8:27—9:1

> But turning around and seeing His disciples, He rebuked Peter, and said, "Get behind Me, Satan; for you are not setting your mind on God's interests, but man's." [8:33]

There is a tendency to view life narrowly rather than as it is. A farmer, engineer, real estate agent, and artist viewing a large tract of land will see possibilities in it according to their individual background and training. Likewise, that which would be punishment for some is pleasure for others. It depends on one's point of view.

Jesus was on Mount Hermon and took the opportunity of that safe recluse from King Herod, the Pharisees, and the Sadducees to teach His followers regarding the crucifixion, which would occur in a few months. He proceeded to clarify in their thinking who He really was. Others had identified Him as John the Baptist, Elias, or one of the prophets. At this point Christ wanted to make sure that His close followers had a true identification. Thus, it was Peter who finally gave the right answer: "Thou art the Christ [the promised Messiah]" (8:29). Christ then asked that they not publicize that fact, since His supporters wanted to make Him king immediately and His opposition wanted an excuse to arrest Him.

Christ then proceeded to unfold the truth about the coming crucifixion. Peter interrupted Him and declared that he would not allow the Master to undergo any such suffering. Jesus rebuked Peter saying, "Get thee behind Me, Satan; for you are not setting your mind on God's interests, but man's" (8:33). Williams's translation of this passage reads: "This view of yours is not from God." The *New English Bible* reads, "You think as men think, not as God thinks." Moffatt translates the statement as, "Your outlook is not God's, but man's."

A contrast of principles (8:35). Man says that life consists of gaining, but God says that life consists of giving. God has written His principles in nature (Rom. 1:20), and a study of nature will reveal it. The rich young ruler had problems at that point (John 19:16-30). He had spent his time getting, and Christ challenged him to go, sell, and give. The Lord Jesus evidenced this principle in His own life (2 Cor. 8:9).

A contrast in persons (8:34). Man says that self should have the preeminence, but God says that the Savior should be first. There should be a rebuke to self-will, self-indulgence, and self-righteousness. We should say "no" to self and let Christ have the preeminence.

A contrast in profits (8:36-38). Man labors for profits in time, but God says that we should labor for profits in eternity. If we could gain the world, how long would it last? Our life is but a vapor. Disease and death can take it from us very quickly. When we invest in eternity by serving our fellowmen in the name of Christ, we are investing in that which time and change cannot erase. If we gain the world but lose the Savior and the forgiveness of sin, which comes through knowing Him, then we really will have lost everything. God has a tomorrow. Plan ahead with Him.

LIFE'S INCONSISTENCIES

John 13:21-30

> Jesus therefore answered, "That is the one for whom I shall dip the morsel and give it to him." So when He had dipped the morsel, He took and gave it to Judas, the son of Simon Iscariot. [v. 26]

The little word *if* is the weakest word in our language. We often hear people say, "If I had only. . . ." But the truth is that they did not, and tragedy resulted.

The sun nourishes the flowers causing them to grow, but it also causes the weeds to grow and the earth to crust. Judas was close to the Son of Righteousness and was outwardly a disciple, but inwardly he was a veritable devil. Calvary became the testing ground, and he failed the test. If he had only done differently.

An evident inconsistency in his occupational life. Six days before the Passover he was in a home at Bethany. While Martha was serving, Mary took an ointment of pure nard, anointed the feet of Jesus, and wiped them with her hair. Judas immediately exclaimed, "Why wasn't this nard sold for sixty dollars and the money given to the poor?" He said that, not because he cared for the poor, but because he was a thief. Since he was the treasurer for the disciples, he had a chance to take out money that was put into the treasury (John 12:6). If it had not been spent, he would have had an opportunity to have it for himself. At heart, he was a thief with a deep love for money. He even came to the point that he was willing to sell his Master for thirty pieces of silver! Considering his occupation, we would think that he would be trustworthy, but actually that was not the case. He was inconsistent in his occupational life.

An evident inconsistency in his social life. Jesus knew that there were those of His disciples who, though they associated with Him, still did not believe. He even realized that one of His associates would betray Him (John 6:46). Outward attention does not mean that there is an inward affection. It seems almost incredible that one who would dip his hand in the dish with Jesus would be the one to betray Him (Matt. 26:23). Unfortunately, those inconsistencies still occur.

An evident inconsistency in his spiritual life. There was an empty room in his life which, when left unguarded, provided a place where Satan could enter (v. 27). Unless Jesus is Lord of all of one's life, He is not really Lord at all. When Satan took control the steps downward were multiplied and hastened. What a descriptive statement is "he went out immediately; and it was night" (v. 30). When Judas allowed that close bond of fellowship with Jesus to be broken, night took over. When we break away with Jesus, we break away with the Light of the World.

Do others see in us that which they expect to find? Our Christian profession lays the groundwork for day-by-day expectancies in our occupational, social, and spiritual living. The inconsistencies can only be removed as we yield to the Lordship of Christ. We must let Him be in charge. Failure to do that was the root of the problem that started Judas on the way "to his own place" (Acts 1:25).

CONTENTMENT

ILLUSTRATIONS

When Saint Theresa was laughed at because she wanted to build a great orphanage and had but three shillings to begin with, she answered: "With three shillings Theresa can do nothing; but with God and three shillings there is nothing that Theresa cannot do."

"Three Shillings and God"

Apart from Me you can do *nothing*. [John 15:5, italics added]

I can do *all things* through Him. [Phil. 4:13, italics added]

It is right to be contented with what we have, but never with what we are.

Sir James Mackintosh

To be content with what we posses is the greatest and most secure of riches.

Cicero

CONTENTED LIVING IN A HARD WORLD
Philippians 4:2-20

I know how to be abased and I know how to abound; in any and all circumstances I have learned the secret of facing plenty and hunger, abundance and want. [v. 11]

The world population will increase by forty-five to sixty million people between 1975 and 1985. Most of that growth is taking place in our cities where an average of three thousand acres of green land is being bulldozed daily. Almost one-third of the population of the United States lives in some fifteen metropolitan areas. The growth in those areas means that every year a new city of two million must be built to accommodate its exploding population.

Tremendous crowds of people living together have not resulted in "community" among those people. Our restless mobility is indicated by the fact that nearly twenty percent of Americans move every year. Our craving for amusement—reflected in the expansion of spectator sports as well as in the less healthy trends toward sensuous movies and literature—is a surface indication that we are not a contented people.

Contentment is not a science with a prescribed formula, it is an art to be learned. We Christians should learn how to be content. "By the help of the Lord always keep up the glad spirit" (Phil. 4:4, Williams). We are admonished to be anxious in nothing, prayerful for everything, and thankful for anything (v. 6).

Paul had learned the secret of contentment even after a flogging while in fetters in prison at Philippi (Acts 26:29), and in spite of being friendless (2 Tim. 4:16). The word *rejoice* appears eleven times in that short letter, and the word *joy* appears five times. Paul learned by experience that you travel third class with Christ present, second class when you have Him prominent, but first class only when you have Christ preeminent.

Contentment demands that we be willing to receive God's peace (Phil. 4:2-7). "And the peace of God, which surpasses all comprehension, shall guard your hearts and your minds in Christ Jesus" (v. 7). There were two ladies in the Philippian church who were not in agreement. The name of the first lady was Euodia, which means "sweet fragrance," and the name of the second was Syntyche, which means "affable." They were certainly not living up to their names or according to their profession of faith. Peace is a legacy of the Lord for the believers (John 14:27) and it is a fruit of the Spirit (Gal. 5:22). In Philippians 4:7, it is a garrison of the soul. "The steadfast of mind Thou wilt keep in perfect peace" (Isa. 26:3).

Contentment demands that we be willing to rely upon God's power (Phil. 4:8-13). "I can do all things through Him who strengthens me" (v. 13). The adjectives found in verse 8 should engage our thinking. Our thoughts should be concentrated upon that which is just, honorable, pure, lovely, and gracious. What we learn and think about, we should also incorporate into our actions (v. 9). However, that cannot be brought to reality through our own strength. Our adequacy comes by attaching ourselves to the adequate One, Jesus Christ. Without Christ we can do nothing (John 15:5).

Contentment demands that we be willing to recognize God's providence (Phil. 4:14-20). "And my God shall supply all your needs according to His riches in glory in Christ Jesus" (v. 19). God often makes providential provision for us through our partners (vv. 16-17). Paul had a solution to the paradox of plenty: "I have received everything in full and have an abundance" (v. 18). That which he really had was not material provision but rather a vital contact with the royal bank of heaven. That made the promise of plenty very real and practical to him. The riches of goodness (Rom. 2:4), the riches of wisdom (Rom. 11:33), the riches of grace (Eph. 1:7), and the riches of glory (Eph. 1:18) are all a part of God's provision for His people.

The poise to bear all circumstances, power to do all things, and plenty to meet all needs blend together to form contentment for the Christian. God's peace, power, and providence are the keys to contented living, even in a hard world.

DESPONDENCY AND DEPRESSION

Depression generally occurs in two varieties: natural and neurotic. Natural depression is situational and is generally triggered by crisis. It can often be "talked out." Natural depression passes with time, but deserves pastoral support while it is running its course. Elijah under the juniper tree and Jonah under the gourd vine are probably biblical examples of situational anger turned inward, causing depression.

Neurotic depression is noted in deep, persistent moodiness. It is locked in and difficult to confront because its causes are not apparent. Occasionally, persistent "blues" are related to physical symptoms such as aging, menopause, or impotence. Another possible cause of neurotic depression is an erroneous view of Christianity. A very strong Christian woman became depressed after reading an article by a "Christian" psychologist. The psychologist had flatly and erroneously said that Christians were never depressed. Since she had recurring spells of depression she feared she might not be a Christian after all, and doubted her worth as a wife and mother. She came to realize Christ was as available to her on "down days" as He was on the days when all was well.

Depressions may range in severity from mild feelings of despondency to a grave mental illness. A depression may be a short and fleeting mood swing, or an extremely obstinate and vicious condition. All of us swing in our moods—we have our highs and lows—but in depression a person swings to depths beyond the normal level, and since he cannot help himself escape he feels that all is lost.

ILLUSTRATIONS

In Psalms 42 and 43 David made use of excellent spiritual therapy. Three times in those two psalms he sank into depressed and hopeless feelings and said, "Why are you in despair, O my soul? And have you become disturbed within me?" (42:11). The answer came back to him as he spoke to his own soul, "Hope thou in God, . . . the help of my countenance, and my God." He did this a second time, as a wave of depression again struck. And then a third time. His final words in Psalm 43 were, "God . . . the help of my countenance." Such a hope gave healing.

William Cowper was a man who struggled much with despondency.

He made several attempts to take his own life. One of his biographers wrote:

> Let those who are assailed by despondency remember that William Cowper lived to write:
>
> > God moves in a mysterious way,
> > His wonders to perform.
> > He plants his footsteps on the seas,
> > and rides upon the storm.[1]

When that persevering traveler Mungo Park was fainting in the vast wilderness of an African desert, naked and alone and considering his days as numbered, a small moss-flower of extraordinary beauty caught his eye.

> Though the whole plant was no larger than one of my fingers, I could not contemplate the delicate confirmation of its roots, leaves and capsules without admiration. Can the Being who planted, watered and brought to perfection, in this obscure part of the world, a thing which appears of so small importance, look with unconcern upon the situation and suffering of creatures formed after his own image? Surely not. Reflections like these would not allow me to dispair; I started up and, disregarding both hunger and fatigue, travelled forward, assured that relief was at hand; and I was not *disappointed*.[2]

> > If every man's internal care
> > Were written on his brow,
> > How many who our envy share
> > Would have pity now.
> >
> > Author unknown

On the shores of the Baltic Sea, after a great storm, fishermen go down into the water and rake the beach for the precious ambergris that has been cast upon the shores by the tumult of the waves. Life's storms bring their treasures with them, and we are wise fishermen if we go out

---

1. Ralph Heynen, *The Art of Christian Living* (Grand Rapids: Baker, 1963), p. 108.
2. Ernest Hemingway, "A Natural History of the Dead."

after the waves and billows have passed over us and gather up the heavenly ambergris with which they have strewn the shores of our life.[3]

For a long time the great Russian novelist Dostoevski was a political prisoner. He once narrowly escaped the firing squad by a last-minute reprieve from the Czar. He has told us that there was a small shutter in his cell door that was mysteriously opened every evening, and through it the voice of an unknown fellow prisoner whispered to him, "Courage, brother, we also suffer."[4]

Sermonic Sources
"Life at the Breaking Point" (Matt. 28:20)
  Roy O. McClain, *If with All Your Heart*
"Isaiah—The Conquest of Despondency"
  Roy L. Laurin, *Meet Yourself in the Bible*

WHEN DESPONDENCY STRIKES

Isaiah 6:1-13

Far from being a nuisance or cruelty, adversity is one of the constituent elements of great living to be finely used. When real adversity comes, a soul true to itself builds new dimensions.

A simple statement may at times hide a multitude of tears. In the first verse of this portion we read, "In the year of King Uzziah's death." He had been the only king Isaiah had known. He was Isaiah's idol and source of inspiration. For fifty years he had ruled Jerusalem and, for the most part, had been one of the best kings. Isaiah had probably said on many occasions, "If I could just grow up to be like Uzziah." Now his hopes were shattered. Uzziah had died and had been removed from the throne room of Isaiah's mind. In his despondency he made his way to the Temple, and there his despondency was dispelled. In fact, he was so stirred that he launched forth on a life of prophetic ministry that lasted some forty years.

Two simple experiences shook his soul. The first of those is recorded in the first verse where it says, "I saw the Lord sitting on a throne, lofty and exalted." Isaiah had gone to a place where he could expect a vision. He had removed personal idols from his mind. God could now take His rightful place of prominence. Moses in earlier years had been captivated at the burning bush by a vision, and Paul in later years had

---

3. Clarence E. Macartney, *Facing Life and Getting the Best of It* (Grand Rapids: Abingdon, 1940), p. 81.
4. Wesley H. Hager, *Conquering* (Grand Rapids: Eerdmans, 1965), p. 22.

been stirred by a vision recorded in 2 Corinthians 12. When one gets a clear picture of Christ in one's mind, life can never be the same again.

That particular vision was one of glory. The fiery beings, the seraphim, who burn up all that is unholy, envelop the vision. The foundations were shaken as one cried to another, "Holy, Holy, Holy is the LORD of hosts, the whole earth is full of His glory" (Isa. 6:3).

The results of this vision recorded in verses 5 through 7 involved personal conviction. When Isaiah beheld the glory of God he could only cry out, "Woe is me, for I am ruined!" That conviction was followed by confession, as he admitted his personal deficiency and the problem of the context in which he was living. As Moses had stood by the burning bush beside empty shoes, so Isaiah awaited with burning lips. The cleansing took place as the seraph placed the live coal on his lips. That vision of God helped him to see himself as he really was.

The second experience that shook his soul is referred to in verse 8: "Then I heard the voice of the Lord." The upward vision had shown him God. It prompted him to look inward and see himself. At the prompting of the voice of God, he looked outward and saw his duty. His call came loud and clear when he was prepared to listen. It prompted a response of consecration on his part. He then said, "Here am I. Send me!" God then clarified Isaiah's task. He was to face difficulties. The ones to whom he would go would be slow to listen, slow to see, and slow to respond. Their predicted unresponsiveness did not remove from him the call to devoted service.

How long has it been since you really had a vision of the glory of God? How long has it been since you have heard His voice calling you to service? When Isaiah saw God, himself, and a needy world, he jumped into the mainstream of life and maintained a testimony for God for forty years. What do the next forty years hold for you? A passage of Scripture that gives great strength and help is found in Philippians 1:6: "He who began a good work in you will perfect it until the day of Christ Jesus."

BLESSINGS IN AFFLICTION
Jonah 1:17—2:10

Jonah and the fish provided one of the favorite objects for Christian art in the catacombs. Representations of Jonah and the fish appeared more frequently than Daniel and the lion's den or Daniel's men in the fiery furnace. Sketching and painting the ceiling in the Sistine Chapel, Michaelangelo made Jonah stand out more prominently than any of the other prophets. It is unfortunate that many have been so intrigued by the great fish that God appointed that they have missed Jonah and Jonah's God.

God's hand of providence reached down and provided a preservation for the prophet. In the midst of that terrifying experience a positive transformation took place in Jonah. Affliction opened the mouth that sin had closed. In Jonah 2:1 we read for the first time in the book that Jonah prayed. The word *prayed* is a strong and forceful word. It refers to habitual praying. That same word is used of Hannah in 1 Samuel 2:1-10 as she poured out her soul to God. Many through the years could testify to the fact that affliction brought them to a place of real prayer. As we study this prayer of Jonah, we will note some of the timeless blessings that came to him through his experience of affliction.

Affliction brings the afflicted to God. "I called out of my distress to the LORD, and He answered me" (2:2). "While I was fainting away, I remembered the LORD" (2:7). This prayer of ten verses is saturated with praise rather than petition. Although he had been cast into the depths (2:3), Jonah could say what Paul said many later years, "We are afflicted in every way, but not crushed, perplexed but not despairing" (2 Cor. 4:8). In everything Jonah could thank God.

Affliction brings God's Word to the mind of the afflicted. There are at least twelve parallels in Jonah 2 and the Psalms and Lamentations. Blessed are they who in "good weather" have stored the Word of God away in their hearts for special help in the "time of storm."

Affliction causes the afflicted to realize his true condition. On the trip to Tarshish, Jonah had been able to sleep. He had not sensed the danger involved from disobeying God. Now he cried out, "I have been expelled from Thy sight. Nevertheless I will look again toward Thy holy temple" (2:4). Later he said, "Those who regard vain idols forsake their faithfulness" (2:8). He, like Isaiah, cried out, "Woe is me, for I am ruined!" which was necessary before being ready to say, "Here am I. Send me!" Jonah, in his disobedience, had only intensified his troubles.

Affliction brings a reality of salvation to the afflicted. Jonah shouted, "Salvation is from the LORD" (2:9). The term *salvation* means "deliverance" and is the intensive form, signifying "mighty salvation." As this greatness of deliverance by the Lord vibrated within his soul there came the utterance of a new vow. "But I will sacrifice to Thee with the voice of thanksgiving" (2:9*a*).

There are some 500 references to prayer in the Bible and some 100 recorded prayers. The second chapter of Jonah should be listed among the great prayer chapters. God spoke to the fish and Jonah was delivered. God's appointed fish had been involved in the making of the prophet. Jonah had learned through those affliction lessons designed to make the prodigal of chapter one the preacher of chapter three. Greatness is born, not just in triumph, but also in adversity.

Disappointment

ILLUSTRATIONS

Disappointment to a noble soul is what cold water is to burning metal; it strengthens, tempers, intensifies, but never destroys it.

Eliza Tabor

Man must be disappointed with the lesser things of life before he can comprehend the full value of the greater.

Bulwer-Lytton

We mortals, men and women, devour many a disappointment between breakfast and dinnertime; keep back the tears and look a little pale about the lips, and in answer to inquiries say, "Oh, nothing!" Pride helps us; and pride is not a bad thing when it only urges us to hide our own hurts—not to hurt others.

George Eliot, *Middlemarch*

William Cowper faced many early discouragements and disappointments. He had received an appointment to a clerkship in the House of Lords, but as soon as he received the appointment he began to conjure up visions of the terrors of an examination and of hostility toward him in the office where he had to study the *Journal*. He became so affected that he tried to take his life with laudanum. When that failed, he resolved to travel to France, change his religion, and bury himself in a monastery. But he turned again to self-destruction. Taking a coach, he ordered the coachman to drive him to the Thames, intending to throw himself into the river. But once again he drew back. On the night before his examination before the Lords, he lay for some time with the point of his penknife pressed against his heart, but could not bring himself to drive the knife home. Then he tried to hang himself, but the rope by which he was suspended broke. Such was the history of the man who lived to write *John Gilpin* and *The Task*, and, what is more, to write *God Moves in a Mysterious Way His Wonders to Perform*.[1]

Two of the world's greatest preachers knew what failure meant. Frederick Robertson of Brighton always aspired to the military life. He wanted to be a soldier but found he was not fitted for it. It was a bitter realization, but he accepted his defeat and disappointment and

1. Clarence E. Macartney, *You Can Conquer* (Grand Rapids: Abingdon, 1954), p. 87.

came to the place where he wrote some of the greatest sermons in the English language. Phillips Brooks taught in the famous old Boston Latin School but failed miserably as a teacher. But through that experience he learned that God wanted him in the pulpit, where he became the voice of American Protestantism in the nineteenth century.

The artist James Whistler, whose famous study in black and grays is popularly known as "Whistler's Mother," also wanted the military life and was enrolled as a cadet at West Point. But he failed a chemistry examination. Later he joked about the wrong answer that meant the difference between passing and failing, saying, "If silicon had been a gas, I would have been a major instead of an artist."[2]

Sermonic Sources
"Getting the Best of Trouble" (Pss. 4:1; 119:71)
Clarence E. Macartney, *Facing Life and Getting the Best of It*
"The Value of Life's Unrealized Purposes" (1 Kings 8:18-19)
George W. Truett, *On Eagle Wings*

FACING LIFE'S DISAPPOINTMENTS
Exodus 15:22–27

And when they came to Marah, they could not drink of the waters of Marah, for they were bitter: therefore the name of it was called Marah. [v. 23]

The shore of life is often strewn with the wreckage from disappointed lives.

Thomas A. Edison wanted to make a nickel-iron-alkaline battery. He performed fifty thousand experiments and failed fifty thousand times. Someone asked him, "Aren't all these failures disappointing to you?" "Not at all," he replied, "for I have learned fifty thousand ways it cannot be done, and therefore, I am fifty thousand times nearer the final successful experiment." Edison used disappointment to his advantage.

In Exodus 15, two million people were on the march from the land of bondage to the land of blessing. For three days they had been walking without water. The first of the three days had probably passed

---

2. Wesley H. Hager, *Conquering* (Grand Rapids: Eerdmans, 1965), p. 17.

as novelty, but as the second and third days of waterless wanderings came their singing turned to sorrow. They had been minstrels, but now they became murmurers. They had left the green fertility of the Nile River, but now faced the silence of the desert. As they trudged from the sea to the land of Shur, along the narrow strip of land about ten to fifteen miles wide, they came face to face with one of the many testings of God as He led them to the land of plenty.

Word was passed back through their lines that water was just ahead. With their throats parched and their feet weary they hastened their step. As the first in line knelt by the water and cupped it to his mouth there came a shout of anguish, "The water is bitter!" What would you have done if you had been there? Or maybe we should ask, What do you do when your expectations are shattered and the water of life is found to be bitter?

These three suggestions may be of help in the future.

Try to discover the purpose behind the disappointment. "There He made for them a statute and regulation, and there He tested them" (v. 25). All the way from Egypt to Canaan God kept testing His people, not for evil but for their good. He was getting them ready for Canaan. Samuel Rutherford of Scotland wrote, "We must try to read God's messages through the envelope in which they come." For example, if Phillips Brooks had succeeded as a schoolteacher the world would have been robbed of one of its greatest preachers.

Try to recognize the person behind the disappointment. "And the people murmured against Moses" (15:24, KJV*). This is quite common. We murmur against the one who is closest to us, though he may not necessarily be the one to blame. Some disappointments do come as a result of the actions of others, but some come as a result of our own actions. We tend to retreat into a cave of luck or chance; but actually there is no result without there first being a cause. Disappointments come through the permissive will of God. God may choose to allow the thorn in the flesh to remain (2 Cor. 12:7), and when He does He reminds us of the abounding grace that is available (2 Cor. 12:9).

Try to employ God's process for overcoming the disappointment. Moses "cried unto the LORD" (15:25, KJV). One is reminded of the stanza from the hymn "What a Friend We Have in Jesus":

*King James Version.

O what peace we often forfeit,
O what needless pain we bear,
All because we do not carry
Everything to God in prayer.

"The LORD showed him a tree" (15:25). Bible commentators say that there were no trees in that district, but God provided one. But God can always provide the impossible. He performed a miracle, and the bitter waters became sweet.

The Lord is our healer (15:26). It was John Tauler who said, "Ills have no weight, and tears no bitterness with God at hand." Just beyond the bitter waters of Marah lay Elim, where there were twelve wells of water and seventy palm trees. Beyond the bitterness, God knows the location of an oasis of refreshment.

DISCOURAGEMENT

ILLUSTRATIONS

Trouble ought to increase our sympathy. It was when Harriet Beecher Stowe sat through the long nights in her home in Ohio watching the struggles of a dying child that she began to think about the sorrows of slave mothers who were parted from their children by slavery. There was born within her the desire to write *Uncle Tom's Cabin*, a book that did so much to bring the wrongs and the sorrows of the slave to the attention of the world.[1]

Over fifty years ago Walt Disney, living in Kansas City and in straitened circumstances, decided that he wanted to be an artist. When he went to see the editor of the *Kansas City Star* and proudly displayed samples of his drawings, he was told that he had no real talent and that he had better go home and forget the whole thing. When some churches hired him to draw, Walt, having no money for the rental of a studio, set up his drawing board in his father's garage. One day a mouse began to play about on the floor. Disney liked the little thing and fed him some bread crumbs. The mouse actually climbed onto the drawing board, looking very wise indeed. A few weeks later, as Walt sat in a rooming house trying to think of an idea for a cartoon, the pert image of the mouse came to mind. He immediately began to sketch the little fellow, and Mickey Mouse was born.

Today Mickey Mouse is known to more people the world over than any other creature. By staying steady in a time of discouragement, Disney eventually got the green light and went on through.[2]

The medieval theologians and preachers made much of what they called the Seven Deadly Sins. These were pride, envy, anger, avarice, gluttony, sensuality, and discouragement. In the old listing of the Seven Deadly Sins discouragement was named sloth, or *accidie*. That surprises us somewhat, for we do not commonly think of discouragement as a sin. We think of it rather as a misfortune or an affliction. But since it results from a lack of faith in God and His providence, it may well be listed among the sins that assail and hurt our souls.[3]

It is strangely true in the physical world that much of the greatest

1. Clarence E. Macartney, *Facing Life and Getting the Best of It* (Grand Rapids: Abingdon, 1940), p. 78.
2. Lewis L. Dunnington, *Power to Become* (New York: Macmillan, 1956), pp. 116-17.
3. Clarence E. Macartney, *You Can Conquer* (Grand Rapids: Abingdon, 1954), pp. 77-78.

beauty is the product of pressure and suffering. The Grand Canyon is the result of the mighty Colorado cutting its way for centuries through the rock. The pearl, one of the loveliest of gems, is the result of pain and irritation within the oyster, where layer upon layer of beauty is laid around the disturbing grain of sand. And the diamond, reflecting the sun's rays in all the sparkling colors of the rainbow, is the result of the pressures and shocks deep within the earth.[4]

Sermonic Sources
"Need for Encouragement" (Haggai 2:4-5)
George W. Truett, *On Eagle Wings*
"The Blessing of Persecution" (Isa. 38:16)
W. Robertson Nicoll, *The Lamp of Sacrifice*
"A Faith to Overcome Pessimism"
Alson J. Smith, *Faith to Live By*
"Elijah—The Conquest of Discouragement"
Roy L. Laurin, *Meet Yourself in the Bible*

OVERCOMING DISCOURAGEMENT

1 Kings 19:1-21

But he himself went a day's journey into the wilderness, and came and sat down under a juniper tree; and he requested for himself that he might die, and said, "It is enough; now, O LORD, take my life, for I am not better than my fathers." [v. 4]

Elijah was one of the most illustrious, unique, and dramatic characters in Scripture. Although we know practically nothing of his background, we do know that he made a mighty stand for the cause of the one true God against terrible odds. That is recorded in 1 Kings 18:1-46, in which he challenged 450 priests and 400 prophets of Baal. Elijah's God answered by fire. When Jezebel heard of the victory, she declared her intention of bringing death to Elijah just as he had been the cause of death coming to her priests and prophets. After running away in search of protection from her wrath, he finally came to the point of feeling that the future held no hope. In his despair, he settled down under a juniper tree and there proceeded to call it quits.

But God had other plans for his life. In fact, God always knows where we are, and it is not His will that His people settle down under a juniper tree. There are two views one can have of God; the first is

4. Wesley H. Hager, *Conquering* (Grand Rapids: Eerdmans, 1965), p. 66.

called "The Cat and Kitten Theory"—that was what Augustine called it—and the other, the "Monkey Theory." The cat always carries around its young by the neck, whereas the monkey clings to its mother and is carried. I suppose all of our theories of God can be divided into those two basic categories. Does God carry me whether or not I resist, or do I cling to God and hold on to Him? Christianity answers, "Both!" *Teneo et teneor*— "I hold, and I am held." That is, I hold Him, and He, in turn, clasps me to Himself, and together we become partners.[5]

In 1 Kings 19:4-8 we have the account of God sending physical refreshment to Elijah. The angel of the Lord came twice to provide food and water and to encourage him to sleep. The first step in God's cure of Elijah's discouragement was to provide for his physical needs.

In verses 9-14 spiritual refreshment is provided. Elijah had strength enough to go into isolation in a cave. He had left his post of duty and become inactive. He had tried once and failed, therefore, he was not interested in trying again. The instruction came to him to go stand on the mount. He was brought to the place where he could recognize the still small voice of God. He had lost his perspective and his soul was shriveling up. He needed to get back into communication with God.

God provided a reinstatement to service. Elijah was to return in the very direction from which he had come. His new commission was an even greater one. A promise was also provided that assured Elijah that he would not be alone, that God would leave more than 7,000 faithful in Israel.

The final step that God took was to provide a helper for Elijah. That provision only came when Elijah needed a helper and when he was in a condition to use him. A busy man by the name of Elisha was challenged to immediate service. It does not take God long to provide help when we need it and are ready to make wise use of it.

Discouragement obscures faith and prostitutes strength. It brings despair and depression so that it is difficult even to see God. God does not want us to stay under the juniper tree.

---

5. George C. Stewart, *The Victory of Faith* (New York: Harper & Brothers, 1935), p. 67.

FAILURE

ILLUSTRATIONS

Albert Einstein was dismissed from a school in Munich because he lacked interest in his studies. He failed to pass an examination for entrance to a polytechnic school in Zurich. He applied later for an assistantship in teaching but was rejected. He did become a tutor for boys in a Zurich boardinghouse, but was soon fired. But failure did not keep him defeated. He kept beginning over again, and in time not only found himself but was recognized as one of the world's greatest geniuses.[1]

Bob Zuppke, former football coach at the University of Illinois, never passed judgment on a new player until he had seen how the fellow reacted to being hit hard. One year at Illinois, a handsome 196-pound running back with a great prep-school reputation came out for the team. The coaches rubbed their hands in glee. "He'll tear the Big Ten apart," they said. But all "Zup" said was, "Wait till he gets hit."

The potential "superstar" made a beautiful running catch of a punt over his shoulder and raced down the field, weaving and dodging skillfully. At midfield he was brought down hard from behind. A couple of plays later, he took a lateral pass and was off again for fifteen yards. But that time, as he was about to be tackled, he slowed up. All afternoon Zup watched him make impressive runs, but slow up before every tackle. After the scrimmage, the other coaches asked Zup where to put the handsome newcomer. "Third team," said Zup. "He stops before he's hit."[2]

About the year 1790, the brilliant German music teacher John Albrechtsberger became outraged because one of his pupils failed to follow the rules of musical composition. A few years later he said of that former student, "That man never learned anything and, what is more, he never will write anything worthwhile." But young Ludwig von Beethoven would not be defeated and kept on writing such things as the Second, Fifth, and Ninth Symphonies in addition to many other compositions that still stir the souls of men.

There is something admirable and inspiring in seeing someone downed by failure rise up and begin all over again. In 1925 an aspiring young rookie baseball player with a shy, boyish grin, an overabun-

1. Wesley H. Hager, *Conquering* (Grand Rapids: Eerdmans, 1965), p. 16.
2. Alson J. Smith, *Faith to Live By* (New York: Doubleday, 1949), p. 106.

dance of muscle, and a reputation for coming apart under pressure looked very much like a hopeless failure. During two years in the minor leagues he had hit a few home runs, but his fielding was pitiful and he seemed to have little more to offer. The great Ty Cobb watched him clumsily field a ball one day and said with contempt, "Look at those piano legs—he'll never last!" But despite his failures he kept getting up and starting over. Eventually, he set the all-time endurance record of 2,130 consecutive games played. Today, Lou Gehrig is called the "Iron Man" of baseball.[3]

Failure is more frequently from want of energy than want of capital.

Daniel Webster

He only is exempt from failures who makes no efforts.

Richard Whately

One should remember that the defeated still have everything if they still have God.

A. J. Cronin

Sermonic Sources
"Destruction By Neglect" (Rom. 13:14)
    J. H. Jowett, *Books by the Traveller's Way*
"Victory Through Defeat" (Gen. 32:28; Gal. 6:14)
    A. W. Tozer, *The Divine Conquest*

DIAGNOSE YOUR FAILURES
Joshua 7:1-15

So about three thousand men from the people went up there, but they fled from the men of Ai. And the men of Ai struck down about thirty-six of their men, and pursued them from the gate as far as Shebarim, and struck them down on the descent, so the hearts of the people melted and became as water. [vv. 4-5]

Failure is a school in which truth always grows strong. Failure sometimes leads to despair, but when it is faced in a wise fashion profitable results can accrue.

The silent majority marched around the great city of Jericho. Only trumpets broke the silence. On the seventh day they circled it seven

3. Hager, p. 16.

times. After a total of thirteen trips around the city, the trumpets were blown and the walls fell. It seems that God had them march long enough to realize that when victory came, it would be His doing and not theirs. The conquest of Canaan took seven years, and during that campaign Israel suffered only one defeat (Ai) and lost only thirty-six men. God wanted victory for His people, but His people brought defeat upon themselves.

Achan had committed a sin, and the anger of the Lord was kindled against the children of Israel (Josh. 7:1). Sin is serious. It brings trouble, separation, and death. God's displeasure is raised against the unrighteousness of man, but it never shuts off His compassion. Israel was made aware of God's displeasure toward sin. He told them that no blessings would come to them until they were sanctified (Josh. 7:13). The presence of Achan's sin in their midst meant that, not only did Achan have to pay the penalty for his sin, but also his family (Josh. 7:24). The sinner's possessions were also to be destroyed with him (Josh. 7:24). A survey of that entire defeat will substantiate the fact that there were some conditions that laid the foundation for the one outward act by Achan.

Overconfidence was one factor in the defeat. "Do not let all the people go up; only about two or three thousand men" (Josh. 7:3). Israel had just come from a victory at Jericho. It appears that they overestimated their own achievements in that victory and forgot that all they actually had done was to march and shout. Great success in the public eye is often followed by failure in private. The victory we won yesterday will not necessarily mean victory today. We must remember that there is nothing so small that we can combat it alone. We need God's help in all that we attempt.

Failure to wait upon God before going forth was another factor in the defeat. Joshua sent the men out, but did not first go back to Gilgal. The venture ended in defeat (Josh. 7:10). The defeated Israelites found themselves in need of action, not meditation. God could have warned them of danger ahead if they had only gone to Him first. Prayer could have revealed the problem posed by Achan's presence in the camp, for there are no secrets before God. He knows the heart of the individual and is acquainted with every circumstance. Before venturing out on our own, we would do well to first wait upon the Lord.

Disobedience to the commands of God was another factor in the defeat. "Israel has sinned, and they have also transgressed My covenant which I commanded them. And they have even taken some of the things" (Josh. 7:11). Joshua followed a very common course when he blamed God for their defeat (Josh. 7:6-9). It is evident, however, that with Achan's great confession, "I have sinned" (Josh. 7:20), that man, not God, should shoulder the blame. The safety of all was dependent on the obedience of each. They were not going to be able to stand against their enemies until they gave up their sin (Josh. 7:13).

The diagnosis of a failure is not a simple matter. There is often an outward sin that becomes clear to observers. Surrounding it, however, are often those elements that have set the stage for that outward sin. Three were evidenced in this incident: overconfidence in oneself, failure to wait upon God, and disobedience to the commands of God.

FEAR

ILLUSTRATIONS

Dr. George Truett, a noted preacher of the last generation, was invited to speak for a week at one of America's most influential colleges. Thoughtfully, he wrote ahead to the president of the college, asking him to circulate a questionnaire among the students to get their suggestions for subjects and themes for his messages. The most often mentioned request was, "Tell us how we can conquer fear."

A doctor was talking to a new patient the other day. In great alarm, the patient mentioned a rare and deadly disease of the liver and claimed to be suffering from it. "Nonsense!" protested the doctor. "You are not suffering from that. In fact, you wouldn't know whether you had it or not. It is a disease which gives no discomfort at all."

"That's just it!" gasped the poor patient. "My last doctor told me that. That is how I know I have it. I feel quite well!"

Alexander the Great, on a campaign with his army from Macedonia to India, rode a beautiful black horse called Bucephalus. The horse had been brought by horse traders to the court of Philip, Alexander's father, for use in his cavalry. But he seemed to be so vicious, plunging and kicking at everyone who came near him, that the king's horseman was about to reject him. Alexander was greatly taken with the animal and asked permission from his father to ride him. When Philip gave his consent, Alexander, who had noted that the horse was frightened by his shadow, took him by the bridle and turned his head into the sun. Then he leaped to his back and galloped up and down before the king.[1]

John Donne's poetic beauty and genuine religious insight is being rediscovered in our day. He knew the ultimate conquest for the fear of death:

> I have a sin of fear, that when I have spun
> My last thread, I shall perish on the shore;
> Swear by Thyself, that at my death Thy Son
> Shall shine as He shines now, and heretofore;
> And, having done that, Thou hast done,
> I fear no more.[2]

1. Clarence E. Macartney, *You Can Conquer* (Grand Rapids: Abingdon, 1954), p. 9.
2. Hillyer H. Straton, *Solving Life's Problems* (St. Louis: Bethany Press, 1954), pp. 40-41.

Freedom from fear and injustice and oppression will be ours only in the measure that men who value such freedom are ready to sustain its possession—to defend it against every thrust from within or without.

Dwight D. Eisenhower
Crusade in Europe

The only thing we have to fear is fear itself.

Franklin D. Roosevelt
Inaugural Address, 1933

Sermonic Sources
"The Fruits of Godly Fear" (Ps. 25:12-15)
  J. H. Jowett, *Brooks by the Traveller's Way*
"Perfect Love Casts Out Fear" (1 John 4:18)
  George B. Duncan, *Wanting the Impossible*
"Getting the Best of Fear" (Gen. 15:1; Rev. 1:17)
  Clarence E. Macartney, *Facing Life and Getting the Best of It*
"When Fear Haunts Our Days" (Pss. 27; 46:1-2; 107; 121:104)
  Charles M. Crowe, *Getting Help from the Bible*
"Not a Spirit of Fear" (2 Tim. 1:7)
  C. Roy Angell, *Baskets of Silver*
"A Faith to Overcome Fear"
  Alson J. Smith, *Faith to Live*
"Daniel—The Conquest of Fear"
  Roy L. Laurin, *Meet Yourself in the Bible*
"The Conquest of Fear"
  Batsell B. Baxter, *When Life Tumbles In*

FREEDOM FROM FEAR
Revelation 1:9-20

When I saw Him, I fell at His feet as a dead man. And He laid His right hand upon me, saying, "Do not be afraid; I am the first and the last." [v.17]

Fear is one of the great spoilers and enemies of mankind. In the opening paragraphs of his book *The Conquest of Fear*, Basil King writes: "During most of my conscious life I have been prey to fear. . . . I cannot remember the time when a dread of one kind or another was not in the air."[3]

John Bonnell points out:

> Psychologists, by means of laboratory tests, have established that at birth two fears are already present: fear of a loud noise and fear of falling. While we begin our lives with only two fears, it is not long before we succeed in accumulating scores of additional ones. The fear of thunder and lightning, of the dark, of people, of life and of death—these have all been taught to children by adults, for they have learned them by watching adult behavior. . . . People are afraid to walk on the streets, afraid to cross a street, afraid to ride in automobiles, or trains, or airplanes. . . . And as for imaginary fear, tens of thousands of people throughout this nation are afraid every time they open a letter, tremble when they see the telegraph boy, or are startled when the telephone rings or even when someone suddenly calls to them. They live in constant fear and feel that some strange, indefinable menace haunts all their days.[4]

Samuel Johnson, the lexicographer, would not pass a post without touching it. It has been said that Professor Leonard of the University of Wisconsin would not go more than five blocks from his home for thirty-five years. Thomas Carlyle built a vault for a study. There was a rooster next door that crowed three times a day, and he just dreaded having to wait for it to crow.

John, the writer of Revelation, was on the Isle of Patmos, incarcerated there because of his testimony for Christ. That little island, only ten miles long and five miles wide, was anchored in the Aegean Sea. On that rocky isle he refused to allow loneliness and fear to spoil his soul. On the "Lord's day" he heard a great voice (Rev. 1:10). He turned and was given one of the most complete and glorious portraits of Christ to be found in the Bible. This sevenfold revelation of Christ was used to dispel his fear. Christ laid His right hand upon John and said, "Don't be afraid anymore." There is freedom from fear when we realize the glory of the presence of Christ.

His body was clothed with a long robe and had a golden girdle about the breast (Rev. 1:13). When Christ was upon the earth, He was the servant with the robe gathered at the waist. John saw Him as the High

3. Batsell B. Baxter, *When Life Tumbles In* (Grand Rapids: Baker, 1974), p. 45.
4. Ibid.

Priest whose robe was gathered at the breast. The servant's work complete, Christ is now the Intercessor.

In the vision, His head and hair were white as wool (Rev. 1:14). He is the ageless One of whom it was said, "He is before all things, and in Him all things hold together" (Col. 1:17). He is the pure one like the lily of the valley. He is the wise one referred to as "the Alpha and Omega, . . . who is and was and who is to come, the Almighty" (Rev. 1:8). His eyes were like flames of fire (Rev. 1:14; Dan. 10:6). Those eyes could pierce the darkest depths. Just a look from Jesus could send Peter, the big fisherman, out into the night to weep after he had denied his Lord.

His feet were like burnished bronze (Rev. 1:15). This metal, having been refined and made pure with terrific heat, comprised the feet. Where they would tread, all the dross would be consumed and holiness would come. His voice was like the sound of many waters (Rev. 1:15). That voice was resistless as at the tomb of Lazarus (John 11:43-44). It has been resounding through the centuries. It is resolute and will not return to God void.

In His right hand He held the seven stars (Rev. 1:15). These are the messengers or ministers and missionaries of the churches (Rev. 1:20). They are kept in the hollow of His hand of power and authority. His face was like the sun shining in full strength (Rev. 1:16). Such glory will certainly dispel all darkness.

Do not be afraid to live, for He is the first and the last (Rev. 1:17). Do not be afraid to die, for He is the One who lives and was dead (Rev. 1:18). Do not be afraid to face eternity, for He has the keys of hell and of death and is alive forever more (Rev. 1:18).

GUILT

In this world of ours no one is completely innocent. Each of us carries some burden of guilt which troubles him and fills him with self-loathing. . . . Where would sympathy, mercy, forgiveness come from if not for our common share of human fallibility?

Friedrich Duerrenmatt and James Yaffe
The Deadly Game

Forgiveness is a beautiful word because it kindles a light in the face of God and in the countenance of man. It is also a costly word. Before God could pronounce it, Christ had to die on the cross. It is a word that is dear to every true believer. It awakens the music of the redeemed in heaven, for that is their song—the forgiveness of God. "To Him who loves us, and released us from our sins by His blood" (Rev. 1:5).[1]

Perhaps the four most beautiful scenes in the New Testament are scenes of forgiveness: the return and forgiveness of the prodigal son; the repentance and forgiveness of Peter; the repentance and forgiveness of the dying thief; and the forgiveness of the woman caught in adultery.[2]

If you have marred or disfigured the day with an unkind word or deed, bring it out before God and seek His forgiveness. If someone has been unkind to you, do not dwell on the grievance but bring it out and allow God's love to play on it until it vanishes from your thoughts. If your work has left you worn and weary and your mind perplexed and troubled, bring it all out before Him until His presence imparts to you the peace you so much need.

Years ago in Winchester, Virginia, lived a boy named Charles Broadway Rousse, the son of a poor, working widow. He went to Sunday school, sang in the choir, and was a useful member in a small church body of poor and inconspicuous people. By and by, the boy fell in with evil associates, was implicated in a crime, and sent to the penitentiary. After a while, the members of the church got up a petition to the governor and had the boy pardoned. They sent a delegation and brought him home. Upon their arrival home they went

---

1. Clarence E. Macartney, *The Greatest Words in the Bible and Human Speech* (Grand Rapids: Abingdon-Cokesbury, 1938), p. 23.
2. Ibid., p. 26.

directly to the little church where all the congregation had gathered, and there in the presence of all the people exercised the divine function that has been committed to the church: they forgave his sins. They said to him, "We want you to come right back into the church and take your place in the Sunday school and the choir. The past is blotted out, *forgiven and forgotten*, and is as though it had never been." Then, one by one, all the members of the church took him by the hand, personally ratifying the action of the church and expressing their confidence.[3]

> Drop Thy still dews of quietness
> Till all our strivings cease;
> Take from our souls the strain and stress,
> And let our ordered lives confess
> The beauty of Thy peace.[4]

Sermonic Sources
"The Forgiveness of Sins" (Eph. 1:17)
  Charles F. Kemp, *The Preaching Pastor*
"The Escape from Guilt"
  Batsell B. Baxter, *When Life Tumbles In*

A CURE FOR A GUILTY CONSCIENCE

Genesis 32:22-32

Dr. Paul Tournier, the Swiss counselor, has said: "There is no worse suffering than a guilty conscience and certainly none more harmful." For some, the present is difficult. For others, it is the dread of the future that is difficult. The worst foe of the soul, however, is the past, because it contains the power to make the present dreadful. While anxiety is dread of the future, guilt is dread of the past.

It was that dread of the past that troubled Jacob in Genesis 32 and made the immediate future foreboding. He had lied and schemed for his birthright (Gen. 25:24) and his father's blessing (Gen. 27:22). In Genesis 32 Jacob is waiting by the River Jabbok as he faces the possibility of meeting his brother, Esau, the next day. He had tricked Esau in the past; now Jacob must meet him face to face. The possible peril ahead and his haunting past keep sleep from his eyes and peace from his soul. A sense of guilt is a deeply rooted emotion that produces discomfort and anxiety. Restlessness and resistance seem to follow it.

3. Edgar DeWitt Jones, *Detroit Daily News*, 12 January 1944, as quoted from Hillyer H. Stratton, *Solving Life's Problems* (St. Louis: Bethany Press, 1954). pp. 71-72.
4. Wesley H. Hager, *Conquering* (Grand Rapids: Eerdmans, 1965), p. 26.

What can we do with a guilty conscience? Some have suggested that we try to suppress or deny it. Others have tried to rationalize it away by claiming that other people are worse. And still others have tried to free themselves from its shackles by projecting the blame on someone else.

There are some practical suggestions in Genesis 32 that may prove helpful to others who like Jacob face a trying circumstance with a guilty conscience. The first suggestion is found in verse 25, which encourages recognition of the limitations of the body. "And when he saw that he had not prevailed against him, he touched the socket of his thigh; so the socket of Jacob's thigh was dislocated while he wrestled." Jacob was good at wrestling, but wrestling brought him no peace. Only when his natural strength was paralyzed did he realize that he needed help from outside himself to get peace.

In the next verse we find the second suggestion: "I will not let you go unless you bless me" (v. 26). We must determine not to leave the place of blessing without the blessing. As Jacob wrestled with the angel, his physical strength was drained and broken. All he could do was to hold on until the blessing that he sought was bestowed. His desire for the blessing stirred his determination to wait until it came.

The third suggestion is that the one seeking a cure for a guilty conscience recognize his true condition. "So he [the angel] said, 'What is your name?' And he said, 'Jacob'" (v. 27). Jacob's name means "trickster." By declaring his name he was at the same time confessing his besetting sin. True forgiveness can never come apart from the recognition of the presence of sin and the need for its forgiveness.

The final suggestion is that we be willing to receive the evidence of a cured conscience. "Your name shall no longer be Jacob, but Israel" (v. 28). There came a change of character and a reconciliation (33:4). He now had a new name, a new power, and a new fellowship.

As Jacob limped away over the hill the sun rose on him (32:21). There is always sunrise when there is surrender. Be willing to yield, cling, confess, and receive. God has a cure for a guilty conscience.

FORGIVEN AND FORGOTTEN

Psalm 103

Some are willing to forgive, but few are willing to forgive and forget. For many the word *forgive* is very limited in meaning. But when its true meaning is surveyed it becomes what Dr. Clarence McCartney referred to as "the sweetest word in the Bible." Forgiveness is the prerogative of God, for we read in Mark 2:7: "Who can forgive sins but God alone?" Of the 14,388 different words in our Hebrew Old Testament and Greek New Testament, few are richer in meaning than the Hebrew and Greek equivalents of the English word *forgive*.

In Psalm 78:38 we read, "But He, being compassionate, forgave their iniquity, and did not destroy them." The word translated "forgave" in this verse means "to cover." It is the same root verb that God used when He gave instructions to Noah in Genesis 6:14: "You shall . . . *cover* it inside and out with pitch" (italics added). When God forgave our sins, He covered them over. Consider Saul, the persecutor in Acts 9, and then Paul, the prophet of love in 1 Corinthians 13. God covered his sins.

Psalm 25:18 says, "Look upon my affliction and my trouble, and forgive all my sins." The word translated "forgive" in this verse means "to lift up or away." This word picture takes us back to Leviticus 14, where we find the procedure for the cleansing of a leper. Two sparrows were taken; one was killed, and the wings of the living sparrow were dipped in the blood of the one just killed. The leper was sprinkled with the blood. Then the priest would "*let* the live bird *go free*" (Lev. 14:7, italics added). When God forgave our sins, He separated them from us.

In Luke 7:43 we read: "I suppose the one whom he forgave more." The word *forgave* in that verse means "to cancel the debt." The verse is included in the parable of the two debtors. One debtor had been forgiven 500 pence and the other 50 pence. The question was asked, Which debtor would love the one canceling the debt more? The reply was, "The one whom he forgave more." Consider our great indebtedness to God, then remember and rejoice that when He forgave our sins, He canceled our debt.

Psalm 103:3 also celebrates God's forgiveness: "Who pardons all your iniquities; who heals all your diseases." The Hebrew word translated "pardons" in that verse means "to send away." For this word picture we need to go back to Leviticus 16. The high priest placed his hands upon the scapegoat, and the sins of the people were laid upon it. The scapegoat was then led out to die in the desert, bearing the sins of the people. Likewise, our sins were forgiven and sent away "as far as the east is from the west" (Psalm 103:12).

What a tremendous contrast between the sadness of sin and the sweetness of forgiveness. Sin with its guilt, helplessness, passion, and slavery is forgiven by God. He covers it, cuts it away, cancels the debt, and sends it away "as far as the east is from the west."

HANDICAPS

ILLUSTRATIONS

Left in solitude, Milton began work on his monumental *Paradise Lost.* It was the work of his declining years. "It was produced," writes his biographer, "when every turbulent feeling of youth had subsided; when experience had had her perfect work, and when his soul could listen in quiet to the voice of the charmer, Wisdom." The work was completed in 1665 when Milton was sixty years old, long tortured by illness, suffering the terrible deprivation of blindness, bereft of his companion, and financially straitened. While most of his writings and those of succeeding ages have been forgotten, Milton's pure lines endure.

The year was 1921. It was near the end of the summer vacation season on Campobello Island, off the coast of Maine. The weather had been hot and dry, and a dangerous forest fire had flamed upon the island, threatening the vacation camps and residences of wealthy New Yorkers who spent their summer there. Most of the men on the island helped fight the fire, among them a certain thirty-nine-year-old politician. When the fire was finally brought under control, this man along with the rest put on his bathing suit and dove into the icy waters of the Bay of Fundy. Later that night, he suffered torturous pain and the next morning was carried on a stretcher to the mainland. There the medical diagnosis came like a sentence of doom—polio.

He had a severe case. It was so bad that he would never walk again. Everybody, including his immediate family, was certain that it was the end of his political career. But for Franklin D. Roosevelt, infantile paralysis was the beginning, not the end. Having been genial, wealthy, and easy-going, he had previously had no need for what now turned out to be his greatest asset—a fighting heart.[1]

Julius Caesar, Alexander the Great, Socrates, Moliere, Richelieu, Dostoevski, and perhaps Napoleon were epileptics; Catherine the Great was horribly deformed and wore a steel brace for twenty-six years; Lord Byron had a clubfoot; Milton and Homer were blind. And even if we are not handicapped physically the chances are ninety-nine out of one hundred that we are handicapped emotionally, economically, or some other way.[2]

Life can be lived gloriously even with tragic handicaps. It can be rich

---

1. Alson J. Smith, *Faith to Live By* (New York: Doubleday, 1949), p. 100.
2. Ibid., p. 101.

despite limiting conditions. William Carey, the great missionary, was a humble cobbler; David Livingstone was a cotton mill hand; Sir Walter Raleigh was a prisoner in the Tower of London, and there wrote his history of the world. John Bunyan would perhaps never have written his *Pilgrim's Progress* had he not endured twelve years in a narrow cell. Although blind, Fanny Crosby wrote hymns of faith that will keep singing in men's hearts forever. Beethoven was deaf, and the apostle Paul had his "thorn in the flesh." Not one of them said: "Because I am poor, I have nothing to give; because I am ignorant I must stay so; because I am unjustly jailed, I will turn sour on the world and give nothing for nothing; because life has never given me a fair chance I will take all I can get for myself."[3]

We can strip off our handicaps and conquer them because God has resources of courage and power for us to use. George Matheson found them and used them, and as a result, lived a victorious life. He was born in Glasgow, Scotland, in 1842. Before he reached the age of two, it was discovered that his eyesight was defective. He, his parents, and the specialists fought a heroic fight, but before George had finished his course at Glasgow University he was completely blind. With courage and faith he graduated with honors in philosophy, studied for the ministry, and in a few years' time became the minister of one of the largest churches in Edinburgh, where he carried on a memorable ministry. In addition to his laborious preparation of his services he did a great deal of parish visitation, wrote numerous articles and twelve books, and continued his own studies throughout his life.

It must have been heartbreaking for George Matheson's parents to have a strange infection in their baby's eyes lead to its blindness. Yet, in that tragic situation George Matheson found God's resources available for him. God poured into his heart the courage, resourcefulness, and grim perseverance that gave him victory over his handicap. Through it all his faith grew stronger, and after twenty years of blindness he wrote:

> O Love that will not let me go,
> I rest my weary soul on Thee!
> I give Thee back the life I owe
> That in Thine ocean depths its flow
> May richer, fuller be.[4]

---

3. Wesley H. Hager, *Conquering* (Grand Rapids: Eerdmans, 1965), p. 65.
4. Ibid., p. 68.

Sermonic Sources
"A Faith to Overcome Handicap"
  Alson J. Smith, *Faith to Live By*
"Paul—The Conquest of Handicap"
  Roy L. Laurin, *Meet Yourself in the Bible*
"The Meaning of Affliction"
  Paul Tournier, *A Doctor's Casebook*

LIVING WITH OUR HANDICAPS
2 Corinthians 12:1-10

> And because of the surpassing greatness of the revelations, for this
> reason, to keep me from exalting myself, there was given me a thorn in the
> flesh, a messenger of Satan to buffet me—to keep me from exalting
> myself! [v. 7]

In 1954 Oberlin College granted an honorary degree to Theodore
Steinway. His piano company had manufactured 342,000 pianos; each
of those pianos had 243 strings, and within each piano those strings
exerted 40,000 pounds of pressure. The citation read at the time of the
granting of the degree stated: "Theodore Steinway has shown the
world that out of great tension, harmony can come."

Louis Pasteur, who suffered a stroke at the age of forty-six, is
remembered as the father of modern science. Mozart composed his
Requiem while fighting a fatal disease. Those and many others like
them have shown the world that greatness is born, not only in triumph,
but also in adversity. They lived out the motto of the Canadian Air
Force, "Through adversity to the stars."

Paul had his limitations. He was possibly the most mobile spirit that
the world has seen. What was his secret of triumph in spite of his trials,
toils, and tempests? The book of Philippians tells us about Paul, the
saint; Romans shows us Paul, the thinker; 2 Corinthians shows us Paul,
the victorious man.

Second Corinthians 12:1-6 tells us of the privilege that came to Paul.
He had been caught up to Paradise and had heard inexpressible words
that a man is not permitted to speak. That experience came to him
fourteen years prior to this time. At that point, he had been preaching
at Lystra and other cities of Galatia (Acts 14:19). They had stoned him
and left him for dead. The heavens had opened up before him and he
had a vision. Paul had eight visions during the course of his lifetime.
This particular experience included an abiding vision of the Lord. Like

Moses before him, he had "endured, as seeing Him who is unseen" (Heb. 11:27).

But there was given to Paul a thorn in the flesh (2 Cor. 12:7). He had now passed from privilege to pain, from the throne to the thorns.

Dr. A. T. Pierson once wrote a philosophy of suffering. He stated that some of it was punitive (Heb. 12:15-17); some of it was corrective (Heb. 12:5-12); and some of it was educative (1 Pet. 1:6-7). Paul's suffering was preventive. It was designed to keep him from having spiritual pride based upon the thrilling visions of his earlier experience. We do not know the nature of that thorn in the flesh. He may have had merely the same bodily limitations that you and I have. He was, however, able to live above those limitations. Paul's example behooves us, with the help of God, to do likewise.

Paul's thorn was a useful gift. Three times he prayed that God would take it away (2 Cor. 12:8). God answered his prayers by saying no. Prayer is not a process whereby we try to change God's mind. Prayer is the process that makes us willing to accept His will. Examine the inside of a clock and you will see little wheels turning forward and backward, apparently in a haphazard manner. Look at the face of the clock and it will tell you the time. You become amazed at the genius that makes the clock work. In a similar way, we often stand on the wrong side of God's providence.

Power came into Paul's life after he had experienced the abiding vision and the abasing thorn. Only grace was sufficient for Paul, "for power is perfected in weakness" (v. 9). Following the privilege and the pain, there came power. When storms come, some trees bend and some break. Paul had learned the secret of not breaking under pressure. In fact, he could say, "I am well content with weaknesses, with insults, with distresses, with persecutions, with difficulties, . . . for when I am weak, then I am strong" (v. 10). He had discovered that God's grace had been made perfect in the midst of his weakness. God wants our weaknesses so that He may work through us for His glory.

There are three secrets to living with one's limitations. The first is to have the privilege of being exposed to an abiding vision. This will center our attention upon Christ rather than upon ourselves. Second, the experience of pain will serve as a "humbling thorn," thus forcing us to seek God's purpose for ourselves in hardship. The final secret is to experience the power that comes from the abounding grace of Christ. Remember, greatness is born not only in triumph, but also in adversity.

INDECISION

ILLUSTRATIONS

He was going to be all that a mortal should be
  Tomorrow
No one would be better than he
  Tomorrow
Each morning he stacked up the letters he'd write
  Tomorrow
It was too bad indeed he was too busy to see Bill,
  but he promised to do it
  Tomorrow
The greatest of workers this man would have been
  Tomorrow
The world would have known him had he ever seen
  Tomorrow
But the fact is he died and faded from view, and all
  that was left when living was through
Was a mountain of things he intended to do
  Tomorrow.[1]

> Author Unknown

To make wise decisions we need a dependable standard of judgment. A basic sense of values must exist. If our standards are those of self-interest, material gain, or simply picking the easiest way out, they fall far below the ideals of the Christian life. Only worthy, God-glorifying, spiritual goals should guide us.

Decisions take courage. That is why there are many in our day who do not make decisions. It is so much more pleasant to be tolerant and open-minded. Such shallow views of living cannot satisfy a thinking man. There are times when we must stand firm and say, "I can do no otherwise, so help me God." That requires all the powers of a strong will.[2]

1. Clarence E. Macartney, *The Greatest Words in the Bible and Human Speech* (Grand Rapids: Abingdon-Cokesbury, 1938), p. 89.
2. Ralph Heynen, *The Art of Christian Living* (Grand Rapids: Baker, 1963), p. 150.

Sermonic Sources
"The Valley of Indecision" (1 Kings 18:21)
  J. Sutherland Bonnell, *Fifth Avenue Sermons*
"Poise Is an Achievement"
  Lewis L. Dunnington, *Power to Become*

LIFE AT THE CROSSROADS
Deuteronomy 1:19

> Then we set out from Horeb, and went through all that great and terrible wilderness which you saw, on the way to the hill country of the Amorites, just as the LORD our God had commanded us; and we came to Kadesh-barnea.

Vacillation is a problem for many. Such people are those the apostle James writes about: "The one who doubts is like the surf of the sea" (James 1:6). An insecure person finds himself constantly on the fence, wondering which way he should go. In fact, most of us have certain areas of our lives in which we find it difficult to make definite choices.

Often, difficulty in making choices has its roots in early life. Some parents insist on making all the decisions for their children. That is fine when they are very young, but early in life children should learn to make simple choices. As the years go by, children must be taught to make up their own minds, to make wise choices, and to make them independently. That is part of the growth and development of character.

It has been said that Kadesh-barnea was the most important location during the period represented by the book of Deuteronomy. By derivation of name, it means "Holy Place." By geographical location, it could be called the crossroads of the Old Testament. It was from Kadesh-barnea that twelve spies went into the Promised Land to survey it prior to its occupation by God's people.

Ten of the twelve returned claiming that it was impossible to go forward because of the insurmountable hindrances. Two of the twelve, Caleb and Joshua, formed God's minority and declared that, though there were giants in the land, God was also there. The majority decision held, and a nation turned back from Kadesh-barnea to die in the desert.

Decision determines destiny. Big doors swing on small hinges. You may be standing now at a modern Kadesh-barnea. Your decision will determine your destiny—the "desert" or the "Promised Land." Do not trifle at the crossroads. Life consists of the sum total of our decisions. Victory comes when the wavering mind sets forth in one direction. We cannot afford to trifle with the choices of a life's mate, an occupation, or especially of a Savior who can save us from sin for eternity. An individual life, career, family, or nation's welfare may be hanging in the balance. Eternity is at stake. Others will be influenced by our decision at the crossroads. No one except Caleb and Joshua were permitted to enter the Promised Land (Deut. 1:34-37).

No one lives to himself. Little feet may be following in large footprints. Achan's covetousness meant that his family also suffered (Josh. 7:1-26).

Decisions should only be made after God has been taken into consideration. One with God is a majority. Two of the greatest words of Scripture are found at the beginning of Ephesians 2:4: "But God." He makes all the difference. Do not go forward unless He is with you. Beware of the foolishness of the rich fool who left God out of his thinking, planning, and philosophy of life (Luke 12:13-34).

It is not wise to delay at an intersection. A decision must be made at the crossroads. A very short time elapses between the change of a traffic light from red to green and the sound of automobile horns blowing. Convictions get weaker, desires dwindle, and the forces of opposition gather while we delay. Now is the accepted time. Lot lingered and lost (Gen. 19:16). Many others have lingered and discovered that they have lost. Satan will try to convince us that there is plenty of time. What if God were to take you in your lingering? To be almost persuaded is to be almost saved. To be almost saved is to be completely lost.

LONELINESS

A clue to what loneliness is can be found in Psalm 142: "No one cares for my soul" (v. 4). Loneliness is the feeling of being cut off from other people, deserted, or banished from their company. It is not merely the fact of being physically alone, it is the result of a breakdown in the emotional giving and receiving between people. We humans need the support of friendly relationships with others as badly as we need food and drink. When we are denied satisfying relaationships with others, the result is loneliness.

ILLUSTRATIONS

Residents of Davenport, Iowa have done something about this universal problem. Some years ago they inaugurated a phone service known as Dial-a-Listener. At the receiving end is a rotating staff of volunteers who keep the number open around the clock. At the calling end are lonely people of Davenport who hunger for the sound of a sympathetic human voice. Unlike the numerous dial-a-prayer switchboards and suicide-prevention centers, the purpose of Dial-a-Listener is neither to deliver canned messages of hope nor to cope with life-and-death crises. It is simply to offer lonely callers a human connection.

> Do you think you can frighten me by telling me that I am alone. France is alone; and God is alone; and what is my loneliness before the loneliness of my country and God? . . . Well, my loneliness shall be my strength too: it is better to be alone with God: His friendship will not fail me, nor His counsel, nor His love. In His strength I will dare, and dare, and dare, until I die.
>
> George Bernard Shaw, *Saint Joan*

In the oration he delivered at the unveiling of the stately memorial built around the lowly birthplace cabin of Abraham Lincoln in Kentucky, President Woodrow Wilson said:

> I have read many biographies of Lincoln; I have sought out with the greatest interest the many intimate stories that are told of him, the narratives of nearby friends, and sketches at close quarters, in which those who had the privilege of being associated with him have tried to depict for us the very man himself . . . but I have nowhere found a real intimate of Lincoln's. That brooding spirit had no real familiars. . . . It was a very lonely spirit that looked out from underneath those shaggy brows and comprehended men without fully communing. . . . In spite of all its genial

efforts at comradeship, it dwelt apart, saw its visions of duty where no man looked on.[1]

Sermonic Sources
"Getting the Best of Loneliness" (Isa. 63:3)
  Clarence E. Macartney, *Facing Life and Getting the Best of It*
"Alone but Not Lonely" (John 14:18)
  David H. C. Read, *I Am Persuaded*
"Loneliness" (Luke 24:15)
  R. E. O. White, *A Relevant Salvation*
"A Faith to Meet Loneliness"
  Alson J. Smith, *Faith to Live By*
"The Problem of Loneliness"
  Batsell B. Baxter, *When Life Tumbles In*
"The Abiding Companionship" (Ex. 33:14)
  J. H. Jowett, *The Silver Lining*

LONELINESS IN CHRISTIAN SERVICE
2 Timothy 4:9-21

For Demas, having loved this present world, has deserted me and has gone to Thessalonica; Crescens has gone to Galatia, Titus to Dalmatia. [v. 10]

Billy Graham says that more people suffer from loneliness than any other problem. Paul Tournier says that it is the most devastating problem of this age. Admiral Richard E. Byrd wrote in his diary: "This morning I had to admit to myself that I was lonely. Try as I may, I can't take my loneliness casually. It is too big. I must not dwell on it; otherwise I am undone."

John R. W. Stott says that this section of Scripture gives the account of Paul's "Gethsemane." He was in prison for the second time. Martyrdom was just ahead. Alexander the coppersmith had opposed his ministry (vv. 14-15). His supporters had forsaken him in his time of need at his first defense (v. 16). Paul, however, was confident that just

1. Clarence E. Macartney, *You Can Conquer* (Grand Rapids: Abingdon, 1954), p. 47.

as the Lord had stood by Him in the hours of trial, He would continue to deliver him from every evil work. In his total experience of testing and trial, Paul was lonely. The three requests that he made to Timothy reveal his needs for combating loneliness in Christian service.

First is a desire for human friendship. "Make every effort to come to me soon" (v. 9). Demas had forsaken him, having loved this present age too much (v. 10). Trophimus was ill and Erastus had remained at Corinth (v. 20). Others were perhaps engaged in the ministry but were away from Paul. Crescens was at Galatia, Titus at Dalmatia, Tychicus at Ephesus, and Carpus at Troas (vv. 10, 12-13). Human friendship is one of God's provisions for the lonely.

Next was the request that Timothy bring the cloak Paul had left at Troas. As he had needed companionship from his supporters, he also needed clothing for his survival (v. 13). Physical discomfort intensified his loneliness. When our bodies are weak, we open ourselves to a multitude of problems. Paul was not ashamed to admit his loneliness, nor was he ashamed to pay attention to his physical needs.

The final request specified the bringing of the books and parchments. It is not enough to care for only the physical and social needs. A provision needs to be made for the nurture of the intellect. William Tyndale's letter, written in prison shortly before his martyrdom, requested that they bring his Hebrew Bible, Hebrew grammar, and Hebrew dictionary that he might spend his time in that pursuit. Paul also wanted to keep his mind busy. An active mind takes one's thoughts off present conditions. The books would occupy his mind and the parchments would feed his soul.

The new birth does not deprive us of our humanities. The trials, troubles, and testings of life are manifold. How would Timothy be able to stand them? Paul prayed that God's presence and power would be his blessed provision. "The Lord be with your spirit. Grace be with you" (v. 22).

THE DISAPPOINTMENT OF DESERTION
2 Timothy 4:9-18

For Demas, having loved this present world, has deserted me. [v. 10]

There are two kinds of loneliness. The first we may call the *isolation of space*. This may be represented by a boy, far from home and loved ones, fulfilling his military obligations in Germany, Iceland, Korea, or Vietnam. How he longs to be home again!

The other kind of loneliness, and far heavier to bear, is the *isolation of spirit*. This is the loneliness of the city and of the crowd. Frederick W. Robertson wrote:

> There are times when hands touch ours, but only send an icy chill of unsympathizing indifference to the heart: when eyes gaze into ours, but with a glazed look which cannot read into the bottom of our souls—when words pass from our lips, but only come back as an echo reverberated without replying through a dreary solitude—when the multitude throng and press us, and we cannot say, as Christ said, "Somebody touched me"; for the only contact has been not between soul and soul, but only between form and form.[2]

Paul had come to the lonely years. He was now sixty-five years of age. Who would stay by his side and provide companionship as he waited in the Mamertime Dungeon in Rome? He had been deserted previously by John Mark. Once again, a trusted friend had faded away. Luke, the doctor, stood by to provide medical help in his hours of need, but where was Demas?

What was the nature of this desertion by Demas? It may have been a gradual development. In Philemon 24 and Colossians 4:14, Demas is named. Paul may have begun to suspect Demas for some time before the incident of the text. We can normally tell who will stand by us in adverse circumstances and who will "leave us in the lurch."

The cause of Demas's desertion is stated as love with the present world. This was certainly not the physical world. Rather, Demas had fallen in love with the world of the secular mind that would not necessarily repudiate the creed but would give first priority to other matters.

It is the mind of the world that gives priority to programs, possessions, pleasures, and popularity. When those are held in unreasonable proportion, they become ruinous. It is pitiful to see one who does not have spiritual strength enough to resist the constant attraction and seductions of the world of things. Faithful followers of Christ would make their way to the catacombs to worship. Apparently, the gaiety, the sight of soldiers with their spoils, and the attraction of the transient charms of surface beauty took their toll on Demas.

The consequences of that desertion bore down on Paul, other believers, and certainly upon Demas. Paul requested that Mark come to help. Certainly, the cloak would warm his body, the books would

2. Batsell B. Baxter, *When Life Tumbles In* (Grand Rapids: Baker, 1974), p. 23.

occupy his mind, and the parchments would feed his soul. But his friend had gone. Colossae had been the city where Demas had accepted Christ and committed his life to service for the Savior. We can wonder how the company of believers felt when they heard that Demas had defected. His close companions had been such men as Luke, Marcus, and Aristarchus. Those close friends had now lost the warmth of a friendship. To whom would Demas turn when trouble came? With whom would he now join in prayer? Paul was in a cold prison and needed a cloak, but Demas was in a cold world and needed peace.

Secularism takes a terrible toll. It erodes convictions, undermines human dignity, and severs friendships. If Demas had been able to win the world, he still could never have really enjoyed it. Someone would cross his path one day and suggest that they go and meet a friend. Listen to what his reply might have been: "Yes, I knew Paul. In fact, some of the best days of my life were spent in his company. I now have palaces and riches, but I really miss my Christian friend more than you will ever know."

> What a Friend we have in Jesus,
> All our sins and griefs to bear!
> What a privilege to carry
> Everything to God in prayer!
> Joseph M. Scriven, "What a Friend We Have in Jesus"

LOSS OF JOY

ILLUSTRATIONS

The little things are often more important than the big things in the cause and cure of unhappiness. James L. Mursell, in his book *How to Make and Break Habits*, gives an interesting example of that. He tells of a group of factory workers who were very unhappy. Their pay was good, their work hours were not unduly long, and the working conditions were excellent. The workers admitted to all of that. Yet, they seethed with discontent. The management was baffled and worried, and finally called in an industrial psychologist. He studied the situation and found that the trouble was in the men's shoes. The workers had to stand for long periods of time on a hard floor. Their feet and legs got very tired because standard-type shoes did not give them proper support. The fatigue that started in their feet spread to their nerves. And soon every molehill was a mountain. The company had special shoes made, and the discontent disappeared.

The same is so often true with us. The smaller things affect us. One bad day spoils the week. An unkind word cancels a friendship. One bad habit ruins a character. One little worry starts a train of worries. A little ache or pain can become enlarged in our minds until it becomes a deadly disease. A dripping faucet can get on our nerves. Indeed, most of us are experts at making mountains out of molehills.[1]

These lines were written by Everard Jack Appleton, who was an invalid for seventeen years. He faced unflinchingly the tragic circumstances that were his. Bedridden for seven years, his room became a place of encouragement and inspiration for many. Said his good friend one day:

"Jack, what do you do when you can't touch bottom?"
"Then I swim," he said.
"And when you can't swim?"
"Then I float," and he added, "underneath are the Everlasting Arms."[2]

An old man was asked what had most robbed him of joy. He promptly replied, "Things that never happened."

Cyvette Guerra, *Joy Robbers*

1. Charles M. Crowe, *Getting Help from the Bible* (Harper & Brothers, 1957), p. 138.
2. Wesley H. Hager, *Conquering* (Grand Rapids: Eerdmans, 1965), p. 67.

Sermonic Sources
"Is Happiness Just a Word?"
  Batsell B. Baxter, *When Life Tumbles In*

INDESTRUCTIBLE JOY

Philippians 1:3-26

> For I know that this shall turn out for my deliverance through your prayers and the provision of the Spirit of Jesus Christ, according to my earnest expectation and hope, that I shall not be put to shame in anything, but that with all boldness, Christ shall even now, as always, be exalted in my body, whether by life or by death. [vv. 19-20]

Do you have joy or are you just happy? At first, such a question seems a bit redundant. Happiness is a pleasurable experience that springs from the possession of good things. It includes good fortune and general prosperity. Joy, on the other hand, is not dependent upon what happens. It comes from sources within the life of the individual. It bubbles forth as water from a spring that never runs dry.

A joyful attitude of mind is valuable. There is an old saying: "We are as old as we feel." Moses was ninety years old before he began his great work as the leader and deliverer of Israel. William Gladstone became the British prime minister for the fourth time at age eighty-three, and completed his translation of Horace at eighty-five. Michelangelo's greatest painting, "The Fresco of the Last Judgment" in the Sistine Chapel at Rome, was completed when he was almost seventy. On the threshold of his ninetieth year he was the chief architect of the Church of St. Peter's, the magnificent dome of which is his noblest monument. When Titian was almost a hundred years old he was still producing paintings of great beauty and merit. The world challenges the Christian to be joyful, and Christ enables His followers to meet that challenge.

When Paul was incarcerated in Rome he waited there like an eagle in a cage. His journeys were halted and his enemies were free to gossip. He had learned, however, that the praising man is the prevailing man. It had been ten years since he had ministered personally at Philippi. Under the inspiration of the Spirit of God, he sent back a personal letter. In it are one hundred personal references and sixteen references to rejoicing within the four short chapters, which can be read by a normal reader in ten minutes. Those few verses reveal how indestructible joy can be the possession of those who put their faith in Jesus Christ. Satan can keep us from traveling, but not from triumphing.

Joy comes through prayer. "Always offering prayer with joy in my every prayer for you all" (Phil. 1:4). Three outstanding sources served as springs from which joy abounded. There was a thankfulness for the past (v. 3). Paul was more sensitive to the mercies of God than to the antagonisms of men. There was also an evident tenderheartedness manifested in his dealings with others (v. 8). The third source was a confidence in the future. He felt certain that God would bring to a glorious completion the work that He had started in the lives of His followers (v. 6).

Three subjects were mentioned in Paul's prayer. He desired that the Philippians' love might overflow but be kept within the limitations of knowledge. It was his hope that they would be able to make a finer evaluation of life, and finally, that they would have a fuller experience of righteousness (vv. 9-11).

Joy comes through keeping a sense of purpose (vv. 12-18). "What then? Only that in every way, whether in pretense or in truth, Christ is proclaimed; and in this I rejoice" (v. 18). It has been said that absorption in a great cause is the secret of success. Paul's difficulties had become doors. The physical limitations and social humiliation really served to advance the gospel (v. 12). He measured his condition, not by hardship, but by the facility it gave for spreading the knowledge of Christ.

Joy comes through the anticipation of glorious prospects in the future (vv. 19-26). "Yes, and I will rejoice. For I know that this shall turn out for my deliverance through your prayers and the provision of the Spirit of Jesus Christ" (v. 19). "For to me, to live is Christ" (v. 21), is possibly the simplest definition of the Christian life. "He who has the Son has the life" (1 John 5:12). Christ turns misery into melody and prisons into palaces.

Paul rejoices over the possibility of death, since all losses would come to an end (vv. 19-24). He also rejoices over the permission to live (vv. 25-26). The direction of his life had been established. He had determined that Christ would be honored in his body (v. 20). He had gone through the valley of indecision (v. 23), but had now arrived at the place of settled conviction. He was to serve through staying (v. 23).

God grant you wisdom in what you do, and us fortitude, courage and peace of heart. He is able—and a wonderful friend in such a time. . . . The Lord bless you and guide you, as for us, may God be glorified whether by life or by death.[3]

That was the note sent back to America by John and Betty Stam before they were martyred in China in 1934. There is an indestructible joy that comes through knowing Jesus Christ as one's Savior and Lord.

3. Mrs. Howard Taylor, *John and Betty Stam: A Story of Triumph*, rev. ed. (Chicago: Moody, 1982), p. 113.

SEARCH FOR SATISFACTION

ILLUSTRATIONS

Samuel Morse is an inspiring example of the inner peace that real prayer can bring. He had spent eleven years working on his telegraph, and had used up all of his money. He persuaded two of his friends in Congress to try to get him a government appropriation for the purpose of building an experimental telegraph line. He was certain that if his friends could get him the money, he could demonstrate the feasibility of telegraphic communication. If they failed, his life's work would be ruined.

The bill had passed the House of Representatives and was awaiting action in the Senate. Unfortunately, the bill was delayed until the last day of the session—March 3, 1843—and, midnight, the fatal hour of adjournment was rapidly approaching. Morse sat all day in the Senate gallery, sending word to his senator friends from time to time asking if there was any hope. They finally told him that the logjam of last-minute bills had forced them to give up his cause.

Morse trudged wearily to his lodgings and made preparations for his departure from Washington. He was fifty-two years old; his money was gone and his invention was supposedly shelved for good. So what did Morse do?

> In this unhappy frame of mind I reached my room and made arrangements to leave Washington on the morrow. Then, knowing from long experience whence my help must come in hours of difficulty, I soon disposed of all my cares, dropped to sleep, and rested the remainder of the night as quietly as a little child.[1]

Morse had built his foundations strong and sure in quieter days. Imagine his joy at awakening the next morning to the glorious news that he had received his appropriation! A few minutes after he had left the Senate Chamber, his friends had an unexpected opportunity to slip his bill into a last-minute omnibus appropriation measure that was hurriedly passed just before the clock struck twelve.

He is well paid that is well satisfied.

Shakespeare, *Henry VI*, Part III

---

1. Lewis L. Dunnington, *Power to Become* (New York: Macmillan, 1956), pp. 180-81.

Sermonic Sources
"The Secret of Hope" (Rom. 15:13)
   J. H. Jowett, *Brooks by the Traveller's Way*
"The Ministry of Hope" (Eph. 2:12-13)
   J. H. Jowett, *The Silver Lining*

SATISFACTION GUARANTEED
Isaiah 55:1-13

> Ho! Every one who thirsts, come to the waters; and you who have no
> money come, buy and eat. Come, buy wine and milk without cost. [v. 1]

When the American Bible Society conducted a survey to discover
the fifteen favorite chapters of the Bible, they found Isaiah 55 to be
among them. Its emphasis on guaranteed satisfaction answers a
common longing of the human heart.

Sir Edwin Arnold, author of *The Light of Asia*, speaking to the
students at Harvard College, said: "In 1776 you conquered your
fathers. In 1861 you conquered your brothers. Now the next great
victory is to conquer yourselves."

The people to whom this chapter was first directed had suffered
many hardships and heartaches. They were disillusioned, disheart-
ened, and at the point of despair. This chapter, with its invitation to
come to God for satisfaction, must have blessed their hearts like a cool
breeze at the end of a hot day. It was Clarence McCartney who
referred to *come* as God's favorite word. He has invited us to come to
Him for safety and satisfaction. His offer of satisfaction is unique.

God's offer of satisfaction is unique in its price (v. 1). We are invited
to buy wine (gladness) and milk (nourishment). An implication of that
verse might be that those items were beyond the reach of money. A
further implication might be that the one selling the items did not need
the money, or that the price had already been paid by someone else.
When God has made such an offer, we wonder with the prophet why
people spend money for that which is not nourishing and labor for that
which does not really satisfy.

God's offer of satisfaction is unique in its proposition (vv. 4-11). The
invitation is made without restriction. Man's part is summarized by six

simple words of action. Three of those words are found in verse one: *come, buy,* and *eat.* Two are found in verse six: *seek* and *call.* The sixth verb, *forsake,* is found in verse seven. Those verbs imply immediacy, initiative, and action. God's part involves the confirmation of His offer through Christ (v. 4), the declaration of that offer by God Himself (vv. 8-9), and the recording of the offer in God's infallible Word (v. 11).

God's offer of satisfaction is unique in its provision (v. 12). The provision is made for their going forth with joy and peace (v. 12). The sharp, piercing, painful thorn will be replaced by the fir tree, the wood of which is used for the making of the frames for harps. The briar, known for its bitter, poisonous sting, is to be replaced by the glossy-leaved myrtle, with its white flowers and graceful perfume.

This whole offer of guaranteed satisfaction is centered in the person of the Lord, for He holds the key. "Seek the LORD while He may be found; call upon Him while He is near" (v. 6). If you want guaranteed satisfaction, accept Christ as Savior and let Him be Lord of your life.

TEMPTATION

ILLUSTRATIONS

Better shun the bait than struggle in the snare.

John Dryden

Temptations are a file which rub off much of the rust of self-confidence.

Fenelon

Some temptations come to the industrious, but all temptations attack the idle.

Charles H. Spurgeon

The last temptation is the greatest treason: to do the right deed for the wrong reason.

T. S. Eliott

Sermonic Sources
"Getting the Best of Temptation" (Matt. 4:3)
    Clarence E. Macartney, *Facing Life and Getting the Best of It*
"Temptation Conquered" (Acts 28:3)
    Clarence E. Macartney, *Strange Texts but Grand Truths*
"The Quest for Wisdom" (Luke 4:8)
    Daniel A. Pohling, *Jesus Says to You*
"Joseph—The Conquest of Fear"
    Roy L. Laurin, *Meet Yourself in the Bible*

MAINTAINING GODLINESS IN UNGODLY SURROUNDINGS
Daniel 6:1-23

Then the king gave orders, and Daniel was brought in and cast into the lions' den. The king spoke and said to Daniel, "Your God whom you serve constantly will Himself deliver you." [v. 16]

Because of the presence of Satan, who desires to turn our minds and hearts away from God, it is never easy to maintain a clear testimony of righteousness and godliness. And there are times when it is a bit harder than others. One of those times is when we are away from our familiar surroundings and friends. It is hard to sing the Lord's song in such a situation.

Ten thousand captives had been taken from their homeland to Babylon. In that group was a lad, then about fourteen years of age, who was to become one of the most influential persons of his day. Few have influenced young men more than Daniel. He was a thermostat that controlled his surroundings rather than a thermometer that merely recorded its temperature without making an attempt to change it.

In the first chapter of the book of Daniel, we find that Daniel met and conquered the physical test. Although expediency would have been easier, he refused to defile himself and compromise his convictions. "But Daniel made up his mind that he would not defile himself with the king's choice food or with the wine" (1:8).

In the second chapter he was faced with the mental test of the interpretation of the king's dream. He asked his friends to pray for him as he proceeded (2:16), and when finally successful, gave the glory to God for his victory (v. 20).

In the third chapter Daniel faced the spiritual test. He was now eighty years old and had long since learned that success would depend on choice, not chance. His physical, mental, and spiritual preparations to that point, as he had allowed God to guide him, were now in special prominence as he took the following steps to maintain his good witness.

He safeguarded his reputation. He realized that character counted. "Then this Daniel began distinguishing himself among the commissioners and satraps because he possessed an extraordinary spirit, and the king planned to appoint him over the entire kingdom" (6:3). His deliverance from the lions' den was wrought by God and His angels since innocency was found in his life (v. 22).

He kept his priorities straight. He realized that regardless of what might be done or said, communication with God through prayer must be maintained (v. 10). Many years later, Henry Drummond wrote, "Don't touch Christianity unless you are willing to seek it first. . . . I promise you a miserable existence if you seek it second." Stones could shut Daniel in the den, but they could not shut God out.

He served God continuously (6:16, 20). The affirmation that was stamped on his life was confirmed in his experience. The king was troubled when he realized the plight of Daniel, but Daniel, having served God continuously, was still serving Him. "No injury whatsoever was found on him, because he had trusted in his God" (v. 23).

It is still true that decision determines destiny. When we are willing to allow Jesus Christ to have first place in our lives, He will help us maintain godliness in ungodly surroundings, for we cannot do it alone. We are partners with God; He does His part as we do ours.

TRIUMPHANT OVER TEMPTATION

Matthew 4:1-11

> Then the devil left Him; and behold, angels came and began to minister to Him. [v. 11]

An individual is as strong as his weakest moment. Satan realizes that and tries to win the battle of the weak moment, thus capturing the individual.

Christ was led by the Holy Spirit into the wilderness to be tempted by the devil. That experience of temptation proved the humanity of Jesus. It was a matter of personal discipline and development, and a preparation for His sympathizing work on behalf of the believers (Heb. 2:18; 4:15). As we survey the temptation of Christ by Satan we find an example we may follow for meeting Satan's attacks on our lives.

It is wise to gain the ability to recognize temptation. Satan is cunning in his attacks. Although he may not be necessarily swift or sudden, he is subtle and systematic. The time of the temptation is emphasized as being forty days after Jesus went into the wilderness (Luke 4:1-2). It was at a time when He was weary and alone. It was also when He stood at the point of special service for mankind.

Temptation is comprehensive. For Jesus, it involved the body, the intellect, and the emotions. It included a doubt of deity, a demand for display, and a deal for delight. First, Jesus was tempted to satisfy lawful needs in unlawful ways (4:3-4). Second, He was tempted to do the spectacular (4:5-7). And third, he was tempted to take a shortcut to world rule rather than the way of the cross (4:8-10).

We can recognize the tempter by his temptations. Satan has three appeals to make. The first is an appeal to the immediate necessity.

What could be more reasonable than to make bread when one is hungry? Satan's second appeal is to encourage the individual to become more religious, even to the point of presumption beyond the rightful limits of faith. The third appeal is to get rich more rapidly than righteousness would allow.

It is wise to gain the ability to resist temptation. No temptation comes to us other than those common to man. God provides a way of escape in order that we may bear each temptation (1 Cor. 10:13). If we are to resist temptation, we will do well to avoid the place of temptation. When experience has shown that there is danger within a context, it is dangerous to remain in that context. Faithfulness in prayer is also helpful in resisting temptation (Matt. 26:41; Mark 14:38).

It is essential that we be prepared with the Word of God. Three times in the first verses of Matthew 4 the phrase "It is written" occurs. In verse 4 Christ quoted Deuteronomy 8:3; in verse 7 He quoted Deuteronomy 6:16; and in verse 10 Jesus quoted Deuteronomy 6:13. For each of Satan's attacks, the Master had a Scripture passage. Jesus knew the Word, believed the Word, obeyed the Word, and quoted the Word. Satan was defeated.

YOUTH IN TURMOIL

"Youth" and "problem" mean about the same thing to some people. Perhaps it is time to begin thinking of the youth opportunity and the youth potential. Of course, teen problems should not be ignored. But it is the privilege and responsibility of the church to discover the nature of today's high school teenager, to work creatively to meet his needs, and to help him achieve his potential for Jesus Christ.

Many young people have made their mark in history. Victor Hugo wrote a tragedy at age fifteen, at seventeen received three prizes at a poetry competition, and earned the title of "master" before he was twenty.

Pascal wrote a great work at sixteen and died at thirty-seven.

Raphael painted his wonderful works as a young man and died also at thirty-seven.

Alfred Tennyson wrote his first volume when he was eighteen.

John Calvin joined the Reformation at age twenty-one, and at twenty-seven wrote the *Institutes of the Christian Religion*, which profoundly influenced the theological thought of subsequent centuries.

Alexander the Great conquered the world when he was twenty-three.

Isaac Newton was twenty-four when he formulated the law of gravity and made some of his greatest discoveries before he was twenty-five.

Charles Dickens wrote his *Pickwick Papers* at twenty-four and *Oliver Twist* at twenty-five.

Jonathan Edwards made five resolutions in his youth and lived by them faithfully. They are worth studying, and anyone who will adopt and follow them will greatly increase his usefulness. The resolutions are as follows:

1. To live with all might while I do live.
2. Never to lose one moment of time, but to improve it in the most profitable way I possibly can.
3. Never to do anything that I should despise or think meanly of in another.
4. Never to do anything out of revenge.
5. Never to do anything which I should be afraid to do if it were the last hour of my life.

Ohio Sunday School Worker

In his autobiography, *My Early Life, a Roving Commission*, Winston Churchill regretted that he did not have a university training. But that regret was tempered by his observation of how college men wasted their time, and he wrote: "But I now pity undergraduates, when I see what frivolous lives many of them lead in the midst of precious, fleeting opportunity. After all, a man's life must be nailed to a cross, either of thought or of action. Without work, there is no play."

Walter Slezak was pleasantly surprised to see his teenage daughter answer the telephone and then hang up after talking for only twenty minutes instead of the usual hour. Slezak congratulated her for keeping the conversation so brief and asked which of her friends had cooperated.

"That wasn't a friend," she said. "It was a wrong number."

American Weekly

A father found this note pinned to the bulletin board by the phone:

Daddy—I am going to wash my hair. If Tom calls, tell him to call back at eight. If Herb calls and Tom doesn't, tell Herb to call back at eight. But if they both call, tell Herb to call at 8:15 or 8:30. If Timmy calls and Tom and Herb don't, tell Timmy to call at eight, but if they both call (Tom and Herb) or one calls, tell Timmy to call at 8:30 or 8:40. Tina.

Advertiser

Nevin C. Harner, in *Youth Work in the Church*, lists these six basic needs of young people:

1. The need for a vital Christian faith
2. The need for self-understanding
3. The need for Christian vocational guidance
4. The need for Christian sex education
5. The need for Christian social education
6. The need for rootage in the Christian fellowship[1]

IS A YOUNG MAN SAFE?
2 Samuel 18:1-33

And the king was deeply moved and went up to the chamber over the gate and wept. And thus he said as he walked, "O my son Absalom, my son,

---

1. Nevin C. Harner, *Youth Work in the Church* (New York: Abingdon, 1942), pp. 31-60.

my son Absalom! Would I had died instead of you, O Absalom, my son, my son!" [v. 33]

In his work *The English Bible as a Guide to Writing*, Charles Baldwin said that this account is one of the best examples of an excellent story. It has suspense (vv. 1-5) as the wartime father battles with the son. No matter which wins, both lose. There is the element of strife (vv. 6-18) as the "fashion plate" of his day becomes the "broken plate." Absalom is caught by his hair in the tree, killed, and lowered into a pit. There is both humor and contrast (vv. 19-32) as Ahimaz the volunteer outruns Cushi the selected messenger. Ahimaz had speed but did not know how to get to the point. Cushi was slower as a runner but carried a valid message. The climax (v. 33) comes in the grief of a wartime father as he bemoans the loss of his son. Absalom had wanted his father killed. David had wanted his son spared. Twenty thousand lay dead on the field of battle, but David was primarily concerned about the welfare of one individual, his son. Absalom was lost in battle, but long before the battle broke the father had lost his son.

The father had failed to develop character in his son. He had given him position and power. There was not a blemish from his head to his toes. But Absalom needed soul cleansing. He had been the son of a busy father. David was evidently so busy with the affairs of state that he had no time to consider the state of his son. If we are to be "thoroughly furnished" (2 Tim. 3:17, KJV), we must not only care for the intellectual, social, economic, and psychological portions of life, but also for the spiritual.

The father had failed to provide a good example for his son. Parents should be aware of the fact that there are little feet following in their footsteps. David committed adultery with Bathsheba (2 Sam. 11:1-5), and then plotted the death of her husband. It was Nathan who was used of God to bring David to the realization of what he had really done (2 Sam. 12:1-15). The declaration was then given that the "sword shall never depart" from his house (2 Sam. 12:10). The law of the harvest is true. "Whatever a man sows, this will he also reap" (Gal. 6:7). The results of sin can be traced through the family of David. Absalom followed in the sinful steps of his father. He became proud

(2 Sam. 15:4), dishonest (2 Sam. 15:7-13), and disobedient to his parents.

The young man can really never be safe when his heart is not right with God and when the guidance provided by parents through their example is misleading. There must be not only social and scholastic concern for the young man, but more important than those, there must be spiritual concern.

Conclusion

You never solve a problem by running away from it. God put us into this world to play our part and it is sheer cowardice to refuse to live simply because it is difficult. It is better to pilot a ship that faces the storms and comes at last, though battered and bruised, with torn sails and damaged rigging, to some fair haven than to beat behind breakwaters with a rigging intact and with the sails flapping in the breeze, not daring to venture forth.[1]

1. Joseph R. Sizoo, *Making Life Worth Living* (New York: Macmillan, 1938), p. 89.

Scripture and Subjects for Meditation and Ministry

The advantage in preparing a sermon with the actual needs of our people in mind is [that] . . . we are dealing with the daily discouragements, the constant frustration and the corroding worries of the people who are before us Sunday after Sunday. We sit where they sit, wear their shoes, and if we are genuinely sympathetic, not merely walk into their hearts and minds, but into their skins! We know what they fear and understand why they are so often defeated.[1]

---

1. Gerald Ray Jordan, *You Can Preach: Building and Delivering the Sermon* (Westwood. N.J.: Revell, 1951), p. 218.

Appendix 1

Numbers

11:17	God's Answer to Despondency
14:17	The Best Way to Overcome Anger
21:4-9	The Case, Consequences, and Cure for Discouragement

Deuteronomy

4:31	The Peace of Fearlessness
28:66-68	Three Reasons for Anxiety
31:6	Courage for Days When Health Fails
31:7-8	Fear's Feared Formula
33:27	The Eternal Cure for Worry

Joshua

4:1-9	Forgetfulness
7:10	Discouragement
14:12	Confidence in Old Age (Caleb)
24:15	Vacillation in Loyalty

Judges

5:15-16	All Discussion, No Action
6:12	Untapped Resources
6:13-14	Complaint
6:15-16	Lack of Confidence (Gideon)
7:11, 15	Fear
9:1-6	Ambition Unwisely Used
10:2	Failure
11:3-31	Rash Vows
15:15-16	Unbridled Strength
15:17-19	Spiritual Thirst
16:28	Revenge
19:15-16, 20	Hospitality

Ruth

2:4	Employee-Employer Relationships
3:12	Fairness
3:12-13	Chastity
3:15	Joys Are Available for Old Age

1 Samuel

1:16-17	Sympathy in Distress

4:27-30	When the Ministry Lacks the Personal Touch
5:25-26	Deceit
7:6	Doubt
16:10-16	Worldliness: Mimicking the Pagans
17:34-41	Divided Loyalties
20:19	Self-Interest

1 Chronicles

4:9-10	Discontent
11:22	Difficulty
22:5	Preparation

2 Chronicles

20:15,17	Fear
21:20	Reputation
26:16	Arrogance
27:2	Missed Opportunity
30:12, 26	Ridicule
36:15-16	Rejection

Ezra

2:63	On Finding God's Will
3:12	Past Glories Gone
9:1-15	Guilt

Nehemiah

5:1-19	Honesty in Government
6:1-19	What to Do with Distractions
6:11	Courage

Esther

3:8-9	Revenge
5:9—6:11	Delayed Commendation
5:13	Prejudice: Leaven of Misery
6:1-11	Self-Interest
7:10	Retribution

Hosea

4:11-19	On Serving Sin
6:4-11	Hypocrisy

7:1-7	A Fatal Domestic Policy
9:10-17	Ingratitude
11:1-11	Forgiveness
12:1—14:9	Faithfulness

Joel

2:12-17	Conditions for Mercy

Amos

3:1-15	Ingratitude
4:1-13	Not Learning from the Past
6:1-13	Indifference

Obadiah

1:1-4	Pride
1:10	On Being a Brother

Jonah

1:1-3	Taking Orders
2:1-10	Feeling Alone
4:1-11	Complaining

Micah

2:1-5	Social Sin
2:6-11	Religious Sin
2:12-13	Mercy
6:1—7:6	Ingratitude and Wickedness

Nahum

1:15	Peace

Habakkuk

2:5-20	Greed; Pride; Cruelty; Drunkenness; Idolatry
3:1-2	Praying for Mercy
3:16-19	Consecration

Zephaniah

2:1-3	Repentance
3:1-4	Rebellion and Disobedience

Haggai

2:4	Encouragement
2:19	Obedience Brings Blessing

Zechariah

1:1-7	Repentance and Obedience
3:1-10	Conditions for Peace

Malachi

1:2-5	Love
1:6—2:9	Irreverence
2:17—3:6	Moral Confusion
3:7-15	Defrauding God

NEW TESTAMENT

Acts

4:32-26	Poverty
5:17-42	Persecution
7:24	Oppression
8:1-40	Persecution
11:1-30	Discrimination, Sectarianism
15:1-41	Discrimination

Romans

1:18-32	Sin
2:17-29	Racial Superiority
5:1-12	Persecution
6:1-23	Christian Liberty
14:1-23	Judging
15:1-2	Hate
16:17-19	Apostasy

1 Corinthians

1:10-15	Disunity
1:19-31	Intellectual Conceit
3:1-9	Spiritual Immaturity
13:1-13	Shallow Love

2 Corinthians

5:1-10	Handicaps

Appendix 2

The following material will provide a beginning list of topics that are covered in life-situation preaching. These topics have been combined with biblical and extrabiblical source material that may prove helpful in the development of messages. The abbreviations enclosed in parentheses refer to books where source material can be found. See the key provided at the end of this section.

Adultery
> Matthew 15:19; Mark 7:21-22 (Bo)
> David—2 Samuel 2 (Bs)

Adversity
> Paul—2 Corinthians 1:1-24; 11:23-27 (Le)

Affliction
> Value of—James 1:2-4

Aggression
> Extrabiblical material (Li)

Alcohol
> Proverbs 20:1; 23:29-31; Romans 14:21; Ephesians 5:18-19 (V)

Altruism
> Luke 6:31; Ephesians 4:25; 1 Corinthians 12:14-26 (Bo)

Amusements
> Extrabiblical material (Ea)

Anger
    Matthew 5:38-48 (Bo)
    Cain—Genesis 4:5 (M)
    Moses—Numbers 20:7-11 (M)
    Balaam—Numbers 22:22-35 (M)
    Naaman—2 Kings 5:12 (M)
    Jonah—Jonah 4:9 (M)
    Extrabiblical material (Sw)

Anxiety
    Psalm 55:22 (B)
    Hebrews 13:6 (Cr)
    Adam and Eve—Genesis 3:1-6, 14-21 (S)
    Disciples—Matthew 6:25-34 (H) (Rp) (Lj)
    Martha—Luke 10:38-42 (S)

Apathy
    Problem of—Hebrews 2:1-4

Backsliding
    Jeremiah 3:22; Hosea 14:4 (Mo)

Body, Caring for
    Snares to—1 Corinthians 9:27 (Mc)
    Belshazzar (Mc)
    Esau (Mc)
    Joseph (Mc)
    Samson (Mc)

Challenge, Reaction to
    Daniel 3:1-30

Choice
    Romans 14:23

Circumstances, Difficult
    Noah—Genesis 6:1-13 (L)

Comfort
    Isaiah 40:1-11

Complacency
  Matthew 6:5 (Ab)
  Luke 17:2 (Ab)
  Paul—Philippians 3:12 (Ab)

Compromise, Overcoming
  Matthew 4:8-10; Luke 4:5-8

Courage, Obtaining
  Psalm 23:4; John 6:20; Revelation 1:17-18

Covetousness
  Achan—Joshua 7:1, 20-25
  Gehazi—2 Kings 5:20-27 (B)
  Baruch—Jeremiah 45 (G)

Cowardice
  Esther—Esther 4:15-17 (B)
  Peter—Luke 22:54-62 (B)
  Thomas—John 11:1-16 (B)

Crisis, Facing a
  Deuteronomy 31:6-8

Crime
  King Saul—1 Samuel 24 and 26 (Bs)

Cynicism
  Luke 9:57-58 (Ab)

Death
  Romans 8:37 (Mc)
  2 Corinthians 5 (Le)
  Lazarus—Acts 7:54-60 (Mc)
  A Christian looks at death (La)
  Jairus' daughter (Mc)

Depression, Antidote for
  Joshua 1:1-9

Despair
  Psalm 88

Despondency
    Isaiah 1:16-20; 6:1-13 (L)

Disappointments
    Psalm 119:67, 71, 75;
        Romans 8:35, 39 (Lw)

Discouragement
    Psalm 42:5 (P)
    Extrabiblical material (Pn)

Dishonesty
    Ananias and Sapphira—Acts 5

Disobedience, Rewards of
    1 Samuel 15:1-31

Divided Loyalties
    Matthew 7:15-29; 12:25-26, 33-34 (Je)

Divorce
    Matthew 5:32; 19:3-9; Mark 10:2-12; Luke 16:18;
        Romans 7:1-3; 1 Corinthians 7:10, 39 (Ea) (Bo)

Doubt
    Disciples—Matthew 28:16-20 (M)
    Healing of a sick son—Mark 9:23-24 (Cr)
    Thomas—John 14:5; 20:24-29 (L)

Envy
    Psalm 73

Evil, Overcoming
    Deuteronomy 30:15, 19; Proverbs 4:23; Ezekiel 18:20;
        Matthew 7:2; Luke 6:45 (D)
    Matthew 15:19; Mark 7:21-22 (Bo)
    Matthew 12:42 (Ce)
    Proverbs 14:12; Matthew 12:45; 18:5-7; Luke 12:1-3;
        Romans 12:21; Philippians 4:8, 13 (D)
    Extrabiblical material (Sw)

Failure
Isaiah 27:3; 41:10, 13; Philippians 1:6; 1 Peter 1:5; Jude 24

Faith, Lack of
Matthew 15:23, 26, 28 (RI)

Family Trouble
Family Life—1 Corinthians 11:8-9; Ephesians 5:22-23 (Ea)
Extrabiblical material (Wy)

Fear
Psalm 27:1 (P)
Genesis 15:1; Judges 6:23 (Ki)
Psalm 56:3; Proverbs 9:10, 10:27; 14:26-27; 2 Timothy 1:7;
Isaiah 12:2; 1 John 4:18 (Lw)
Psalm 56:4; Isaiah 41:10; Luke 12:22, 25; 2 Timothy 1:7 (Cr)
John 14:26-27; Romans 8:38-39; 2 Corinthians 4:16-18;
Philippians 4:5-7; 1 Peter 1:21 (0)
Psalm 27:1-5; Proverbs 1:33; 3:23-26; 29:25; Isaiah 30:15; 33:24;
Matthew 8:26 (Je)
Abraham—Genesis 15:1 (M)
Daniel—Daniel 1:8-16; 2:1-49; 6:1-23 (L)
David—1 Samuel 17 and Psalm 56 (J)
Gideon—Judges 6:1—7:25 (Cr)
Israelites—Psalm 53:5 (J)
Nehemiah—Nehemiah 6:10-19 (B)
Extrabiblical material (Pr) (Sw)

Foes, Overcoming
Mordecai—Esther 7:10 (M)

Forgiveness
David—1 Samuel 24 (B)
Jesus—Luke 23:34 (B)
Joseph—Genesis 50:20 (B)

Frustration
Psalm 23 (O)
Luke 11:21 (RI)
Jeremiah—Jeremiah 5:31-32; 8:18-22; 9:1-2; 17:5-8 (L)
Overcoming—1 Corinthians 9:24-27; 1 Timothy 6:11-12 (Je)

Futility
  Gideon—Judges 6:11-24 (L)

Giving
  Romans 15:3 (Rc)

Gossip
  Proverbs 13:3; 14:3; 26:22; Matthew 12:36-37; 17:9; 21:23;
    James 1:26; 3:5-8; 1 Peter 3:10

Guilt and Guilt Feelings
  Adam and Eve—Genesis 3:7-15 (S)
  Cain—Genesis 4:8-11 (S)
  Judas—Luke 22:3-6, 47-53 (S)
  Prodigal son—Luke 15:11-24 (S)

Handicap, Overcoming
  Sarah—Genesis 16 (G)
  Paul—1 Corinthians 15:10; 2 Corinthians 12:1-11 (L)

Happiness, Finding
  Matthew 5:12; 6:33; 28:20; John 1:12; Galatians 5:22-23;
    Romans 12:9 (Bg)

Hate
  Joseph's brethren—Genesis 37:1-28 (S)

Hypocrisy
  Scribes and Pharisees—Matthew 23:25; John 21:22;
    Romans 2:1, 3; 14:10-12; James 4:12

Idleness
  2 Thessalonians 3:6-14

Illness
  Psalms 6; 28; 91

Immorality
  Judah—Genesis 38 (H)
  Tamar—2 Samuel 13 (H)

Inconsistency
Unforgiving servant—Matthew 18:23-35

Indifference
Parable of the Good Samaritan—Luke 10; Psalm 85:6 (P)

Inferiority Complex
Leah—Genesis 29 (G)
Moses—Exodus 3:1—4:17 (L)
1 Corinthians 1:26-29; 3:21-23; 2 Corinthians 8:11-12 (Je)
Extrabiblical material (Sw)

Ingratitude
Israelites to Gideon—Judges 8:28-35
The nine lepers—Luke 17

Insecurity
Wise and foolish builders—Matthew 7:24-27 (J)

Insignificance
Aaron—Exodus 7 (G)
Andrew—John 1:40-42; 6:8; 12:22 (L)
Baruch—Jeremiah 45 (G)
Elisha—2 Kings 2:1-15 (D)
Mary and Martha—Luke 10:38-42; John 12:1-3 (L)
Rehoboam—1 Kings 12:6-15 (B)

Intellectuality
Athenian philosophers—Acts 17

Intolerance
Peter—Acts 10

Irresponsibility, God's cure of
Psalm 119:9-16

Jealousy
Sarah—Genesis 21:9-21 (M)
Extrabiblical material (Sw)

Juvenile Delinquency
    Luke 15:11-32 (V)

Language, Poor
    Psalm 141:3; Proverbs 12:22; Matthew 5:33-37; 12:35; 26:74
    (Kn)

Loneliness
    Believers—Matthew 18:19-20 (J)
    Isaiah—Isaiah 63:1-19 (M)
    Israel—Deuteronomy 33:26-29 (J)
    Jesus—Matthew 14:22-23 (J)

Lying
    Acts 5:1-11

Maladjustment
    King Saul—1 Samuel 28 (Bs)

Melancholy
    Psalm 139

Mental Disturbance
    Peace of mind—Philippians 4:7 (K)

Nervousness
    Psalm 55:22; Proverbs 28:12; Isaiah 30:15; 40:27-31; Matthew
    6:25-34 (Lw)

Opposition
    Nehemiah—Nehemiah 4:1—6:19 (L)

Overwork
    Luke 10:38-42

Pain
    Psalm 139; John 15:1-16 (Si)

Patience, Developing
    Christian—James 5:7-11

Perplexity, Victory over
    Hebrews 3

Persecution
    Matthew 5:11-12; 10:36; Acts 5:41; Romans 8:18; Philippians
        1:29; 2 Timothy 2:12; Hebrews 11:24-25; 1 Peter 2:20, 4:14

Poverty
    Widow and the mite—Mark 12:42

Prayer, Hindrances to
    Psalm 66:18; Isaiah 59:1-2; Hosea 6:3; Mark 11:23-26;
        Ephesians 4:32; James 4:3; 1 Peter 3:1-7; 1 John 3:20-22; 5:14
        (I)

Prejudice
    Boaz—Ruth 2:1-23 (B)
    Egyptians—Genesis 43:32 (B)
    Nathanael—John 1:45-51 (L)

Presumptuousness
    Uzzah—2 Samuel 6
    Rich fool—Luke 12

Pride
    King Saul—1 Samuel 13:24-46 (Bs)
    Pharisee—Luke 18:9-14

Procrastination
    Hebrews 3:7-13

Profanity
    James—James 5:12

Rebellion
    Absalom—2 Samuel 15:4-12

Reputation, Poor
    Matthew—Matthew 9:9-13; Mark 2:14; Luke 5:27-32 (L)
    Woman at the well—John 4:1-42 (B)

Resentment
>   Extrabiblical material (Sw)

Self-centeredness
>   Mark 8:34; Romans 15:1; 1 Corinthians 10:24; 2 Corinthians 5:15 (Je)

Self-control
>   Proverbs 5; 7; 2 Peter 1:6; 1 Corinthians 9:25

Self-denial
>   Matthew 5:29-30; 19:29; Luke 9:23-24; 14:33; 18:28-30; Galatians 5:24; Philippians 2:5-7

Selfishness
>   Dinah—Genesis 34 (H)
>   Demas—2 Timothy 4:10 (G)
>   Jacob—Genesis 32:24-32 (L)

Self-righteousness
>   Adam and Eve—Genesis 3

Separation
>   2 Corinthians 6:17; Revelation 18:4 (Me)

Sorrow
>   Jacob—Genesis 37:31-35 (B)
>   Jesus—John 11:34-40 (P)
>   Job 35:10 (Mc)
>   Mary Magdalene—John 20:2 (B)
>   Psalms 23; 40; 43; 107; 116; 130
>   Ruth—Ruth 1:19-21; 2:13; 2:20-23; 4:13-15 (L)

Stewardship
>   Luke 16:9 (Rl)

Success, Achieving
>   Luke 12:15 (Ce)

Suffering
>   2 Corinthians 7 (Le)

Philippians 4:6; 1 Corinthians 12:26; Hebrews 13:8; 1 John 1:9
(Ln)

Suicide
King Saul—1 Samuel 31 (Bs)

Surroundings
Paul—Philippians 4:22 (Mc)
Daniel (Mc)
Woman in adultery (Mc)

Temper
Luke 15:28

Temperance
Proverbs 20:1; 21:17; 23:19-21; 23:29-32; Daniel 1:8;
Galatians 6:l9-21; Ephesians 5:18

Temptation
Joseph—Genesis 39:7-21 (L)
Satan—Luke 22:31 (Mc)
1 Corinthians 10:13 (Mc)

Tension
Apostles—Mark 6:30-32 (J)

Timidity
Woman with issue of blood—Matthew 9:20-22

Unbelief
Apostles—Matthew 17:14-21

Unity, Lack of
Ephesians 4:1-16

Weariness
Exodus 14:13; Psalm 42:5

Will of God
John 7:17; Acts 22:14; 1 Thessalonians 4:3;
Hebrews 10:9-10; 1 Peter 1:15-16

Willfulness
Jonah—Jonah 1:3; 2:7-9; 4:1-11 (L)

Witnessing
Andrew—John 1:42 (Rc)

Worry
Matthew 6:34 (Lj)

Zeal, Misguided
James—Mark 3:17; 10:35-40; Luke 9:54 (L)

Ab	*The Parables of Jesus*, George A. Buttrick
B	*Biographical Preaching for Today*, A. W. Blackwood
Bg	*The Secret of Happiness*, Billy Graham
Bo	*University Lectures on Ten Commandments*, G. Boardman
Bs	*Preaching from Samuel*, Andrew Blackwood
Ce	*Sermons on the Parables of Jesus*, Charles M. Crowe
Cr	*Getting Help from the Bible*, Charles M. Crowe
D	*Power to Become*, Lewis L. Dunnington
Ea	*The Christian, His Creed and Conduct*, William Evans
G	*A Galaxy of Saints*, Herbert F. Stevenson
H	*How to Solve Your Problems*, Faris D. Whitesell
J	*How to Preach to People's Needs*, Edgar N. Jackson
Je	*Abundant Living*, E. Stanley Jones
K	*Crossing the Border*, Guy King
Ki	*Acres of Rubies*, LeBaron Kinney
Kn	*New Order*, Guy King
L	*Meet Yourself in the Bible*, Roy L. Laurin
La	*Acts*, Roy L. Laurin
Le	*Life Endures*, Roy L. Laurin
Lj	*Sermon on the Mount*, D. Martyn Lloyd-Jones
Lw	*What the Bible Says*, Roy L. Laurin
Mc	*You Can Conquer*, Clarence Macartney
M	*Facing Life and Getting the Best of It*, Clarence E. Macartney
O	*The Bible in Pastoral Care*, Wayne E. Oates
P	*Planning a Year's Pulpit Work*, A. W. Blackwood
Pn	*A Guide to Confident Living*, Norman Vincent Peale
Pr	*Release from Guilt and Fear*, Gordon Powell
Rc	*Christian Commit Yourself*, Paul Rees
Re	*Victorious Christian Living*, Alan Redpath

RI	*Learning to Live*, Alan Redpath
Rp	*The Hard Commands of Jesus*, Roy Pearson
S	*Psychiatry and the Bible*, Carrol A. Wise
Si	*Make Life Worth Living*, Joseph R. Sizoo
Sw	*The Secret of Radiant Life*, W. E. Sangster
V	*Christian Faith in Action*, Fay Valentine
Wy	*How Christian Parents Face Family Problems*, J. C. Wynn

Appendix 3

The following material presents suggestions for sermon titles and outline sketches that deal with life situations.

The Confidence Crisis (Exodus 3:1—4:17)
    The presence of God gives confidence   Ex. 3:12
    The promises of God give confidence   Ex. 3:14
    The power of God gives confidence   Ex. 4:3

Feeling Inferior? (Exodus 3:1—4:18)
    Lack of reputation   Ex. 3:11
    Lack of information   Ex. 3:13
    Lack of persuasion   Ex. 4:1
    Lack of elocution   Ex. 4:10

Christ and the Inferiority Complex   Ex. 3:11

The Curse of Complaining   Num. 11

How to Face a Crisis   Deut. 31:1-8

Hidden Sin Hurts (Joshua 7)
    The individual   Josh. 7:21
    His family   Josh. 7:24-25
    His nation   Josh. 7:4-5
    His God   Josh. 7:25

Discouragement (Nehemiah 4:1-23)
    Commit the situation to God   Neh. 4:4-5

Remember God	Neh. 4:10-11
Do all you can, trusting God for the rest	Neh. 4:14
Poverty	Job 1:13; Prov. 16:8; 19:1; 28:6
Discouragement	Job 3; 10:1; Pss. 88; 93; 95-100; 102-5; 137
Triumph over Tragedy	Job 42:1-10
Devotion	Ps. 1:1—3:8
The Cure for Sleeplessness	Ps. 4:8
Lack of Leadership	Ps. 5:8
Integrity	Ps. 5:8
Weakness	Ps. 6
Wickedness	Pss. 10; 11:6-7; 12; 50; 109; Prov. 2; 3:24; 28:1
Faults	Ps. 19:7-14
Fear	Pss. 23; 27:1-3; 46:1-3; 64; 118:6
Sorrow	Ps. 25:15-22; Eccles. 7:2-6
The Cure for Fear	Ps. 27:1

The Cure for Sin	Ps. 32:1
Happy Is the Man (Psalm 32)	
Rebellion is forgiven	Ps. 32:1
Misdirection is straightened	Ps. 32:1
Deviation is righted	Ps. 32:2
Deception is removed	Ps. 32:2
Benefits of Confession (Psalm 32)	
Forgiveness	Ps. 32:5
Protection	Ps. 32:7
Direction	Ps. 32:8
Sin	Pss. 26; 32; 52; 58; 74; 80; 83; 89:38-52; 110
Meaning in Life	Ps. 39; Eccles. 1:2-11; 2:1-26; 3:1-22; 4:4-11; 5:15-16; 6:1-12; 8:6-17; 9:4-10; 12:8-14
The Cure for the Blues	Ps. 42:5
Guilt Feelings Gone	Ps. 51:1-19
Dealing with Sin (Psalm 51)	
Praying in confession	Ps. 51:3
Pray for God's cleansing	Ps. 51:2
Pray for God's restoration	Ps. 51:12
Forgiveness	Pss. 51; 85; 130

The Cure for Worry	Ps. 55:22*a*
Defeat	Ps. 60
Trouble	Pss. 69-70; 79; 120-21; Prov. 3:11-20

The End of Envy (Psalm 73)
    Refrain from hasty emotional reactions   Ps. 73:15
    Enter the presence of God   Ps. 73:17
    Understand the end of the wicked   Ps. 73:18-22, 27
    Be occupied with God   Ps. 73:23-26, 28

The Cure for Doubt	Ps. 73:16-17
Unbelief	Pss. 78; 106:23-47
The Cure for Indifference	Ps. 85:6
The Cure for Nerves	Ps. 91:1

Feeling Insecure? (Psalm 91)
    Realize your position   Ps. 91:1
    Realize His provision   Ps. 91:15

Vengeance	Ps. 94

The Chill of Loneliness (Psalm 102:1-28)
    Remember that God is eternal   Ps. 102:12
    Remember that God is active   Ps. 102:13
    Remember that God can be contacted   Ps. 102:17

Godly Living in an Ungodly Society
    (Psalm 119:9-16)
    Apprehend God's law   Ps. 119:11

Declare God's law	Ps. 119:13
Meditate upon God's law	Ps. 119:15
The Cure for Restlessness	Ps. 121:1
Self-Confidence	Pss. 127-28
Greed	Prov. 1:10-19
Correction	Prov. 3:11-12
Envy	Prov. 3:31; 24:1-4
Laziness	Prov. 6:6; 13:4; 20:4; Eccles. 7:10-18
Hypocrisy	Prov. 11:1-31
Obedience	Prov. 15:26; 16:3
Pride	Ps. 10; Prov. 16:18- 22; 22:24
Happiness at Home	Prov. 17:1; 21:1; 23:25-36
Friendship	Prov. 24
Discrimination	Song of Sol. 1:5-7
The Dangers of Hypocrisy	Isa. 29:11-24
Sufficiently Satisfied	Isa. 55:1-13
Meeting the Lord's Requirements	Micah 6:1-8

The Age of Anxiety (Habakkuk 3:1-19)
    Admit our fear   Hab. 3:16
    Rejoice in the God of our salvation   Hab. 3:18
    Look only to God for our strength   Hab. 3:19

Jealousy   Matt. 2;
                                       20:20-28;
                                     Mark 10:35-45;
                                     Luke 7:36-50

The Problem of Temptation   Matt. 4:1-11;
                                     Luke 4:1-13

The Problem of Anger   Matt. 5:21-26

The Problem of Retaliation   Matt. 5:38-42

Hypocrisy   Matt. 6:1-
                                     18;
                                     7:21-28;
                                     11:1-8;
                                     12:33-36;
                                     15:1-21;
                                     23:1-12;
                                     Mark 2:23-38;
                                     7:1-23;
                                     12:38;
                                     Luke 11:37-54;
                                     20:45, 47

The Problem of Materialism   Matt. 6:19-21

Overcoming Anxiety (Matthew 6:19-34)
    Treasure eternal values   Matt. 6:20
    Trust God to provide   Matt. 6:31
    Put God first   Matt. 6:33
    Avoid needless speculation   Matt. 6:34

Anxiety (Matthew 6:19-34)
    Transfer your trust   Matt. 6:33
    Transfer your treasures   Matt. 6:20

God's Cure for Anxiety	Matt. 6:25-34; Luke 12:22-31
Antidote for Anxiety (Matthew 6:25-34)	
Take positive action against anxiety	Matt. 6:25*a*
Replace anxiety with positive trust	Matt. 6:33
Take one day at a time	Matt. 6:34*a*
God's Provision for Anxiety (Matthew 6:25-24)	
Recognize God's care	Matt. 6:26
Recognize God's knowledge	Matt. 6:32
Recognize God's promise	Matt. 6:33
The Problem of Judging	Matt. 7:1-5
Critical Attitude	Matt. 7:1-6; Luke 6:37-45
Persecution and Fear (Matthew 10:16-33)	
Remember Christ's own persecutions	Matt. 10:25*b*
Remember your real enemy	Matt. 10:28
Remember your value	Matt. 10:30
Remember your reward	Matt. 10:32
Discouragement	Matt. 10:24-33; 11:25-30
The Problem of Traditionalism	Matt. 15:1-9; Mark 7:1-13
Selfishness	Matt. 16:24-28; 26:6-14, 16; Mark 14:3-9; John 12:1-8
Temptation	Matt. 18:7-9; Luke 4:1-13;

Christ and Doubt	John 20:28
Overcoming Prejudice	Acts 10:1—11:18
Defeating Doubt	Acts 12:1-24
Conquering a Critical Attitude	Rom. 14:1-23
Encouragement in Temptation	1 Cor. 10:13
Race and Brotherhood	Gal. 3:23-29; 5:13-26; Eph. 4:1-6, 23-32; Col. 3:1-15
Personal Character	Gal. 5:19-24
Family Relationships	Gal. 6:1-18; Eph. 5:18-33; 6:1-4; Col. 3:18-21; 1 Tim. 5:1-16; Titus 2:1-8
Peace	Eph. 2:13-22; 6:10-16; 1 Thess. 5:11-15; 1 Tim. 6:11-17; 2 Tim. 2:1-4; 4:1-8
Personal Rights and Responsibility	Eph. 2:13-22; 6:5-9; Phil. 2:3-13; 4:11-13; Col. 2:6-10; 3:8-15; 1 Thess. 3:11-13;

1 Tim. 6:17-21;
2 Tim. 2:15-19;
Philemon 1-25

Anger (Ephesians 4:26, 31-32)
    Express righteous anger   Eph. 4:26
    Deal with anger immediately   Eph. 4:26
    Avoid malicious anger   Eph. 4:31
    Remember God's forgiveness   Eph. 4:32

A Cure for Procrastination   Eph. 5:15-17

A Recipe for a Happy Home   Eph. 5:22—6:4

Protection and Security   Eph. 6:10-20;
2 Tim. 2:14-26;
3:12-17

God's Cure for Unhappiness (Philippians 1-4)
    Have a single mind   Phil. 1:21
    Have a submissive mind   Phil. 2:3
    Have a spiritual mind   Phil. 3:20
    Have a secure mind   Phil. 4:6

Saved from Selfishness (Philippians 2:1-8)
    Look at the worth of others   Phil. 2:3*b*
    Look at the needs of others   Phil. 2:4*b*
    Look at the example of Christ Phil. 2:5

Facing Anxiety (Philippians 4:4-7)
    Rejoice in God   Phil. 4:4
    Pray to God   Phil. 4:6*b*
    Allow the peace of God to live within you   Phil. 4:7

Overcoming Anxiety   Phil. 4:6-9

Prosperity   Phil. 4:8-19

Contentment   Phil. 4:11

Avoiding Destructive Controversy
   (2 Timothy 2:1-26)
      Proclaim God's Word   2 Tim. 2:15
      Practice kindness   2 Tim. 2:24
      Purify your heart   2 Tim. 2:22

Worldliness   2 Tim. 4:10

Unbelief   Heb. 3:7-19

Temptation   Heb. 4:15

Discouragement   Heb. 4:15-16;
                                         12:1-4

Guilt   Heb. 10:1-22

Poverty   Heb. 13:5-6

Facing Trials (James 1:2-8)
      Understand the reasons for trial   James 1:3-4
      Realize God's provisions   James 1:5
      Correct our attitude in trials   James 1:6-8

The Rewards of Trouble   James 1:12

The Plague of Partiality   James 2:1-13

Winning over Worldliness (James 4:1-10)
      Resist the devil   James 4:7
      Submit to God   James 4:7

Patience   James 5:7-11

Living Through Adversity (1 Peter 1:3-25)
      Remember God's provision   1 Pet. 1:3-12
      Redefine your relationship to God   1 Pet. 1:13-21
      Renew your love for one another   1 Pet. 1:22-25

Steadfast in Suffering   1 Pet. 4:12-19

Bibliographies

SERMON CONSTRUCTION AND HISTORY

Blackwood, A. W. *The Preparation of Sermons*. New York: Abingdon-Cokesbury, 1948.

Bryson, Harold T., and Taylor, James C. *Building Sermons to Meet People's Needs*. Nashville: Broadman, 1980.

Caldwell, Frank. *Preaching Angles*. Nashville: Abingdon, 1954.

Dargon, Edwin Charles. *A History of Preaching*. 3 vols. New York: George H. Doran, 1905.

Doniger, Simon, ed. *The Application of Psychology to Preaching*. Great Neck, N.Y.: Pastoral Psychology Press, 1952.

Eggold, Henry J. *Preaching Is Dialogue*. Grand Rapids: Baker, 1980.

Erdahl, Lowell O. *Preaching for the People*. Nashville: Abingdon, 1976.

Fant, Clyde E. *Preaching for Today*. New York: Harper & Row, 1975.

Fasol, Al. *Selected Readings in Preaching*. Grand Rapids: Baker, 1979.

Gonzalez, Justo L., and Gonzalez, Catherine G. *Liberation Preaching*. Nashville: Abingdon, 1980.

Haselden, Kyle. *The Urgency of Preaching*. New York: Harper & Row, 1963.

Jackson, Edgar N. *How to Preach to People's Needs*. New York: Abingdon, 1956. Reprint. Grand Rapids: Baker, 1970.

Jefferson, Charles. *The Minister as a Shepherd*. New York: Thomas Y. Crowell, 1912.

Jones, Ilion T. *Principles and Practice of Preaching: A Comprehensive Study of the Art of Sermon Construction*. New York: Abingdon, 1956.

Jordan, Gerald Ray. *You Can Preach: Building and Delivering the Sermon*. Westwood, N.J.: Revell, 1951.

Kemp, Charles F. *Life-Situation Preaching.* St. Louis: Bethany Press, 1956.

Linn, Edmund Holt. *Preaching as Counseling: The Unique Method of Harry Emerson Fosdick.* Valley Forge, Pa.: Judson, 1966.

Luccock, Halford E. *In the Minister's Workshop.* New York: Abingdon-Cokesbury, 1944.

MacLennan, David. *Pastoral Preaching.* Philadelphia: Westminster, 1955.

McBurney, J. H., and Hance, K. G. *Discussion in Human Affairs.* New York: Harper & Brothers, 1950.

McCracken, Robert. *The Making of the Sermon.* New York: Harper & Brothers, 1956.

Oates, Wayne. *The Christian Pastor.* Philadelphia: Westminster, 1951.

Perry, Lloyd. *Biblical Preaching for Today's World.* Chicago: Moody, 1973.

Sangster, W. E. *The Approach to Preaching.* Philadelphia: Westminster, 1952.

Teikmanis, Arthur L. *Preaching and Pastoral Care.* Englewood Cliffs, N.J.: Prentice-Hall, 1964.

Tizard, Leslie J. *Preaching: The Art of Communication.* New York: Oxford U., 1959.

Volbeda, Samuel. *The Pastoral Genius of Preaching.* Compiled and edited by Robert Evenhuis. Grand Rapids: Zondervan, 1960.

Webber, F. R. *A History of Preaching in Britain and America.* 3 vols. Milwaukee: Northwestern, 1953.

Wiseman, Neil B. *Biblical Preaching for Contemporary Man.* Grand Rapids: Baker, 1976.

ARTICLES IN JOURNALS OR MAGAZINES

Adams, Theodore F., and Holman, Charles T. "Preaching Versus Counseling?" *Pastoral Psychology,* January 1964, pp. 41-44.

Bartlett, Gene E. "The Preaching and Pastoral Roles." *Pastoral Psychology,* March 1952, pp. 21-28.

Belgum, David. "Preaching and the Stresses of Life." *The Lutheran Quarterly* 20 (November 1968): 352-59.

Bowman, Howard L. "Counseling Can Improve Preaching." *Pastoral Psychology,* February 1957, pp. 13-15, 65.

Burkhart, Roy A. "Preaching with Counseling Insight." *Pastoral Psychology,* May 1957, pp. 21-26.

Burns, James H. "The Application of Psychology to Preaching." *Pastoral Psychology,* March 1952, pp. 29-33.

Caplan, Harry, and King, Henry H. "Pulpit Eloquence: A List of Doctrinal and Historical Studies in English." *Speech Monographs* 22 (special issue 1955): 5-159.

Casteel, John L. "Homiletical Method for Pastoral Preaching, Part I." *Pastoral Psychology*, November 1955, pp. 11-15.

———. "Homiletical Method for Pastoral Preaching, Part II." *Pastoral Psychology*, December 1955, pp. 27-34.

Curran, C. A. "Psychological Reactions to Sermons." *Theology Digest*, Winter 1962, pp. 40-44.

Dawson, Joseph Martin. "The Preacher and Current Events." *Church Management*, November 1942, pp. 46-47.

Fosdick, Harry Emerson. "Personal Counseling and Preaching." *Pastoral Psychology*, March 1952, pp. 11-15.

———. "What is the Matter with Preaching?" *Harper's Magazine*, July 1928, pp. 133-41.
See reprint of this article in Crocker, Lionel, and Eich, Louis M. *Oral Reading*. New York: Prentice-Hall, 1947, pp. 216-26.

Furgeson, Earl H. "Psychology and Preaching." *Pastoral Psychology*, October 1963, pp. 5-7.

Greeves, Frederick. "Preaching and Suffering." *The Preacher's Quarterly*, December 1956, pp. 335-60.

Halvorson, Arndt L. "Preaching Is for People." *The Lutheran Quarterly* 20 (November 1968): 359-63.

Hiltner, Seward E. "On Preaching." *Pastoral Psychology*, April 1961, pp. 7-9.

Hodges, Graham R. "Counseling from the Pulpit." *Pulpit Digest*, February 1962, pp. 21-24.

Hudson, R. Lofton. "Preaching and Mental Health." *Pastoral Psychology*, October 1953, pp. 3-39.

———. "Therapeutic Preaching." *Review and Expositor*, July 1952, pp. 295-303.

Hulme, William E. "Effective Preaching Includes Counseling." *The Pulpit*, July 1952, pp. 2-4.

Jackson, Edgar N. "The Therapeutic Function in Preaching" *Pastoral Psychology*, June 1950, pp. 36-39.

Kemp, Charles F. "Life-Situation Preaching and Pastoral Work." *Pastoral Psychology*, October 1956, pp. 35-46.

Long, Thomas G. "Therapeutic Preaching: Three Views." *The Princeton Seminary Bulletin* 68 (Winter 1976): 80-93.

Luccock, Halford E. "What Preaching Owes to Pastoral Counseling." *Pastoral Psychology*, March 1952, pp. 9-10, 66.

MacLennan, David A. "Preaching and Pastoral Counseling Are One Task." *Pastoral Psychology*, March 1952, pp. 16-20.

Meiburg, Robert L. "The Preaching Pastor." *Review and Expositor*, October 1953, pp. 430-33.

Montgomery, John Warwick. "Book Review of *Sola Scriptura: Problems and Principles in Preaching Historical Texts*, by Sidney Greidanus." *Journal of the Evangelical Theological Society* 14 (Fall 1971): 253-54.

Morlan, George K. "Preaching and Psychological Research." *Pulpit Digest*, January 1952, pp. 15-17.

Oates, Wayne. "Evangelism and Pastoral Psychology." *Pastoral Psychology*, June 1956, pp. 7-9.

Peters, Frank C. "Counseling and Effective Preaching." *Bibliotheca Sacra* 126 (April 1969): 99-108.

Rees, Paul S. "The Minister's Workshop: Preaching That Confronts the Times." *Christianity Today*, 10 April 1964, p. 35.

Reid, Clyde H.; Howe, Reuel L.; and Gene E. Bartlett. "A 'Give and Take' on Psychology and Preaching." *Pastoral Psychology*, February 1964, pp. 53-59.

Robson, C. Lewis. "The Preacher as Pastor." *The Pulpit*, June 1961, pp. 7-8.

Ruopp, Harold W. "Preaching to Life Situations." *The Christian Century Pulpit* 6 (January 1935): 20-21.

———. "Life Situation Preaching." *The Christian Century Pulpit* 12 (May 1941): 116-17.

———. "Life Situation Preaching (Part II)." *The Christian Century Pulpit* 12 (June 1941): 140-41.

Stackel, Robert. "Pastoral Preaching." *The Lutheran Quarterly* 20 (November 1968): 364-72.

Starenko, Ronald. "Preaching and Counseling." *Concordia Theological Monthly* 42 (October 1971): 630-40.

General Counseling

Adams, Jay E. *Competent to Counsel*. Grand Rapids: Baker, 1970.
Probes the relationship between Christianity and psychiatry. A strong argument for the relevance of Scripture to man's needs.

Adolph, Paul E. *Release from Tension*. Chicago: Moody, 1956.
Written by a Christian physician and formerly published under the title of *Health Shall Spring Forth*.

Allen, Charles L. *God's Psychiatry*. Westwood, N.J.: Revell, 1953. Reprint. Old Tappan, N.J.: Revell, Spire, 1963.

Views the healing of mind and soul from the standpoint of Psalm 23, the Ten Commandments, the Lord's Prayer, and the Beatitudes.

Blaiklock, David A. *Release from Tension*. Grand Rapids: Zondervan, 1969.
The author is a medical doctor who practices in New Zealand. Chapters include topics on suffering, worry, anger, and guilt.

Collins, Gary T. *A Psychologist Looks at Life*. Wheaton, Ill.: Key, 1971.
The author takes a look at numerous psychological disorders and presents Christian solutions.

———. *Living in Peace: The Psychology of Interpersonal Relations*. Wheaton, Ill.: Key, 1970.

———. *Man in Transition: The Psychology of Human Development*. Carol Stream, Ill.: Creation House, 1971.
First book in a "Psychology for Church Leaders Series." Shows how psychology can be applied to the work of today's church ministering to people enmeshed in the stresses of life.

———. *Search for Reality: Psychology and the Christian*. Wheaton, Ill.: Key, 1969.
Collins considers such topics as these: the nature of man, neurosis, and the causes and treatment of mental illness. See chapter eleven, "Preaching, Brainwashing and Behavior Manipulation," pp. 144-58.

Dicks, Russell L., ed. *Successful Pastoral Counseling Series*. Englewood Cliffs, N.J.: Prentice-Hall, 1964.

Hallesby, Ole. *Temperament and the Christian Faith*. Minneapolis: Augsburg, 1962.

Hiltner, Seward. *The Christian Shepherd: Some Aspects of Pastoral Care*. New York: Abingdon, 1959.

Howe, Reuel L. *Partners in Preaching: Clergy and Laity in Dialogue*. New York: Seabury, 1967.

PASTORAL CARE

Adams, Arthur Merrihew. *Pastoral Administration*. Philadelphia: Westminster, 1964.

Adams, Jay E. *Pastoral Leadership*. Grand Rapids: Baker, 1975.

———. *The Pastoral Life*. Grand Rapids: Baker, 1974.

Brister, C. W. *Pastoral Care in the Church*. New York: Harper & Row, 1964.

Dale, Robert D. *Growing a Loving Church*. Nashville: Convention, 1974.

Dicks, Russell. *Principles and Practices of Pastoral Care*. Philadelphia: Fortress, 1966.

Evans, Erastus. *Pastoral Care in a Changing World*. London: Epworth, 1961.

Gray, Robert M. and Moberg, David O. *The Church and the Older Person*. Grand Rapids: Eerdmans, 1962.

Griffith, Earle G. *The Pastor as God's Minister*. Schaumburg, Ill.: Regular Baptist Press, 1977.

Hughes, Thomas Hywel. *The Psychology of Preaching and Pastoral Work*. New York: Macmillan, 1941.
See Part 1, "The Psychology of Preaching," pp. 57-142.

Hulme, William E. *How to Start Counseling: Building the Counseling Program in the Local Church*. New York: Abingdon, 1955.
See especially chapter 6, "Preaching and Counseling," pp. 65-76.

Ishee, John, ed. *When Trouble Comes*. Nashville: Broadman, 1970.
A compilation of eight case studies written by individuals who had particular problems in their life experience. Suggested activities for use in groups. Book is coordinated with a record by the same title.

Jackson, Edgar N. *The Pastor and His People*. Manhasset: Channel, 1963.

Jefferson, Charles. *The Minister as Shepherd*. Manila, Philippines: Living Books for All, 1973.

Johnson, Paul E. *Pastoral Ministration*. London: James Nisbet & Co., Ltd, 1955.

Killinger, John. *The Centrality of Preaching in the Total Task of the Ministry*. Waco, Tex.: Word, 1969.
See especially chapter 3, "Preaching and Pastoral Care," pp. 54-71.

LaHaye, Tim. *Spirit-Controlled Temperament*. Wheaton, Ill.: Tyndale, 1966.
Based in part on Hallesby's book. Excellent treatment on the ministry of the Holy Spirit in personality change.

————. *Transformed Temperaments*. Wheaton, Ill.: Tyndale, 1971.
Written from his experience in counseling people in trouble. Explains the transformations of temperament in the lives of four biblical personalities with application to Christians today.

Luccock, Halford E. *Christianity and the Individual in a World of Crowds*. Nashville: Parthenon, 1937.

Mickey, Paul; Gamble, Gary; and Gilbert, Paula. *Pastoral Assertiveness: A New Model for Pastoral Care*. Nashville: Abingdon, 1978.

Mobbs, Bernard. *Our Rebel Emotions*. New York: Seabury, 1970.
Chapters on hostility, frustration, irritation, anxiety, depression, jealousy, and other problems of the inner life.

Narramore, Clyde M. *Encyclopedia of Psychological Problems*. Grand Rapids: Zondervan, 1966.
Contains a glossary of terms, a bibliography, and encyclopedic articles on all the major psychological problems people face. Suggests spiritual causes and solutions as well as the medical and traditional aspects of problems.

Oates, Wayne E. *Protestant Pastoral Counseling*. Philadelphia: Westminster, 1962.

————. *New Dimensions in Pastoral Care*. Philadelphia: Fortress, 1970.

————. *The Bible in Pastoral Care*. Philadelphia: Westminster, 1970.

————. *The Christian Pastor*. Philadelphia: Westminster, 1946.

Oglesby, William B., Jr. *Biblical Themes for Pastoral Care*. Nashville: Abingdon, 1980.

Schaller, Lyle E. *The Pastor and the People*. Nashville: Abingdon, 1973.

Sugden, Howard F., and Wiersbe, Warren W. *When Pastors Wonder How*. Chicago: Moody, 1973.

Teikmanis, Arthur L. *Preaching and Pastoral Care*. Englewood Cliffs, N.J.: Prentice-Hall, 1964.

Tournier, Paul. *The Meaning of Persons*. New York: Harper & Row, 1957.

SERMONS PREACHED TO PEOPLE WITH PERSONAL PROBLEMS

Fosdick, Harry Emerson. *Living Under Tension*. New York: Harper & Brothers, 1941.

————. *On Being a Real Person*. New York: Harper & Brothers, 1943.

Gilkey, James Gordon. *When Life Gets Hard*. New York: Macmillan, 1945.

Hastings, Robert J., Jr. *How to Live with Yourself*. Nashville: Broadman, 1966.

Heimarck, Theodore. *Preaching for Tethered Man*. Minneapolis: Augsburg, 1962.

Kemp, Charles F. *Life-Situation Preaching*. St. Louis: Bethany, 1956.
Appendix I contains 100 sermon titles that deal with life situations. All the sermons have appeared in print either in preaching journals or books of sermons, and Kemp tells where they can be found.

————. *Pastoral Preaching*. St. Louis: Bethany Press, 1963.
A book of eighteen sermons, including biographical sketches of preachers. Published as a sequel to *Life-Situation Preaching*. The first three chapters give background to this kind of preaching. Book shows relationship between preaching and pastoral care.

————. *The Preaching Pastor*. St. Louis: Bethany Press, 1966.
Part I shows the close relationship between preaching and pastoral work. Part II is the main section of the book and gives recent and older sermons in eight areas that illustrate desired kinds of growth.

Laurin, Roy L. *Meet Yourself in the Bible*. Chicago: VanKampen, 1946.
Analyzed for methodology.

Macartney, Clarence Edward. *Facing Life and Getting the Best of It*. New York: Abingdon, 1940.

————. *You Can Conquer*. Grand Rapids: Abingdon, 1954.

McCracken, Robert J. *Questions People Ask*. New York: Harper & Brothers, 1951.

More Sermons from Life. New York: Cokesbury, 1939.

Mountains and Mountain Men of the Bible. New York: Abingdon, 1950.

Mueller, J.T. *Problem Sermons for Young People*. Grand Rapids: Zondervan, 1939.

Pentecost, J. Dwight. *Man's Problems-God's Answers*. Chicago: Moody, 1971.
Analyzed for methodology.

The Power to See It Through. New York: Harper & Brothers, 1935.

Redpath, Alan. *Victorious Christian Living*. Westwood, N.J.: Revell, 1955.

Rees, Paul S. *Things Unshakeable, and Other Sermons*. Grand Rapids: Eerdmans, 1947.

The Secret of Victorious Living. New York: Harper & Brothers, 1934.

Sermons from Life. New York: Cokesbury, 1933.

Sizoo, Joseph R. *Make Life Worth Living*. New York: Macmillan, 1938.

Sockman, Ralph W. *Live for Tomorrow*. New York: Macmillan, 1942.

Weatherhead, Leslie. *This Is the Victory*. New York: Abingdon, 1941.

Scripture Index

Page numbers printed in boldface are found in Appendix 2, pages 235-47.

Moody Press, a ministry of the Moody Bible Institute, is designed for education, evangelization, and edification. If we may assist you in knowing more about Christ and the Christian life, please write us without obligation: Moody Press, c/o MLM, Chicago, Illinois 60610